Losing the Plot

Losing the Plot
Crime, Reality and Fiction in Postapartheid Writing

Leon de Kock

WITS UNIVERSITY PRESS

Published in South Africa by:

Wits University Press
1 Jan Smuts Avenue
Johannesburg, 2001
www.witspress.co.za

978-1-86814-964-3 (Print)
978-1-86814-967-4 (PDF)
978-1-86814-965-0 (EPUB – China, North & South America)
978-1-86814-966-7 (Rest of the World)

Copyedited by Inga Norenius
Proofreader: Lisa Compton
Index by Clifford Perusset
Cover design: Riaan Wilmans
Typeset by Newgen Knowledge Works
Printed and bound by Creda

For Jeanne-Marie

CONTENTS

Acknowledgements

I am indebted to Jeanne-Marie Jackson and Ashraf Jamal, who twisted my arm one afternoon in 2013 and convinced me to write a book on postapartheid literature. In the three years of reading and writing that followed, Jeanne-Marie proved to be a consistently outstanding interlocutor, loving friend and partner, and so this book is dedicated to her.

I owe debts of gratitude both big and small to Michael Titlestad, Darryl Accone, Jean and John Comaroff, Dawie Malan, Frederik de Jager, Imraan Coovadia, Donald Brown, Jonny Steinberg, Kavish Chetty, Willem Anker, Marlene van Niekerk, Niq Mhlongo, Francis Galloway, Fourie Botha, Roshan Cader, Veronica Klipp, Catherine du Toit, Colette Knoetze, Sally-Ann Murray, Pete Colenso, Dawid de Villiers, Tilla Slabbert, Michiel Heyns, Dominique Botha, Christo van Staden, Etienne van Heerden, Maria Geustyn, Wamuwi Mbao, Charis de Kock, Jane Rosenthal, Cuthbeth Tagwirei, Eben Venter, Adi Enthoven, Paul Voice, Peter Midgley, Craig MacKenzie, Tommaso Milani, Henrietta Rose-Innes, Raymond Suttner, Corina van der Spoel, John Eppel, Hettie Scholtz, Ingrid Winterbach, Sandra Platt-Tentler, Kerneels Breytenbach, Luke de Kock, Peter Wilhelm, Ned Sparrow, Gareth Cornwell, Hans Pienaar, Veronique Tadjo, Lesley Cowling, Gary de Kock, Dirk Klopper, Stephen Clingman, and still many others. At Johns Hopkins University (JHU) over the course of 2015 and 2016, I benefited from my association with The Writing Seminars and the Department of English. I am grateful to Eric Sundquist, Christopher Nealon, Douglas Mao, Sharon Achinstein, Sally Hauf, Tracy Glink, Mary Jo Salter, David Yezzi, Amy Lynwander and Yvonne Gobble for making my work at JHU yield such rich rewards.

Lynda Gilfillan's first round of editing the manuscript constituted a formidable engagement and led to many substantial improvements to the text, for which I am more than usually grateful. I feel thankful, also, for Inga Norenius's perspicacious second round of editing.

This work is based on the research supported in part by the National Research Foundation of South Africa, and by the Academic and Non-Fiction Authors' Association of South Africa (ANFASA). Opinions and conclusions expressed are those of the author.

Some of the chapters published here are more developed versions of previously published material. Chapter 2 is derived, in part, from the article 'From the Subject of Evil to the Evil Subject: "Cultural Difference" in Postapartheid South African Crime Fiction', published in *Safundi: The Journal of South African and American Studies* Volume 16, Issue 1, 2015, available online: http://www.tandfonline. com/10.1080/17533171.2014.950483. It is published here with the permission of Taylor and Francis Group.

Chapter 3 grew out of the article 'Freedom on a Frontier? The Double Bind of (White) Postapartheid South African Literature', first published in *ariel: A Review of International English Literature* Volume 46, Number 3, July 2015, pp. 55–89, DOI 10.1353/ ari.2015.0022. This version is published with the permission of Johns Hopkins University Press.

Part of Chapter 6 was first published as 'Postapartheid as wondkultuur binne 'n patologiese openbare ruimte: Mark Gevisser se *Lost and Found in Johannesburg*' in *LitNet Akademies*, Jaargang 13, Nommer 1, Mei 2016, available online: http://www.litnet.co.za/wp- content/uploads/2016/05/ LitNet_Akademies_13-1_DeKock_272-293.pdf.

1

Introduction

This is not a study *of* postapartheid South African literature. Rather, it is study *in* that vast field of writing. I do not believe a coherent a study *of* this dizzyingly heterogeneous corpus is possible, short of the encyclopaedic method (a curated series of topics written by many different writers, or alphabetical listings). Such a 'companion' approach remains the default option, and it is duly taken by David Attwell and Derek Attridge, along with their 41 fellow contributors to *The Cambridge History of South African Literature*, and by Gareth Cornwell, Dirk Klopper and Craig MacKenzie in *The Columbia Guide to South African Literature since 1945*. And still, as these compilers might themselves acknowledge, there will be significant gaps. This book, in contrast to such works of general coverage, proposes a way of examining the distinctive features of South African literature after apartheid. Put differently, it delineates certain through-lines that characterise postapartheid writing.[1] Although these lines are, in my view, prominent and important, they remain a partial set of concerns. This relation of single study to corpus may be viewed via the analogy of a hologram. Take this angle of view, and the shape emerges thus; tilt the hologram surface, or change your own angle of looking, and the object under view suddenly looks quite different. All the shapes brought into view, in their provisional wholeness, have validity – call them alternative manifestations of the complexity of the entity under examination. Such an approach allows the making of bold conceptual propositions without resorting to the fixity, and the closure, of all-consuming metanarratives. It means that in advancing a theory about the corpus of work under scrutiny, or more accurately within that body of work as a whole, one's conceptual model is acknowledged as partial (e.g. Shaun Viljoen, *Richard Rive: A Partial Biography*). Like Viljoen, one acknowledges, in addition, one's own partiality too: this is *my* reading of things, or my *reading*. Other readings are possible, indeed necessary. Please join the party. Write your own study. But for a moment, consider this one. Perhaps it will influence your own perspective on the field we share, though from different angles of view. This book, then, in full awareness of the risks inherent in such an undertaking, proposes a set of related ideas as a way of conceptualising certain emphases, perhaps, in South African literature after apartheid.

In the course of this study, I mention, and discuss, many writers and, in selected instances, this book offers readings of particular works. These readings lie at the heart of *Losing the Plot*, as they both instantiate and elucidate major threads of argument. In all such cases, however, the particular work so discussed serves to illuminate the larger idea to which it is yoked, and the reading of the work concerned should be seen as suggestive of trends. There are many worthy writers who are not mentioned in the pages of this study, and a great number of instructive works that do not get the readings they deserve. However, to include everything, and to discuss all works of importance, is both impossible and undesirable. Such an undertaking would result in a shapeless monster, so vastly populated is the field of postapartheid writing, and so varied the directions in which the literature goes.

Still, one particular line does suggest itself quite emphatically, and this is the key notion, or moment, captured in the term 'transition' – that putatively transformative shift from one 'state' to another in which an entire nation found a form of secular redemption from purgatorial political conditions in the first half of the 1990s. Following this line, *Losing the Plot* proposes a way of looking at the field of South African writing in the 1990s, 2000s and the current decade that pivots around a continuingly problematised notion of transition. In the contextual, if not immediate, background of most postapartheid writing, as much as in the popular South African imagination, the transition or *switch* to a 'new dispensation' serves as a founding marker in the 'new' nation's collective consciousness. The putative 'transition' – a word defined as a 'movement, passage, or change from one position, state, stage, subject, concept, etc., to another' (Dictionary.com) – ushered in the resplendent idea of a 'rainbow nation', a catchphrase coined by Nobel Peace Prize laureate Desmond Tutu,[2] who also chaired South Africa's public (and symbolic) transitional gateway mechanism, the Truth and Reconciliation Commission (TRC). The promise of the rainbow nation rapidly became popular mythology, replete with multicultural adverts projecting racial bonhomie. It led also, and inevitably, to an energised counter-discourse which followed the epochal events of 1994, a dialectical, many-sided engagement typical of the combative South African civil sphere, gaining force as the new democracy gradually appeared to lose its lustre, especially after the Mandela presidency of 1994–1998.

This study, then, proceeds from the premise that an initial wave of optimism, evident in the early phase of upbeat transitional ferment,[3] was followed by a gradual and deepening sense of 'plot loss'[4] among South African writers and intellectuals of all stripes. That much was conceded even by the man that now serves as the country's deputy president, Cyril Ramaphosa, who commented near the end of Thabo Mbeki's reign as president that the democratic project was not a dream deferred but 'a dream betrayed'.[5] From the early 2000s, escalating service-delivery protests in poor communities across the country – led by the very people meant to be the primary beneficiaries of liberation – suggested that a wide-ranging sense of dismay had taken root.[6] The middle classes – by no means exclusively white – gave fulsome expression to such disappointment, too. Whether this general public disillusionment proceeded from a left-wing point of view, a nonracial stance, an anti-corruption position, or a sense of insecurity as crime statistics rose, the signs were ominous. Neoliberal economic policies were perceived as blocking economic transformation and severely impeding the social-democratic revolution of the liberation struggle. A new racial exclusivism emblematised by Thabo Mbeki's 'Native Club' ushered in a resurgence of what Xolela Mangcu in 2008 described as 'racial nativism'.[7] Alarming disclosures about crime and corruption in a wobbly criminal justice system all contributed to the belief that the longer-term transition was going off the rails.[8] In Anthony O'Brien's words, the post-1994 years saw a 'normalization of the political economy' which he typified, following Graham Pechey, as 'the neocolonial outcome of an anticolonial struggle' (3).[9] Such looming disillusionment, if not disorientation, rooted in a social imaginary that continues to hold dear the founding tenets of the 'new' democracy, effectively sets the scene for postapartheid literary culture. It creates the conditions for a wide-ranging investigation into the causes of the perceived inversion, or perversion, of the country's reimagined destiny, a derailing that has widely come to be regarded as criminal. Hence the remarkable efflorescence of crime writing in the post-liberation period, in both fictional detective stories and nonfiction works of 'true crime', not to mention critical analyses of this work.[10] In various chapters in this study, I consider the manner in which crime authors Antony Altbeker, Angela Makholwa, Deon Meyer, Sifiso Mzobe, Mike Nicol, Margie Orford, Roger Smith, Jonny Steinberg and Mandy Wiener seek to redefine the locus of public virtue in a context in which the boundaries between right and wrong have blurred. It is a context of social disorder, typical of the late-modern postcolony, in which the signs by which we read the social have, in Jean and John Comaroff's description, become 'occulted',[11] i.e. obscured by contending regimes of information and legitimation. Unlike the situation during apartheid, when all good, or even half-good, writers knew who was right and who wrong, the postapartheid milieu is less easily legible.[12] As in other postcolonies in Africa, Latin America, South Asia and elsewhere, this is a context in which, as the Comaroffs write, 'social order appears ever more impossible to apprehend, violence appears ever more endemic, excessive, and transgressive, and police come, in the public imagination, to embody a nervous state under pressure' ('Criminal Obsessions' 803).[13]

Such wayward, hard-to-read social conditions require exacting and forensic examination, which is what crime writing sets out to do, holding up to the light South Africa's reconstituted public sphere and finding it riddled with symptoms of criminal pathology. Crime writing's generic inclinations come conveniently to hand, since the crime story typically sets out to pinpoint the culprit, or, in the tale's implicitly wider terms, the sources of social and political perversity. I see such acts of writing as works of social detection; the underlying context that gives rise to them may be related to both immediate pressures on the ground and more extensive transnational conditions. The diagnostic works of crime writers refract a real but perverted transformation in which the postcolonies of the late-modern world are awash with criminality despite a heightened preoccupation with law and (dis)order.[14] In particular, the 'criminalisation of the state' is hardly peculiar to South Africa but rather a common feature of postcolonial polities, of which the postapartheid state is but a belated example.[15]

While many postapartheid writers choose to write about anything they like, a large number of authors seem compelled to chronicle the grit of urban existence in South Africa. This may be an aspect of a transnational impulse to narrate the textures of disorder in the global south (not to mention the faltering north), charting African destinies more widely now that Azania had come about (except it was still called South Africa) and was no better or worse than other developing regions. Some academics began seeking broader connections in the global south, including the Antipodes, while nonfiction scribes like Steinberg found stories of displacement and reconnection both inside and outside the once 'beloved country', from Liberia to New York to Somalia and back to Johannesburg and Cape Town. A new wave of crime writers and speculative fiction innovators sought answers in a dystopian, entangled global scene where individual destinies traverse connected cities. The post-millennium hangover was not confined to any one place, and the exceptionalism (famously outed by Mahmood Mamdani[16]) that apartheid had once conferred on South Africa was now really gone for good. As South African writers and scholars, we found ourselves tainted by the more general rot of a neoliberal world order of hyper-capitalism.[17] But we also found an almighty stink at home, where venality had taken root, not only in the place where political virtue had once seemed to reside, but everywhere else, too. The scramble for position, privilege and wealth was the new contagion, and writers were overwhelmed with an abundance of ready-to-hand plots.

The shift towards social forensics was more than mere opportunism or clever marketing, and from the 2000s, the quest to uncover *what's going on* in an obscured public sphere became a consuming obsession for many writers. Ventures into the heart of the country, exemplified by Steinberg's *Midlands*, reveal rebarbative forms of social interaction, a disorienting return to the violence of the frontier. Public levels of distress rise (and fall) with predictable regularity as each new media exposé uncovers the latest instance of state corruption, cronyism or, worse still, criminal neglect of and violence against citizens. Lately, the hashtag wars (such as #RhodesMustFall and #FeesMustFall) have come into play as a means of social mobilisation via broad and instantaneous dissemination of information. Government's counter-efforts in the information wars include the Secrecy Bill,[18] as well as growing influence over the South African Broadcasting Corporation (SABC), the Independent newspaper group, and the *New Age* newspaper. Hence Meyer's acute fictional analysis of warring information regimes in *Heart of the Hunter*, and Orford's *Gallows Hill*, which may likewise be read as a form of fictionalised reconnaisance, a quest to uncover reliable, inside information.[19]

Postapartheid writing constitutes an investigation into, and a search for, the 'true' locus of civil virtue in decidedly disconcerting social conditions, in an overall context of transition.[20] I have chosen not to follow this line through Gordimer and Coetzee, the latter's 1999 novel *Disgrace* rendering problematic any easy notion of transformative reconciliation in the South African body politic, as does Gordimer's final opus, *No Time Like the Present*. In this novel, her main characters, 'having worked so hard to install democracy…see its fragile stability threatened by poverty, unemployment, AIDS, government scandal, tribal loyalties, contested elections and the influx of refugees from other African countries'.[21] One could equally take a view of Marlene van Niekerk's *Triomf* and *Agaat* as twisted love stories, respectively on the cusp of, and beyond, transition. Likewise, one might read the novels of Mandla Langa – *The Lost Colours of the Chameleon*, in particular – as telling parables about the ambiguities of power in post-liberation conditions, along with similar novels by Zakes Mda, while the works of Zoë Wicomb reveal the enduring intractability of race and gender issues, despite constitutional freedom (*David's Story*, *Playing in the Light* and *October*). And so one could go on, including Etienne van Heerden's complex meditations on the slippage between past and present in works such as *In Love's Place*, *30 Nights in Amsterdam* and *Klimtol*; Breyten Breytenbach's reflective lyricism in *Dog Heart*, with its focus on ambiguous transformations that give the lie to notions of communitarianism implicit in rainbow-ism; Ivan Vladislavić's articulation, via Aubrey Tearle in *The Restless Supermarket*, of the persistence of the old despite the new; Achmat Dangor's wry depiction of the torsions of power in *Bitter Fruit*, which sees a post-liberation state 'bargaining, until there was nothing left to barter with, neither principle nor compromise'(154). More, too: Nadia Davids, Rayda Jacobs, Antjie Krog, Sindiwe Magona, Njabulo Ndebele, Eben Venter and still others, too numerous to mention let alone discuss equally within the confines of a single study. All of them, in one way or another, can be seen to be testing the limits, and the possible breaches, of a reconfigured sense of probity in a public sphere so bewilderingly remixed, and so seemingly in a state of 'plot loss', that almost nothing can be taken for granted.

Rather than conduct a Cook's tour through postapartheid literary works on the basis of how they unsettle the founding myth of transition, this study seeks to trace some of their internal dynamics. It asks the question: what formal patterns emerge from postapartheid writing, in relation to a widespread sense that the transition has been derailed?[22] While such writing includes diverse forms, including popular and nonfiction, the field is limited mainly to narrative. (In selected cases, I include Afrikaans works.) A more general bifurcation seems to have taken place on the formal level of plot and plotting in postapartheid narratives: one strain – particularly genre fiction and incident-heavy nonfiction – tends towards a playing up of plot, while another tends to downplay this aspect, as in much literary fiction. In underplotted work, writers seem to take the position that, given the refractoriness, and the unpredictability, of the unfolding post-apartheid experiment, the writer acts as a kind of camera or projector, throwing images onto a screen – for example, the eye of Milla in *Agaat*, and the news clippings in Van Niekerk's convulsive play *Die Kortstondige Raklewe van Anastasia W*; the various photographers in Vladislavić's *Double Negative*; the imprint of gender and race upon Zoë Wicomb's characters; the autobiographical 'I' introjected into the subject of Phaswane Mpe's *Welcome to Our Hillbrow*, K Sello Duiker's *The Quiet Violence of Dreams* and Niq Mhlongo's *After Tears*. In works such as these, plot plays a lesser role. For Peter Brooks in *Reading for the Plot*, the 'ambitious hero…stands in as a figure of the reader's efforts to construct meanings in even larger wholes, to totalize his experience of human existence in time, to grasp past, present and future in a sentient shape' (48). Such plotting, implying as it does an near-omniscient grasp that is capable of totalising experience in time, is eschewed by certain writers, often the more 'literary' ones. Of course, there is imaginative invention of events purely for the sake of entertainment, and there is plotting, as in putting together a frame or adding to a palimpsest for the recovery, or rendition, of that which is perceived to be the ground of the insistently 'real'. Rita Barnard notes that significant postapartheid novels like Anne Landsman's *The*

Devil's Chimney, Etienne van Heerden's *The Long Silence of Mario Salviati*, Zakes Mda's *The Heart of Redness*, Van Niekerk's *Agaat* and Wicomb's *David's Story* 'have multilayered plot lines'. Barnard argues: 'Their forms, one might say, are palimpsestic: the narrative oscillates between contemporary events and parallel (or originary) events in the past' ('Rewriting the Nation' 660). The layerings of plot, in Barnard's argument, serve to inscribe the mark of the real (events) on the palimpsest of the aesthetic/cultural record.[23] Barnard reminds her readers, too, that the 'most characteristic and pervasive tropes' in postapartheid writing, unearthed by Shane Graham in his study *South African Literature after the Truth Commission*, are the archive, the palimpsest, and excavation, along with digging and holes (657).

At a deeper level, the impulse to under-invent can be read as a *yielding to the real*, in this case because the meaning of *what's going on out there*, as well as the substance – increasingly the single most urgent issue in public life – is perceived to have been occulted. To a large extent, this precludes the need for, indeed possibility of, imaginative reconstruction. Conversely, genre practitioners, crime writers in particular, overplay plot, dealing with the experience of occultation by turning it into a process of search and discovery, and often exaggerating for effect. This 'solving the crime' approach acts as an analogy for detecting the source of public misgovernance or private malfeasance, or (as often occurs) both. These, of course, are very real problems. The thickly plotted crime novel, then, seeks to capture the perverse details of plot loss in its search for representational adequation[24] of actual, lived conditions. This is a feature not only of genre fiction but also of 'true crime' stories, a dynamic form of writing in postapartheid conditions.

The inclination to yield to the real, apart from its salience transnationally,[25] also picks up from the TRC's emphasis on witnessing and (re)discovery, and from the perceived need to excavate and confront previously concealed or repressed forms of truth, as Graham suggests. Narrative forms, especially post-2000, continue the TRC ethos of investigating perversities by folding these into a past-present conjunction. This is done either in nonfiction writing that follows an 'evidential paradigm', implicitly following the example of Carlo Ginzburg in his work *Clues, Myths, and the Historical Method* (see Chapter 3), or in generic fictions founded on decidedly real conditions: human trafficking in Andrew Brown and Diale Tlholwe (*Refuge* and *Counting the*

Coffins, respectively); farm murders and their complex causes in Karin Brynard (*Plaasmoord*, translated as *Weeping Waters*); inter-gender violence and abuse in Angela Makholwa (*Black Widow Society*); abuse of women and children in Margie Orford's novels; public corruption in Mike Nicol (the Revenge Trilogy); corrupt policemen exploiting civil violence in Roger Smith (*Wake Up Dead* and *Mixed Blood*). In nonfiction, a slew of writers cut to the quick about law enforcement, among them Antony Altbeker and Kevin Bloom.

My argument is structured around the following set of concepts: Chapter 2, crime fiction; Chapter 3, nonfiction; Chapter 4 focuses on the influence of, and ferment among, literary-cultural analysts, from the 'spring is rebellious' phase in the early 1990s and the critical reception of Zakes Mda's *Ways of Dying* to the dialogue between Ashraf Jamal and JM Coetzee concerning South Africa as a 'pathological' space. Chapter 5 traces the accelerating sense of derailment and its effect upon the ailing body of the no-longer-new South Africa, with a focus on the noir-like detachment of Roger Smith, and Makholwa's 'chick-lit' neo-noir frame in a tale of revenge against patriarchal abuse. The next part of this chapter follows nonfictional investigations into crises of policing and corrupt dealings in the criminal justice system, taken up by Steinberg, Altbeker and Mandy Wiener. Chapter 6 traces the powerful influence of the new media on reading as well as writing. Here, I examine recent nonfiction by Mark Gevisser and Mzilikazi wa Afrika as well as the journalism of Greg Marinovich. Chapter 7 dwells on fiction's implicit response to this onrush of the real, examining Ivan Vladislavić's 2010 novel *Double Negative*, and then looking at a series of recent fictional works that have reported on states of public pathology, as relayed through the perceptual registers of fictional subjects.

In summary, current South African writing is characterised by the rise of both genre fiction and creative nonfiction as ways of responding to a widely perceived sickness in the body politic, where the plot, metaphorically speaking, is thought to have been lost, and there is a premium on uncovering actual conditions. The real issue, for writers, is to find the right story, or to get the story right.

Conceptualising the 'transition': Ambiguity and temporality

This study proposes that the concept of transition – its uptake, problematisation and forensic-diagnostic investigation – serves as a pivot in postapartheid literary culture. In view of this emphasis, the term itself needs to be unpacked. Whether it references a sceptical 'transition' to democracy or an optimistic 'democratic miracle', this moment indubitably signals a shift in post-1994 South African literature from the centrality of apartheid.[26] The process most commonly described as the 'transition to democracy' has been well documented across several disciplines.[27] It is common cause that the year 1994, when South Africa finally became a fully inclusive political entity, serves as a decisive marker in the country's history, similar to the shorthand of 1910 and 1961, when the country became a Union and a Republic, respectively, or 1948, when the National Party rose to power and proceeded to consolidate colonial segregation into the notorious ideology of apartheid.

The historic elections in 1994 ushered in a remarkable series of changes, bringing reforms in social welfare, housing, electrification, and the like, although terms such as 'silent revolution'[28] and tags like 'Mandela's miracle'[29] suggest a bloodless turnaround, a 'quiet coup'. The changeover of power was there for all to see in the structures and make-up of government, along with the superstructure of the new Constitution, though it was far less discernible on the ground, where there was little evidence of the elimination of severe economic disparities. The transition was of course manifestly, and symbolically, dramatised in the public domain by means of the TRC, from which flowed a quintessential postapartheid work, Antjie Krog's *Country of My Skull*. This work is key because it inaugurates major trends, both in its content and its forms of address. It brings into stark relief what Mark Sanders calls the 'ambiguities of witnessing' as a through-line in postapartheid discourse, including the 'new' South Africa's reinvented literary culture. At once testimony and witnessing that might enable national healing, the TRC also set a precedent for *writing up the real*, disclosing and uncovering, as an urgent priority. For Sanders, testimony is neither 'fiction' nor 'truth' but both: fundamentally unverifiable, it '[facilitates] both a narrative and a counternarrative' (8). Essentially productive, this ambiguity strikes a bass note in postapartheid writing, and in considerations about the nature of the transition. It is as if the TRC inaugurated a quest for establishing the truth of 'what really happened' – and what continues to happen – in relation to a past that is itself subject to continual revision. In their introduction to *Beyond the Threshold*, Hein Viljoen and Chris van der Merwe write about the 'dilemma of being stuck between past and present'

(2), and 'the impasse of being caught on the threshold between past and present' (3). Similarly, Meg Samuelson suggests that the concept of transition in South African literary culture can be seen to enable 'thinking about being-at-home that is at the same time inherently liminal…entering the house that locates one on a perpetual threshold' ('Walking' 134). In a sense, the new literature serves as a measure of an unreadable present and an unplottable future, appraised in relation to an eternally unsettled past.[30] All in all, this is a mission of (re)discovery which, nevertheless, plays havoc with the teleological thrust implicit in the notion of a transition to democracy. So, for example, Jacob Dlamini's *Native Nostalgia* speaks to this imperative of rediscovery, and to the ambiguities of witnessing, in its blending of memoir and essayistic journeying into finer calibrations of conceiving both current and past lived experiences in relation to established narratives. Dlamini's work retrospectively confirms a line of similar postapartheid works in which reflective, literary nonfiction emerges as a reverberant form of expression about who and where 'we' are, now, and how we have come to be in this place. This is a line of writing that, in keeping with global trends,[31] begins to surge under postapartheid conditions. Inaugurated, in a sense, by Nelson Mandela's *Long Walk to Freedom* and, earlier, Charles van Onselen's epic oral history *The Seed is Mine*, postapartheid nonfiction comprises powerful writing[32] that in one way or another addresses the problematic nexus of past and present, as concentrated in the notion of transition.

Despite the efflorescence of postapartheid writing, its apparent release from the straitjacket of political themes,[33] it is also true that much of the new writing consists of narratives and counter-narratives that set up a dialectic around the very notion of a fresh start. That is to say, the idea of *transition* itself, in its denotation as a process or period of change from one state to another, a linear path that somehow yields the telos, or end point, of postapartheid – Desmond Tutu's multicultural rainbow nation, the 'democratic miracle' of popular discourse – is questioned, problematised, cast in doubt or rendered ironic.[34] While scholars such as Graham Pechey rightly warn that the term postapartheid 'defines a condition that has contradictorily always existed and yet is impossible of full realisation' (153), writers remain aware of the persistence of founding myths, the bedrock mythography of 'new' South Africans. The foundational event was instantly memorialised in *SA, 27 April 1994: An Author's Diary | 'n*

Skrywersdagboek, edited by André Brink, and it continues to infuse political commentary, invoking the promise – and disillusion – of the rainbow nation as a standard trope.[35] Indeed, it remains a serviceable trope for all manner of writers.

One of the most generative areas of such troubling has come, as suggested above, in delineations of temporality after apartheid. Introducing a special issue of *English Studies in Africa* on post-transitional literature, Ronit Frenkel and Craig MacKenzie note the caveat issued by Michael Chapman on the 'convenience' and provisional nature of 'phases of chronology' such as 'post-transitional' and his own coinage, 'post-postapartheid' (3–4). In his essay 'Conjectures on South African Literature', Chapman writes as follows:

> If post-apartheid usually means after the unbannings of 1990, or after the first democratic elections of 1994, or in/after the transition, then beyond 2000 begins to mark a quantitative and qualitative shift from the immediate 'post' years of the 1990s to another 'phase'. (1–2)

The various descriptions used to typify this second phase, the time beyond the immediate transition of the 1990s, include Chapman's 'post-postapartheid', Frenkel and MacKenzie's 'post-transitional', and Loren Kruger's 'post-anti-apartheid'. For Kruger, writing in 2002, the solidarity of the Black Consciousness movement in South Africa has waned because its chief antagonist, white supremacism, no longer enjoys official sanction. This ushers in 'post-*anti*-apartheid – post-anti-apartheid because the moral conviction of and commitment to anti-apartheid solidarity have waned, while in their place has come postcolonial uneven development rather than radical social transformation' ('Black Atlantics' 35). Kruger's refinement of familiar terms usefully covers both a temporal and a conceptual shift: if the immediate years of transition were post-apartheid, with a strong emphasis on reckoning with the past, the 2000s roughly mark a period ('post-transitional', perhaps) in which many writers begin to conceive of themselves beyond the *immediate* aftermath of apartheid, and certainly free of the need to reckon with it.

Regardless of how one conceives of the chronology of postapartheid, its temporality remains contradictory and complex, as Grant

Farred argues in his introduction to a special issue of the *South Atlantic Quarterly* entitled 'After the Thrill is Gone: A Decade of Post-Apartheid South Africa'. For Farred, temporality in postapartheid is necessarily doubled, rendering all 'post' descriptions internally ironic, encoding both the idea of a (virtuous, desired) teleology and its persistent rupture. Farred argues that

> [t]he propensity for the teleological, to think post-apartheid South Africa as the disarticulation (and possibly even evacuation of) and triumph over its apartheid predecessor, the narrative of 'progress' from a racist past to a nonracial present (and future), is a critical modality that has significant purchase in the post-1994 society. ('The Not-Yet Counterpartisan' 592)

For Farred, the event of the nation's first democratic elections 'signals the "end" of one era and the beginning of a new, democratic one that aligns South Africa – almost half a century later – with a global post-1945 nomos', although with the provisos 'that past economic inequities, cultural differences, and racial tensions, to mention but three, would have a (powerful) residual life in the new, post-apartheid nomos' (592). Farred continues:

> [T]he old illegitimacy has been replaced by a new, substanceless legitimacy, a formal equality that simply displaces social hierarchy from race into economics; the white/black distinction is transfigured into rich/poor, or 'creditor/debtor'. There is already a tension inherent within the new legitimacy: the marking of epochal progress, from apartheid to post-apartheid, quickly showed itself to be less a march toward an ideal political future – let alone present – than a new democracy living in a double temporality. (592–593)

Farred's insights are on point, especially with regard to fractured or doubled temporalities and economic stasis. Other contributors to the *South Atlantic Quarterly* issue[36] are similarly coruscating about the notion that the transition has seen a transformation in material conditions after ten years of democracy. In particular, the new government's adoption of neoliberal macro-economic policies that effectively maintain or worsen oppressive economic conditions, creating a present and a future that looks and feels like the apartheid past, is held up to scrutiny. For Farred, South Africa after 1994

> is a nation living with a dual orientation: it looks, sometimes simultaneously, sometimes discretely, to its past and its present; it has a historical vision that is alternately bifurcated and cyclopean – split in its visual outlook or too trained on a single moment. The new nomos of the South African earth is haunted by the old nomos; the old nomos is inveterately part of the new one, a source of concern, regret, and anger to some, a source merely of chagrin and inevitability to others. (594)

Another way of describing such a double temporality is to adopt Hal Foster's notion of a 'future-anterior'.[37] In the 'future-anterior', a 'will-have-been' mode of seeing and feeling makes a mess of linear temporalities or easy assumptions about periods that are 'post' anything.

Terms such as 'postapartheid' and, occasionally, 'post-liberation' and 'post-transitional' are used to cover the nominal understanding of literature that has succeeded South African writing during the time of apartheid, with the necessary conceptual caveats about the paradoxes of both 'transition' and 'transformation'. One might argue that postapartheid pertains to the 1990s, and post-transition (or post-anti-apartheid) more accurately describes the 2000s, while post-postapartheid emerges around and after 2010. Although these designations may have merit, the internal dynamics of the literature, in my view, remain similar regardless. The foundational social significance of the transition, and its sceptical treatment in writing, remain on track throughout, although the entire period also yields up works that refuse any relation to transition and postapartheid, or to any 'politics' at all. That, too, should be seen as part of the new literature's anti-exceptionalism, its newfound normality, allowing it to be anything it wants, if it so desires. Nevertheless, in its weightier instances it all too often returns to the moral fate of the country and its subjects after apartheid, as Coovadia does in his 2014 novel *Tales of the Metric System*.

Transition, the putative mid-point of postapartheid culture, is frequently shown to be a paradoxical cross-temporal knot, an ateleological threshold replete with ambiguity. Michael Titlestad's phrase 'mezzanine ontology'[38] ('Afterword' 189) captures this sense as the incomplete transition leaves the country's citizens 'caught up in a world of contradictions and ironies'. For Titlestad, the mezzanine is the post-1994 version of Gramsci's interregnum, or the 'the historical moment when apartheid was dying-but-not-dead' (as described by Thurman 181). Titlestad calls into question the 'teleological rumbling forward' he espies in the idea that authors should 'put their shoulders to the wheel of history'; the lives of authors, as much as the subjects they write about, are 'caught in-between' the old and the new as they themselves face the 'uncertainties of the future' (188). In similar vein, Samuelson ('Scripting Connections' 116) argues that post-transition literature is 'characterized more by its rearrangement than its abandonment of the chronotopes of South African literature and its expanding field of enquiry'.

Postapartheid as a phase of events, an identifiable period, is, as Titlestad suggests, marked by routine indeterminacy, in which a ready-to-hand telos gets twisted out of shape and doubles back on itself. Dialectically, the conceptual nexus suggested by the term 'transition', including its wayward temporality and deep ambiguity, has proved useful in critiquing popular rainbow discourse. It has broadly served as a kind of grammar for contextualising contentious events, culminating in the corrupt crony-capitalist administration of Jacob Zuma, and the concomitant economic empowerment of party loyalists. Unsurprisingly, therefore, the country swings between extremes of optimism and disappointment. The events of 1994 were nothing less than epochal. Uniquely, more than 350 years of bloody contestation over land and resources, over power and ideology, seemed to be settled in a way that was acceptable to everyone, both inside and outside the country. A violent revolution was forestalled, disaster averted. There could be no doubting the historic shift, the switch to democracy. South African Air Force jets performing a fly-past at Nelson Mandela's inauguration as head of state in Pretoria on 10 May 1994 signalled the birth of a new South Africa, and people all over the world bore witness to an event that many had long believed impossible. The seeming loss of such a wondrous breakthrough, its gradual dismantling, and the subsequent critique and lamentations constitute a churn in which postapartheid and its subjects remain entrapped.

The reclamation of narrative

If the 'forward march' version of transition has been conclusively derailed, leaving indeterminacy and plot loss in its place, then one of the unambiguous success stories emerging from the transition is the restorative value of story itself, or, more broadly speaking, narrative. In postapartheid writing, a great diversity of form and content emerges, constituting a body of work that is itself significantly transformed, despite its subject matter often being about the failures of transformation. This is a key point. For, regardless of the perceived loss of plot in political and social terms, the space of postapartheid is one in which a great many voices have found their pitch in public discourse, in more conventional as well as new media forms. Such speaking out, self-validation and identity reclamation, not to mention public position-taking (or posturing), is surely one of the most notable achievements of postapartheid writing, and of the 'silent revolution' in general.

Njabulo Ndebele's essay 'Memory, Metaphor, and the Triumph of Narrative' underlines the regenerative power of story, and the link between testimony, memory and narrative. 'Time has given the recall of memory the power of reflection associated with narrative' ('Memory' 20), Ndebele argues. This reflective capacity, 'experienced as a shared social consciousness', is posited as the 'lasting legacy of the stories of the TRC' (20) – one that gives 'legitimacy and authority to previously silenced voices' (20), and functions as an 'additional confirmation of the movement of our society from repression to expression' (20). Whereas the state attempted, in the apartheid era, 'to compel the oppressed to deny the testimony of their own experience, today that experience is one of the essential conditions for the emergence of a new national consciousness', Ndebele writes, adding that '[t]hese stories may very well be some of the first steps in the rewriting of South African history on the basis of validated mass experience' (20).

Ndebele here captures one of the core impulses of transitional and post-transitional narrative in general: the restoration of 'legitimacy and authority' to previously silenced voices, and the emergence of a 'new national consciousness'. In concluding his essay, he argues that a 'major spin-off' resulting from the 'stories of the TRC' is the 'restoration of narrative'. He sees this event as a rare opportunity to take narrative beyond testimony, towards imaginatively creating what he calls 'new thoughts and new worlds' (28). Writing in the year 2000, Ndebele sets a challenging agenda for postapartheid writing as a whole. The criterion, as he sees it, is that the narratives resulting from 'a search for meanings' (20) in the wake of apartheid 'may have less and less to do with the facts themselves and with their recall than with the revelation of meaning through the *imaginative combination of those facts*' (21, emphasis added); for, at that point, Ndebele writes, 'facts will be the building blocks of metaphor' (21).

It is striking that Ndebele's sense of the imagination follows an arc that traverses fiction and nonfiction, testimony and invention, fact and fable. Accordingly, postapartheid's many sources of (formerly muted) self-expression and storytelling condense into metaphor, into an imaginative amalgam, whether the writing is autobiography or poetry, whether it bears witness to or fictionalises a lived reality; the pressing need is an imaginative reconstruction of experience via memory, which has regenerative 'moral import'. This proves a testing criterion as many works engage in a 'search for new meanings'.

In particular, the capacity for newfound self-affirmation, the recuperation of formerly repressed and often still-marginalised voices, positions and identities, has been one of the more emphatic, and unambiguously affirmative, yields of postapartheid literary cul-ture. A culture of authentic self-expression in response to centuries of patriarchy and racism has emerged, as evidenced by a work such as Samuelson's *Remembering the Nation, Dismembering Women? Stories of the South African Transition*. Andrew van der Vlies argues that 'Samuelson's project...is informed by a desire to "restore" to these his-torical women [Krotoa-Eva, Nongqawuse and Sarah Baartman] some of their strangeness and challenging heterogeneity, that which does not necessarily serve the purposes of normative, naturalising national discourses' (954). Similarly, Pumla Dineo Gqola's *What is Slavery to Me?* seeks to problematise appropriations of slave heritage in order to reconfigure group identity, just as Gabeba Baderoon's *Regarding Muslims* tracks South African cultural expressions of Muslim iden-tity. The reclamation or recuperation of formerly repressed identities and subject positions, coincident with the transition and its aftermath, also involves the politics of appropriation and the dangers of being subsumed into larger, newly repressive, or normalising, narratives. In an important sense, the post-transitional literary-cultural sphere is a locus of contending scripts, characterised by keen vigilance about who speaks for, and about, whom, and under what authority.

If there is a golden, affirmative thread in postapartheid writing, one might find it in narrative reclamations of identity, the excavation of buried or repressed selves, in unfolding self-expression. Such speaking out satisfies, in spirit at least, Ndebele's vision of narrative as giving 'legitimacy and authority to previously silenced voices', confirming the 'rewriting of South African history on the basis of validated mass experience' ('Memory' 20). Further, as Ndebele notes, it is the revelation of meaning through the 'imaginative combination of...facts' (21) so that 'facts will be the building blocks of metaphor' (21) that is important. Hence the prevalence of memoir-type or confessional/autobiographical writing by a wide range of South African subjects, whether from township streets or prisons – or universities. Indeed, academics are more likely nowadays to write their own variants of memoiristic witnessing or reflection than pen 'appreciations' of 'great writers', as earlier generations were inclined to do. Notable recent examples of this trend include Stephen Clingman's *Birthmark*, Mamphela Ramphele's *A Life*, Steven Robins's *Letters of Stone and* Leslie Swartz's *Able-Bodied*. Sarah Nuttall and Cheryl-Ann Michael argue that the 'flourishing of the autobiographical voice has emerged alongside the powerful informing context of South Africa's Truth and Reconciliation Commission, but it is also a symptom of the decompression, relaxation, and cacophony of the post-apartheid moment in general' (298). They contend that the 'autobiographical act' is 'more than a literary convention'; it 'has become a cultural activity'. In a multiplicity of forms, including 'memoir, reminiscence, confession, testament, case history and personal journalism', such 'biographical acts or cultural occasions' see narrators take up 'models of identity that have become widely available'; these have 'pervaded the culture of the 1990s and have spread into the new century' (298). Nuttall and Michael continue:

> Particularly since the political transition of 1994, personal disclosure has become a part of a revisionary impulse, part of the pluralizing project of democracy itself. The individual, in this context, emerges as a key, newly legitimized concept. South Africa becomes a 'recited' community...[t]alking about their own lives, confessing, and constructing personal narratives – on the body, on the air, in music, in print – South Africans translate their selves, and their communities, into story. (298)

These points are well made. However, it is not just that, in the wake of the TRC, everyone has a story to tell, and should tell it, reclaiming selfhood, dignity and difference, or providing still more diverse and variable perspectives on past and present. It is also that the transitional zone – where lines became blurred by different reckonings of value, different invocations of legitimacy – has become a space of contest between individuals and groups via the valence of storytelling. In that sense, the post-liberation era has seen an acceleration in the *politics* of stories and storytelling, where significant stories generally bear a strong relation to the 'real', narrating people's lived experience. This current of connection to the detail of the actual is not quite the 'stenographic bent' that Louise Bethlehem ('A Primary Need' 365) identified in pre-1994 literature, with its 'rhetoric of urgency'. It reveals, rather, an insistence on both the real *and* the right way of viewing this, as people insistently express their own versions of themselves. Stories of survival, a thriving line of oral rendition, as Jonny Steinberg's *The Number* amply illustrates, encode identity in highly particularised ways, contributing to self- and group-validation as perhaps the single biggest symbolic reward of democracy. (The controversies over Steinberg's own appropriations of his subjects' stories ironically confirm how keen the contention over stories, their nature and their ownership, continues to be.) Particularised and contentious gambits, however, implicitly question the idea of a universal measure of reclaimed identity; they reopen 'grounds of contest'[39] in ways that render precarious any cosy metanarratives or settled identity politics on the basis of victimhood in the world of postapartheid. To conclude this introduction, I offer, below, an extended reading of *The Number* as an instantiation of the stakes involved in contending lines of storytelling in post-transitional culture.

The politics of (true) stories

Steinberg's *The Number* is indubitably one of the most suggestive works of postapartheid South African writing. The narrative itself is a dense, analytical weave of stories told, scrutinised, picked apart, reconsidered and retold. When all else fails, *The Number* suggests, narrative accounts – stories – are what South Africans cling to. Here, the double entendre in the term 'accounts' is apposite, for there is the all-important matter of accounting for oneself, and laying accounts at the door of history, if not other people. Steinberg is acutely sensitive to the charge and importance, in postapartheid society, of stories. His mission is to excavate layers of narrative as a means of understanding various postapartheid 'others' in a country where, as Steinberg has commented, writing continues to be a business of 'coordination between deaf people'.[40] Not only does Steinberg retell stories told to him, and read by him, in the course of the book, but he also retells the story of how the stories told to him, and read by him, have been shaped by earlier histories. Somewhere in this entanglement of storylines, data originally perceived to be true 'transmogrifies' (a word often used by Steinberg) into myth, or philosophy, or law, either written or unwritten. And these articles of belief, resting on the foundation of perceived truth, with origins in real events, are decisive for the people about whom Steinberg writes, because they live by such lore. In Steinberg's work, and in the wider domain of postapartheid writing, stories therefore gain a secular prominence of critical proportions.

Steinberg's telling example of this, in *The Number*, is gang mythology in South Africa's prisons. The 'Number' bands derive their sense of origins from the densely worked and reworked story of Nongoloza Mathebula, a late-nineteenth and early-twentieth-century bandit figure who straddled the boundary between law and its abrogation amid oppressive social conditions. Mathebula's tale was first recounted in book form by Charles van Onselen in *The Small Matter of a Horse: The Life of 'Nongoloza' Mathebula, 1867–1948*, published in 1984. At one stage in *The Number*, Steinberg turns Van Onselen into a character in his book by relating the venerated historian's version of Nongoloza to his interlocutor-subject, Magadien Wentzel. One must remember here that, academic accounts aside, rival versions of the Nongoloza story, in the country's prisons, can have life-or-death consequences because they are allied to what Steinberg' calls 'competing doctrinal positions'; moreover, competition of any kind between the Number gangs often leads to killings. Whether or not, for example, sex with men is validated by the Nongoloza story depends on a doctrinal difference between different Number factions, a difference that might well have deadly consequences.[41] So, when Steinberg brings Van Onselen's account of the Nongoloza story into confrontation with the understanding of it held by long-term prisoner Wentzel, this Numbers gang leader is not impressed:

'There is the black man's story and the white man's story. Go to any prison in this country, you will hear the black man's story – exactly the same in every prison. You go there with Van Onselen's story, they will kill you. Serious. How can you say Nongoloza spoke to a white man?' (*The Number* 236)

Steinberg tries to explain how Van Onselen came into legitimate possession of the story he tells, but Wentzel interrupts him:

'Van Onselen is fucking with something very fucking important. You look at Shaka's history, you look at Piet Retief, at Jan van Riebeeck. This is history people believe. It is like a power. People are prepared to die for their stories.' (238)

Here, we witness a turn in the politics of knowledge production. In this instance, intellectual jousting in the cloistered halls of the university is rendered relative by contention over stories in another hothouse of competing narratives, another enclosure in which understanding is forged via the giving and taking of accounts: the South African prison, with its marked cultures of institutionalised violence. Van Onselen, himself widely known for his gloves-off style of argument (in his years at the University of the Witwatersrand, especially), would be at something of a disadvantage in this debate with Wentzel, who seems capable of giving the term 'visceral engagement' a wholly new twist. The democratic space of postapartheid writing, via story-aggregator Steinberg, opens up a dialogic zone in which such unlikely bedfellows are allowed to share the privilege of open, public dialogue, even if it is reconstructed after the event. This is what one might call a Bakhtinian moment, a dialogic zone never available in quite the same measure before 1994. Steinberg, and writers like him, stitch together stories from irreconcilably polarised realms because real communication and real listening remain an urgent need despite – or because of – the gains of postapartheid. Recall Steinberg's statement that writing in and about South Africa 'is a question of coordination between deaf people'. Steinberg's raison d'être as a writer seems to be to act as a collector of accounts, and to scrutinise them with an unsparingly sharp eye, while also embedding himself inside his interlocutor's felt world, his felt life. Anyone who has read Steinberg, whether it is *The Number, Three Letter Plague, A Man of Good Hope* or any of his other books, is likely to agree that his ability both to listen to, and to elicit from, his subjects what one might call 'heartfelt' stories is quite extraordinary. These subjects open up to him, entering into a bond in which the right, or best possible, telling of the story becomes an objective of the utmost importance because, always, the stories matter deeply; on these accounts hang someone's sense of self, or at least their own understanding of it.

Clearly, then, this is serious business, involving the most intimate textures, or layers, of people's lives, their self-making and identity construction, their aversions and resentments, and their most prized memories. There is little place in such a highly sensitive process for 'fiction', or for fictionalising life stories, and yet there is much fictionality in these accounts; here, one might talk about the fictions that underlie – in some cases make up – much of what is taken to be the real. This kind of 'fictional' content almost always enters into Steinberg's stories at a secondary level, as he disentangles truth from half-truth, perspective from fact. Despite such blending of non-fiction and fiction, however, the emphasis remains squarely on the primacy of an impeccable standard of accuracy, and of reported actuality. Steinberg frequently refers to himself as a 'journalist', despite the fact that his books are a hybrid of investigative journalism and scholarly research, achieving a quality of social history that is, in South African studies, unique, though he does acknowledge, in *The Number*, a great debt to Van Onselen. In this regard, Steinberg, like Dlamini, is unique to postapartheid writing, and his mission as a discoverer of deep stories, excavated with due regard for both their surface feel and their below-the-radar complexity, gives his work an edge over writing that is merely imagined or made up. Perhaps this is what Krog means when she says, 'I want to suggest that at this stage imagination for me is overrated', and Van Niekerk, too, when she opines that a reading of the best South African nonfiction (in this case, Antony Altbelker's *Fruit of a Poisoned Tree*) 'almost convinces one that fiction has become redundant in this country' (Twidle, 'Literary Non-Fiction' 5).[42]

It is as if the analytical edge of nonfiction, in its commitment to establishing a baseline account and its dedication to getting the story right, is necessary precisely because the 'right story' can only be achieved, or nearly achieved, in a continuous weighing up of the value of the stories people tell themselves, which are likely to have varying degrees of usefulness. That is to say, Steinberg deploys a mode of nonfictional investigation, akin to journalism in the best sense of that term, to discriminate between orders of information folded into stories. Steinberg is alert to the fact, always, that subjects use stories strategically and pragmatically, so he cannot take them at face value. Much of the information gleaned in the course of a Steinberg-type book, although based on fact, often verges on a kind of fictionality in its arrangement of elements. For example, Steinberg writes, at one stage, that

> [Wentzel's] identification with Sidney Poitier in *To Sir with Love* is almost certainly a retrospective memory. It is the product of a conciliation he has made with the world during the last three years. It is also the symptom of a peace he has made with himself. (*The Number* 138)

Explaining this, the author suggests that

> [watching *To Sir with Love*] wasn't his first experience of black and white. Away from the screen, in his real life, he was watching his mother give her maternal love to two white children. And the feelings this spectacle invoked had made him a virulent racist. He hated the Sampsons in particular, the entire white population in general. Even the 'pseudo-whites', the coloured middle class, with their domestic workers and their family cars, he hated with a vengeance. (138)

On the basis of this evaluation of what Steinberg has deduced about Wentzel's sense of things, over the longer term and in view of the stories he typically tells himself, the author is able to identify his subject's current storyline as a 'retrospective memory', a reconstruction (or fiction, of a sort), in the present, of a memory that, Steinberg concludes, must have had a different charge in the past: 'Back in the mid-seventies, he must have watched *To Sir with Love* with ambivalence at best: a toxic mix of longing and envy' (138).

Such meta-reflexive recalibrating in the face of a superfluity of oral and researched data represents the real work of Steinberg's (and Dlamini's) brand of nonfiction. In *The Number*, as elsewhere in his corpus, the importance of such work is evident in the consequences attendant upon narratives of self-understanding, or delusion. The very destiny of Steinberg's interlocutors is intricately bound with their stories of origination and validation. This can be seen on both an individual and a collective level. Socially, the prisons become a site in which the political narrative of transition after 1994 gains a sharpened focus. The early years of Mandela's presidency saw riotous conditions inside gaols like Pollsmoor in the Cape after unrealistic expectations of mass amnesty and 'freedom' on an exaggerated scale were not met (*The Number* 271–276). However, white bosses in the command structure gave way to people of colour fairly quickly, and the new prison directors had their own ideas about running institutions of incarceration. One new manager in particular, Johnny Jansen, decided to turn the prison around, from an authoritarian, violent and mistrustful institution to a place where the governors and inmates might forge a common language. As a man of colour himself, Jansen had experienced the humiliation of racial discrimination at the hands of his former white bosses, '[s]o he believed that he knew why the men in his charge had murdered and raped; their psyches had been mangled by the collective humiliation of apartheid' (319). 'I don't think the solution to crime is so complicated,' Jansen says to Steinberg in the course of *The Number*. 'Human beings are supposed to be simple. They didn't become what they are by choice, but by their circumstances. If you expose them to different ways of doing things, it is like giving a child a new toy' (319). Steinberg continues:

> It was all charmingly romantic. Human beings are naturally good: apartheid had deformed their souls. Jansen himself had almost succumbed to the cancer of racial humiliation; he had wanted to kill. But he was better now, a fully-fledged human being, and he was going to shepherd his flock back to goodness: one victim of apartheid taking the rest by the hand. (319)

Romantic it may well have been, but at this point, Jansen as a senior prison boss is engaged in something quite astonishing in any prison environment, let alone one inextricably linked with apartheid – he is structuring a management revolution in a discourse associated with redemption. It is surely not accidental that healing discourse of this kind was also being used, at the same time, by the TRC, which was in fact sitting in the period that Jansen launched his initiative (1997–1998). The redemptive version of the transition story so key to post-apartheid mythography, then, is played out inside Pollsmoor, one of South Africa's biggest prisons. And, given the confined space of prison, its urgent pressures, Pollsmoor witnesses a dramatic, larger-than-life version of the promise, and outcome, of the transition narrative. Is it fiction or reality? Can it be made to work? What is more, Steinberg's interlocutor, Wentzel, comes to internalise this redemptive promise (for reasons that are skilfully narrated in *The Number*), and so his story – and *The Number* – gain an enhanced significance as postapartheid documents: alongside the TRC, they bear witness to momentous currents of change, and the power of narrative to reconstitute the self.

In the course of Jansen's ambitious programme, he recruits the Centre for Conflict Resolution (CCR) to come to Pollsmoor. Jansen wants the CCR to conduct conflict resolution workshops for warders and inmates. 'These were heady days at Pollsmoor,' Steinberg comments. 'Its young coloured managers wanted to reinvent the prison; they were searching hungrily for ideas' (323). The CCR people succeeded in changing the prison 'profoundly', Steinberg writes, 'at least for a while' (323). During their first 18 months at Pollsmoor, the CCR consultants established a workshop involving inmates and warders 'in an endeavour to unstitch the coarse and violent practices apartheid had bequeathed to the prison' (323). The 18 inmates in the workshop consisted mostly of Number gang leaders and members of the inmate committee. The workshop was based on psychological research around 'human dynamics'. A second course involved 'creative and constructive approaches to conflict', while another on trauma debriefing was conducted by clinical psychologist Stephen van Houten (326). 'It was the first time ever for some prisoners,' Van Houten reported, 'that they were able to verbalise their traumatic childhoods and/or their crimes.' Steinberg sees in this a transformative moment:

> That, indeed, is much of what the workshops were about for Magadien. At the age of 39 he learned a foreign language, a language of self. It opened the door to an entirely new universe. The idea that one can make of one's life a project, an internal and inward-gazing project, that one can retrieve the most intimate of one's memories, work on them, shape them into a single narrative of meaning – this was radically foreign, and a revelation. (326)

There is a clear similarity between Ndebele's 'restoration of narrative' and Steinberg's 'narrative of meaning', both of which enable affirmative reclamation of previously distorted and mangled senses of self. In addition, the correspondences between this 'foreign' notion of trauma debriefing and self-shaping in Pollsmoor, on the one hand, and similar processes going on in the TRC, on the other, cannot go unremarked. During the optimistic, early phase of transition, public discourse about the project of democracy seized the language of healing and reparation, of making good, all of it involving what one might call projects of reoriented selfhood. The late justice minister Dullah Omar regarded the Commission as 'a necessary exercise to enable South Africans to come to terms with their past on a morally accepted basis and to advance the cause of reconciliation'.[43] For Omar, healing the 'wounds of the past' (a common phrase in public discourse at the time) and avoiding further conflict meant building 'a human rights culture', for which 'disclosure of the truth and its acknowledgement are essential'. Omar went further, declaring 'truth' the fulcrum of the public healing process: 'The fundamental issue for all South Africans is therefore to come to terms with our past on the only moral basis possible, namely that the truth be told, and that the truth be acknowledged.'[44] This publicly enshrined, redemptive understanding of 'truth' struck home forcefully as the TRC hearings and their media reverberations echoed in the public imagination. This was the secular redemption[45] of postapartheid at work, and it paralleled the remarkable literary event of Krog's *Country of My Skull*, published in 1998. As suggested earlier, Krog's amalgam of reporting and lyrical writing, drawing on testimony and, to a lesser extent, memoir – some of it fabricated for effect – established 'creative nonfiction' as an ascendant form of literary intermediation in postapartheid writing. 'Truth' – the real thing, wheat that had been sifted and gleaned from the chaff of lies and 'fictions' – became a discursive imperative in both the more general public sphere and in the delimited literary realm. It ushered in a widespread public emphasis on embracing an unadulterated brand of scrupulous, ethical communication after decades of official prevarication and private denial. Such utterance of bare truth, such painful unearthing of repressed psychic material, is clearly of a different category to the notion of a reified 'real' – a category that literary scholars correctly dismiss as simplistic or banal, citing the interpenetration of fictional and real elements in both fictional and nonfictional utterances. Certainly, even TRC testimony is likely to contain storytelling elements that are constructed after the fact, ingredients that might be seen as 'fictive', but the categorical insistence on the primacy of a discourse of truth and truth-telling – in contradistinction to lying and repressing, withholding and twisting – should be seen for what it was in the late 1990s, going into the 2000s, in postapartheid time and space: an urgently revelatory, cleansing process.[46] At least, that was the aim, if not always the outcome. Fiction, until the mid-1990s the pre-eminent form for intermediating higher 'truth' in South African culture, now had to take a back seat, finding its place in the internal registers of a discourse of 'healing', a revelatory brand of truth containing the much-needed 'real' content of what had happened, and what was still going on, out there.[47] This was a discourse that borrowed from the conventions of storytelling, but which saw its main business as excavating repressed registers of selfhood and community.

Postapartheid, then, becomes a voluminous, many-tiered space of stories, a house with many rooms, one might say. At the TRC, the stories came in the form of testimony and witnessing, often in broken registers of language that seemed inadequate to the task of expressing the trauma at hand. In the process, what Krog would later come to call the country's new common language of 'bad English' came into prominence.[48] In the prisons, the 'foreign language' that Steinberg talks about, what he calls 'a language of self', opening the door to 'an entirely new universe' in which 'one can retrieve the most intimate of one's memories, work on them, shape them into a single narrative of meaning', coincided also with the adoption of English. 'It was foreign,' Steinberg continues, 'not only in the sense that the language of self is largely a bourgeois language, a million miles from the way a man of the ghettos thinks about himself. It was quite literally spoken in a different language: the workshops were largely conducted in English.' So, Wentzel, a mother-tongue Afrikaans-speaker, comes to use English as 'a significant part of his internal dialogue; many of his most intimate thoughts he could only think in English' (326).

Exactly the same thing was happening in the public sphere at large, and it is exemplified in the way in which Krog, a formerly Afrikaans poet, was partly transformed into an English writer of creative non-fiction. In 'Antjie Krog, Self and Society', Anthea Garman has written suggestively about how overlapping public 'fields' such as the media field, the literary field and the political field exerted pressure on Krog to produce *Country of My Skull*.[49] First, in her capacity as a radio reporter on the TRC hearings, Krog was invited to write long-form

pieces for the *Mail & Guardian* by that weekly's then editor Anton
Harber. These harrowing pieces had a strong political impact, and
Krog was approached by Random House. She supplemented the
pieces, and *Country of My Skull* has come to rival even Alan Paton's
Cry, the Beloved Country in its global reach. Just as Paton's book stood
as a masterpiece that captured the pain of racial conflict for all the
world to see and feel, so *Country of My Skull* spoke to the world of the
new drama in postapartheid South Africa – its reckoning with Truth.
In the wake of significant international uptake, both works eventually
became Hollywood movies. Both, in a sense, inaugurated a certain
tradition of writing: Paton set the tone for the liberal novel (and realism in general) as a leading form for relaying apartheid conditions,
while Krog's work stood as a major example of how a new form of
nonfiction might mediate postapartheid conditions;[50] as life-writing, it
is a lyrical blend of the real and its retelling, making free use of fictive
devices. Such writing conjoined the perceived need to unveil truth, on
the one hand, and, on the other, to reconstruct a viable 'language of
the self' for traumatised South Africans – a by no means simple task.

The 'language of the self' under the spotlight here, conducted
mostly in English, amounted to what Steinberg calls the working
and shaping of memories into a 'narrative of meaning' in the wake
of democracy. This specifically *narrative* capacity was perceived as a
revelatory opening, a rupture of enormous significance. Despite the
'language of self' being bourgeois, 'a million miles from the way a
man of the ghettos thinks about himself', it took hold in literate public
discourse. Moreover, it stuck, not only in Steinberg's own remarkable
series of memory-shaping true stories – books that came to be seen as
the cutting edge of postapartheid writing, winning a slew of prizes –
but also in a run of 'truth' books displaying the diversity of forms
characteristic of postapartheid literature.[51]

The 'language of self' that Steinberg captured in prison discourse
was, moreover, also key to the rise of identity politics in public contestations, as witnessed in the heated exchanges about Pippa Skotnes's
Miscast exhibition, soon followed by similarly bruising arguments
over Brett Murray's satirical painting *The Spear*.[52] In academic discourse, too, the politics of identity found strong expression in partisan critical readings of writers like Zoë Wicomb, Gabeba Baderoon
and Yvette Christiansë, among others, whose work has been taken
as affirming the agency of subject positions marginalised in the past

on the basis of gender and race. In a broader sense, life-writing as a genre became a means to self-discovery, self-expression and self-affirmation on the basis of ethnicity/race, gender or sexual orientation. Creative writing programmes in the postapartheid years confirm this trend. 'Everyone has a story to tell' was a common refrain in the new culture of bearing witness, the opening up of self and past. Fiction often seemed irrelevant, even meretricious. There were too many stories waiting to be told, and a strong conviction that such stories needed to be given utterance, 'voiced' in a wave of speaking out and talking back to decades of power abuse and of silencing; all this for the sake of healing a traumatic and troubled past, of restoring agency to citizens. Who would wish to argue with such virtuous uses of culture, such powerful possibilities of restitution in the aesthetic forms of a scarred country? One only had to attend a poetry reading at Wits University or the Poetry Africa festival, or listen to the InZync poets of the Stellenbosch Literary Project (SLiP), to hear self-making in full flow, talking back sharply, and with verve, to earlier histories of denigration and dehumanisation.[53] The works of 'spoken-word' poets such as Lebo Mashile, Jitsvinger, Koleka Putuma, and the Botsotso Jesters energetically took up the language of self-making and celebration, bringing into being an assertive new lyricism: We are here; This is who we are; This is how we speak; We will not go away. For many, not forgetting the growing legions of spoken-word poets and their fans, this brand of self-assertive speaking out is the core, the real point, of postapartheid life, whether in 'bad' English, 'Kaaps', 'Boland rap' or any other 'creolisation'.[54] This new performance culture has little to do with rarefied literary fiction. The spoken-word performances almost always conjoin individual experience with hip-hop and rap avowals of gender politics, self-discovery in challenging conditions, and the remaking of identity in the unstable conurbations of twenty-first-century metropolitan living. Whether one likes it or not – and many don't – these challenging, defiant forms constitute a powerful and insistent force in the locales of cultural reception.

For Magadien Wentzel – alias 'JR', 'William Steenkamp', 'Darryl' – the TRC-style language of self, rooted in reckonings with the real rather than the denials and fabrications of apartheid and its aftermath, gave him something of inestimable value: the ability to consolidate his various, spurious identities. Here was an opportunity to story himself into a new being, for if Mandela's revolution itself wasn't able to open the prison gates, then individual subjects could take hold of their memories and experiences and reshape them into something of worth, a story with dignity and purpose. Wentzel switches from Afrikaans to English for this encounter. This is true also for Krog in *Country of My Skull*, as she embraces the redemption narrative of postapartheid in English, for her a second language. Steinberg writes of Wentzel: 'And so everything about his new experience smacked of revelation, of a radical rupture, just as certain Christians describe the sudden presence of God in one's life' (326). In his conversations with Steinberg, the 'jargon of psychology' slips into Wentzel's language, in his use of phrases such as 'I need closure' (327). Steinberg realises he is witnessing something remarkable:

> Journeying with him back to his past, I felt we were two outsiders looking into the world of a stranger. The tools he used to think about his history were not available to him when he lived it. There is a sense in which he was re-inventing his past when he spoke to me, using his new knowledge to write a history of himself. (327)

The question, of course, is whether the rewritten history of self can hold up in the face of adverse material conditions once Wentzel is finally released from prison. In Wentzel's case, the narrative of mostly secular redemption (he does align himself with religion from time to time) wears thin as actual circumstances make it difficult for him to maintain an adequate standard of living outside of crime. Wentzel does, however, succeed in resisting the invitations of various former crime partners to take the easy way out. Despite the tough conditions and relative poverty he faces once out of prison, he holds onto the riches of what one might call symbolic deliverance. At a Sunday religious service held in Pollsmoor in the early 2000s, Wentzel 'got up and denounced the gangs in the name of Jesus', something 'he remembers…as one of the bravest actions he has ever taken' (327). Johnny Jansen's prison reforms, even in the sceptical view of Steinberg, prove to be 'astoundingly successful' (328), and Wentzel himself becomes, before his release, a 'minor celebrity at Pollsmoor'. He would be 'wheeled out for all visitors' because 'Pollsmoor was doing well, beyond the wildest expectations, and the change managers wanted to show off their good work', inviting all and sundry to the prison to come see for themselves (331). By late 2002, Steinberg writes, Wentzel 'was being booked out of Pollsmoor to meet the world' (331). The 'relentlessly energetic' Jansen co-founded a modest community-based organisation called Ukukhanya Kwemini Association (UKA) (331). Jansen felt he needed to take the message outside prison, to the communities from which the inmates came. And so, in October 2002, Jansen takes Wentzel with him on a car trip into the Klein Karoo to visit the town of Ladismith. They meet with members of the UKA board of directors and, that night, Magadien addresses a packed Ladismith community hall. The next day he speaks at the local school's morning assembly.

> The way he tells it, he was the town's hero for a day. 'I spoke straight to their hearts. To the kids I described the horrors of prison. I told them prison does not make you a man, it fucks you up and rapes you and then throws you out. I said that no human being who cares for himself will want to go to prison. To the parents, I said how I had fucked up the task of bringing up my own kids. I said that in some homes, you have three generations sitting around smoking drugs together. I said we had to rebuild some sanity in our communities.
>
> 'They all crowded round me after my speech in the town hall. A woman came up to me and hugged me and burst into tears. She explained that her son was in prison.
>
> 'It was one of the greatest moments of my life. The Uka delegation all had dinner in a restaurant that night. I was served by a waiter for the first time in my life. I ordered chicken livers for starters. It was my first taste of food outside the prison since 1998. I savoured every mouthful. I felt I could learn to eat properly again.
>
> 'I looked round the restaurant, and looked at myself eating in the restaurant. I thought to myself: "I am somebody now. I am a decent human being, someone a waiter takes an order from."
>
> 'I laughed at myself. I thought: "I have dignity now...".' (332)

This is a significant moment, on several levels. The restitution of dignity via the power of narrative is a high point for Wentzel personally, and it provides an example of postapartheid discourse delivering the tangible, felt benefit of self-reclamation. This is a yield that might come in various ways: in the form of self-storying (richly evident in the passage above); in the repossession of dignity via identity solidarity (for example, as a victim of male abuse; a Xhosa poet; a Rastafarian; an urban, hip-hop spoken-word artist from the townships); or in any of the other positions that were becoming available, both in the public space of liberated political discourse and in the spaces opening up on the internet and in the new media. Anyone could set up a website, start blogging, publish their own writing, post on Facebook and start aggregating an audience. The forms of public expression available to formerly silenced people seemed similar to TRC-style reckonings, potentially freeing the body politic of its psychic horrors, and helping to reconstitute people as full citizens rather than mere 'subjects' (see Mamdani).

Wentzel holds out, against the odds, in the story narrated in *The Number* – and it is important that this is indeed a true story. However, the story outside of Steinberg's narrative, the story of self-recovery, wears thin as Wentzel's 'minor celebrity' status slowly evaporates after his release from prison and his work with UKA runs aground. Still, Wentzel clings to his story as he gets poorer and more desperate, begrudgingly accepting charity from his hard-up in-laws, in whose backyard 'Wendy house' he lives in Manenberg, estranged from his wife, Faranaaz, and increasingly at odds with her family. He manages to hold out, right to the end, when he phones Steinberg to declare that he has found the love he has spent his life searching for (416). Whether this love will hold out or not is less the issue than the fact that the story of it – a redemptive narrative – at one point nourished Wentzel's sense of self.

Wentzel's story, folded into a larger discourse of truth reclamation, is individually empowering, speaking to the power of narrative as a means for constructing a truth about oneself, a story that one can live with. Such narrative also functions as a potent social force, as Jane Taylor – who collaborated with William Kentridge in the production of *Ubu and the Truth Commission* – suggests:

> What has engaged me as I have followed the Commission, is the way in which individual narratives come to stand for the larger national narrative. The stories of personal grief, loss, triumph and violation now stand as an account of South Africa's recent past. History and autobiography merge. This marks a significant shift, because in the past decades of popular resistance, personal

suffering was eclipsed – subordinated to a larger project of mass liberation. Now, however, we hear in individual testimony the very private patterns of language and thought that structure memory and mourning. *Ubu and the Truth Commission* uses these circumstances as a starting point. (ii)

Echoing Ndebele and Steinberg, Taylor contends that the merging of 'history and autobiography' in the making of 'the larger national narrative' speaks directly to a discourse of self. The latter is a means to achieve a level of truth that is potentially redemptive, a means of deliverance from the past. The terms 'reality' and 'fiction' in this book's subtitle gesture to the strong urge, identified here by Taylor, towards merging stories of self-making and 'history', and they also point to the productive tensions between 'fiction' and 'reality' with their multiple meanings.

2

From the subject of evil to the evil subject

Cultural difference in postapartheid South African crime fiction

One of the more energetic debates about postapartheid South African literature revolves around the question of why genre fiction, and more particularly crime fiction, so heavily saturates the book market. This debate has often been conducted anecdotally or superficially in reviews and comments on literary websites, despite scattered journal articles and one or two special issues on the topic.[1] Particularly contested has been my own suggestion that crime thrillers may have come to stand in for what used to be seen as political or engaged fiction, in response to which some academics have argued that the generic or formulaic nature of detective novels precludes them from a nuanced treatment of sociopolitical issues.[2] A common strand has been the contention that it is far-fetched to assume that genre fiction can engage with political themes in the manner of Gordimer, Langa, Mda or Serote. A great deal of this commentary appears in the form of stabs of opinion in the comment threads of digital media, and as such does not penetrate much beyond provisional position-taking.

An exception to this trend is Michael Titlestad and Ashlee Polatinsky's essay 'Turning to Crime: Mike Nicol's *The Ibis Tapestry* and *Payback*', in which the authors argue that Nicol's own turn from serious fiction (as exemplified by his 1998 novel *The Ibis Tapestry*) to the popular form of crime fiction (as in his 2008 novel *Payback*) represents an unfortunate withdrawal from more serious literary writing in which matters are, fittingly, in a state of unresolved tension.

Instead of keeping faith with the open-form novel, Nicol gives way to the temptation of neat but ultimately superficial gestures of closure. Although Titlestad and Polatinsky do not say so explicitly, there is in their argument a strong sense of disappointment that an outstanding South African author, in the older, more serious vein of South African writing, should 'sell out' to the seductions of a popular market where trite 'answers' are laid out in accordance with the norms of the genre. For Titlestad and Polatinsky, the intense grappling of pre-2000 writing with the challenges of cultural difference – how to give people of all ethnic, gender and class variations their due – appears to have given way to 'thriller' computations of the social totality. Nicol's neo-noir[3] palette, for Titlestad and Polatinsky, amounts to premature closure, as if the new democracy is little more than a motley gangland version of the rainbow nation. Reading Titlestad and Polatinsky, one finds it difficult not to agree that, if it is indeed true that crime fiction mostly dishes out cheap closure, such totalisation would be premature, to say the least. The sense of disinvestment so brought about, a divestiture of multilayered texture and imponderable complexity for the sake of superficial resolution and easy entertainment, is helped along by some of Nicol's own statements. These utterances (as disingenuous, perhaps, as Athol Fugard's protestations that his writing is 'not polit-ical') make the case that Nicol has abandoned serious fiction to write 'commercial fiction' because he supposedly enjoys it more, and it sells better.[4] So, in a sense, Titlestad and Polatinsky's article reads as a kind of parable for a literature that has 'lost the plot', abandoning its moral compass and its sense of direction. This, indeed, is a common theme in discussions of postapartheid writing (see Frenkel and MacKenzie). One might argue that, being lost, this new writing has surrendered to the quick fix of genre fiction, though with a patina of political content in its preoccupation with social violence, or 'crime'. Given the subtext of Titlestad and Polatinsky's argument, one is invited to read the story of a once-great literature, with redoubtable names like Breytenbach, Brink, Coetzee, Gordimer, Hope, Langa, Leroux, Matshoba, Mda, Mphahlele, Ndebele, Serote, Van Heerden, Van Niekerk and Vladislavić, against an alarming recent trend of 'dumbing down'. The post-transitional genre writers are seen as copping out of the real deal, i.e. complexity and openness, for the sake of quick-sell entertainment. These supposedly cheap tricks, in addition, feed off a still-volatile soci-ety in a manner which, some might claim, borders on the unethical.

Titlestad and Polatinsky's argument is generally sound and well executed, though Christopher Warnes ('Writing Crime' 983) detects a 'popular' and 'highbrow' binary in their reasoning. Without going into the merits of an argument that compels one to choose between 'high' and 'low' forms, I would like to suggest that there may be a different way of looking at Nicol's work, and that of other crime writers. This chapter, then, asks a different question of crime fiction, one which might be introduced as follows: what if one were to read the large (although by no means universal) shift from, let's say, social-realist 'complexity' to crime-detective 'genre', as something else entirely? This would involve reading the genre as symptomatic of a bigger movement, of a seismic social shift. What if the upsurge in South African 'crime writing', in all its forms,[5] rather than selling out on intricate 'entanglement' (see Nuttall, *Entanglement*), is in fact prising open the workings of a genuinely transformed social condition? This is a condition, moreover, that is no longer just national, just 'South African', but transnational in its dimensions, and global in its derivations.

The question, then, might be posed thus: why this obsession, in the new millennium, with law and (dis)order, and more particularly with the spectacle of 'crime', as presented in mediated forms such as fiction and nonfiction writing? Articulated in this way, the question leads us away from the ultimately futile war of opinion about whether or not crime fiction is sufficiently 'literary', or adequately complex as an object of formal literary architecture. Instead, it concentrates attention on the questions: what is this fiction about? And what is it doing out there? This, indeed, is the issue to which Warnes also directs scholars of South African writing, suggesting that writers such as Meyer and Orford 'keep faith with some of the core features of "serious" South African literature: its capacity to document social reality, to expose injustice, and to conscientise readers into different modes of thought and action' ('Writing Crime' 983). I would add a further set of 'core' questions which the literary scholar might address: why the relatively sudden, and major, shift in circulation and reception from liberal-humanist and late-modern forms of fiction to genre-based novels? To what larger socio-historical complex might this be attributed, as a more general syndrome? This is a by no means uninteresting question, and one that Warnes seems not to probe sufficiently, merely resting his case on the argument that 'the postapartheid crime thriller should be read as negotiating – in the ambivalent sense of the word – the threat and uncertainty that many feel to be part of South African life, creating fantasies of control, restoration and maintenance, and reflecting on the circumstances that gave rise to this unease' ('Writing Crime' 991). But what of the greater complex of circumstances that underlie the 'threat and uncertainty' that Warnes identifies?

Cultural difference in a postapartheid frame

My argument commences with an overview of the changing role of cultural difference before and after the political transition of the 1990s. For several decades now, postcolonial theory, not to mention grassroots cultural politics, has encouraged an emphasis on cultural difference as a modifier of political subjectivity and identitarian position-taking. More general studies of cultural difference in its many dimensions, such as those by Homi Bhabha, Edward Said, Gayatri Spivak and Robert Young,[6] in addition to local ones by, inter alia, Attwell, Duncan Brown and Wylie,[7] have tended to place the spotlight on the many ways in which cultural difference has been misrecognised, in the colonies and the Orient, within reductive epistemic frames of reference. The centuries-long discourse around the 'wild man',[8] primitivism, exoticism and other categories, including the fixations of social-Darwinist thought and biological racism,[9] found a rebuttal in postcolonial theory and revisionist cultural history, most emphatically perhaps in Said's *Orientalism*, and stretching beyond literary and cultural criticism to empirically founded historical works of epistemic redress such as Dipesh Chakrabarty's *Provincializing Europe*. JM Coetzee's South African novels may be said to deal with the politics of cultural difference in one way or another. The same is true for Nadine Gordimer and legions of other novelists working in the pre-2000 period. A common strain is the sense that cultural difference has been mismanaged in both colonial and neocolonial contexts, not to mention neoliberal conditions; also, vigilance regarding all forms of difference – whether relating to race, gender, ethnicity, language or culture – remains an important ethical task. It is also fair to suggest that South Africa's negotiated settlement put in place (at least via the justice system and the Constitution) a process of remediation. By 1994, racial discrimination and the mismanagement of difference came to be seen by all except the far right as a universal evil, as the very subject of evil. By this time, apartheid, solidly based on the segregationist foundation laid by more than three centuries of colonialism, had been declared a crime against humanity; now, after the advent of full democracy, even the insiders of apartheid, the privileged whites, were persuaded to accept that 'rainbowism' – a symbolic figuration of 'good' or equitable cultural difference peculiar to South Africa's late 'revolution' – was a virtuous state of being.[10] For a short while during President Nelson Mandela's five years of rule, rainbowism was enthusiastically promoted, not least by its originator, Archbishop Desmond Tutu, and Mandela himself, who will be remembered for, among other things, magnanimously taking tea in the white 'homeland' of Orania with Betsy, widow of apartheid's architect, Dr Hendrik Frensch Verwoerd.

The cultural-difference rainbow, in its fresh phase, was fleeting. Starting around the ANC's second term of office in 1999, and the ascension to the presidency of the remote, less conciliatory Thabo Mbeki, a pervasive current of disillusionment set in. This occurred amid widespread perceptions of, first, the consolidation of a neoliberal form of 'class apartheid' in a 'choiceless democracy' (Bond, 'Mandela Years' n.p.) and, second, an emerging political discourse which was race-inflected to a degree that many found uncomfortable. One example of the new focus on race – particularly the valorisation of 'pure' blackness – was the controversy over the Mbeki-supported 'Native Club',[11] which was part of a bigger pattern that Finlay describes as typifying the Mbeki presidency up to 2008: '[A] polarity in public exchanges dealing with race that, for many, felt quite different from the spirit of the preceding period, where notions of nonracialism and inclusivity were the guiding ideology of state decision and the *zeitgeist* of public discussion' (Finlay 36).

To the ire of many long-standing nonracialists, the Native Club, closely affiliated with President Mbeki's office, was open to black intellectuals only. Such exclusionary discourse and practice was widely perceived to signal the emergence of an unwelcome racial essentialism. It was perceived as abrogating the very nonracialism for which the ANC had fought; the latter had grown out of the concept of equality, a key principle in the 1955 Freedom Charter. It was felt that here, once again, a particular race was being valorised. The spectre of a resuscitated variant of exclusionary preferment, and the hardening of this scab on the body of the 'new' South Africa, galled many 'new'

South Africans. Not least among such perceived defacements of the ideal of freedom and equality were the neoliberal economic policies which, combined with state corruption, were making conditions ripe for what Bond refers to as the 'crony-capitalist, corruption-riddled, brutally securitised, eco-destructive and anti-egalitarian regime' that South Africa today endures (Bond, 'Mandela Years' n.p.).

Bond's version is, of course, one strand in a complex story about what has gone 'wrong' in South Africa's transition to democracy. However, the fact that the widely held belief that democracy was 'failing' gained broad traction in the 2000s (see, for example, Xolela Mangcu's *To the Brink*). A 2008 conference at the University of the Witwatersrand had as its theme 'Paradoxes of the Postcolonial Public Sphere: Democracy at the Crossroads'. At this gathering, political analysts Ivor Chipkin and Mangcu, among others, sounded warnings about a disturbing narrative of 'national identity' that seemed to be increasingly normative, and exclusionary on a racial basis, in the ranks of the governing party. In his book, Mangcu critiques what he describes as the 'racial nativism' (*To the Brink* xiii ff.) of the Mbeki government, calling for a renewed acceptance of 'irreducible plurality' and a return to the traditions of nonracialism (*To the Brink* 119).[12] Such Mbeki-era 'racial nativism' landed with a threatening thud among South African cultural and political analysts, many of whom were familiar with Kwame Anthony Appiah's cautionary remarks on the 'topologies of nativism' (*Father's House* 47–72). Appiah and other postcolonial thinkers in Homi Bhabha's *Nation and Narration* perceived essentialised versions of 'national identity,' especially racialised national identity, as running counter to trends that had prevailed in critical theory since the Paris upheavals of 1968. It could no longer be assumed that the 'new' South Africa was on board in the larger progressive project of dismantling hegemonic and/or foundational fixities of identity. This is not to mention the bad taste such a return to ethnic fixations left in the mouth of Fanonites who feared the emergence of corrupt ruling elites, a comprador class wont to lose the plot of its own self-made 'revolution'. Yet far from being unique in this regard, postapartheid South Africa was merely a late entrant to a global club, from north to south and west to east, in which newly constituted democratic regimes have suffered routine 'breakdown' (see Linz and Stepan).

It is not my purpose here to test and probe such positions or their prior historical conditions, but rather to note the resurgence of alarm about new orthodoxies of national identity, and new forms of differential preferment, perceived as contradictory to the promise of the negotiated South African settlement. Mbeki's promised African Renaissance has been followed by the era of Zuma: instead of rebirth and restoration, there is a new clamour demanding the fall of villains, from Rhodes to Zuma. It is common cause that the democratic ideal has been profoundly compromised, culminating in a system of patrimonialism with President Zuma at its apex.

In a 2013 commentary, Achille Mbembe remarks on the state of the country:

> South Africa has entered a new period of its history: a post-Machiavellian moment when private accumulation no longer happens through outright dispossession but through the capture and appropriation of public resources, the modulation of brutality and the instrumentalisation of disorder. ('Our Lust for Lost Segregation' n.p.)

For Mbembe, South Africa in 2013 is not immune from the 'mixture of clientelism, nepotism and prebendalism' common to African postcolonies, and he observes that an 'armed society' such as South Africa is 'hardly a democracy'; it is, he writes, 'mostly an assemblage of atomised individuals isolated before power, separated from each other by fear, prejudice, mistrust and suspicion, and prone to mobilise under the banner of either a mob, a clique or a militia rather than an idea and, even less so, a disciplined organization'.

'Bad' difference – a new evil?

My focus is the relationship between crime stories and a growing public disquiet about social disorder. The new wave of fiction works on the assumption that a fresh and perverse form of officially sanctioned 'bad' cultural difference has become a justification for civil mismanagement, perhaps even for what Mbembe refers to as the 'instrumentalisation of disorder'. 'Bad' difference is coming to be perceived as a sinister recuperation of elitism, so that detection, as spun into detective stories by a new generation of writers, has become a matter of exposing 'bad' difference and its legitimating rationalisations, its postures and pretexts, marking it as the shadow side of legitimate cultural difference. Such socially 'conscientising' writing, in Warnes's words ('Writing Crime' 983), seeks to demonstrate how 'bad' difference goes about its disingenuous work. If the 'transition' itself is opaque and barely credible, with so little apparent social change, in hard economic terms, especially for the poor,[13] then such detection and exposure is – perhaps inevitably – the task of the writer. In such an understanding of the writer's role, the author seeks to show what's actually going on, or at least to suggest a theory, a revised version of the lost plot, where a calculated guess is made. The task for the writer (and the critic), then, is to make the transition – or the myth of transition – visible and tractable by plotting its characters, their sphere of operation, their motives and modus operandi, and, ultimately, their actions and their social meaning. Political operatives who were 'good' in the past, under conditions of disenfranchisement, now often become 'bad' holders of power. At least, this would often appear to be the hidden meaning of the transition. Power is perceived as a motor of corruption. The implicit question is: has South Africa, beset with resurgent violence and disorder, truly moved on from apartheid? The answer, it seems, is dubious, to say the least.

Racial and cultural difference, as affirmed by the South African Constitution, particularly in its clauses guaranteeing equality, suggests a symmetry whereby the component parts of a diverse society enjoy equal rights. This may be termed 'good' difference. On the other hand, however, conditions in South African society have, since 1994, produced what may be termed 'bad' or corrupt difference, which uses the legitimising politics of cultural difference (identity politics) to achieve asymmetrical gain, often at the expense of others. 'Bad' difference is, then, the abuse of political privilege in order to leverage preferment, often under the guise of egalitarian practice. One example of this is the South African arms deal, while another is President Jacob Zuma's relationship with the Gupta family, which enables privileges such as the use of a military airfield for private purposes. 'Bad' cultural difference in such cases enables corrupt collaborative practices in state as well as private-sector dealings characteristic of comprador societies. Materialist critics like Bond see government's role in this as a form of class betrayal, with the postapartheid order constituting 'class apartheid' ('Mandela Years' n.p.); in this system, advocates for the poor gain capital leverage based on an 'empowerment for all' ticket. This chimes with what the new generation of Black Consciousness proponents, such as Andile Mngxitama, claim.[14]

For crime writers, the existence of corrupted or 'bad' difference is detected in a range of public and private spaces: within government itself (more specifically, its corrupt officials and their cronies, as in Nicol's works); among criminals, which often includes (degenerate, sold-out) members of the South African Police Service, formerly the South African Police Force (as in Roger Smith's *Mixed Blood*); or in civil society, where 'bad' alliances between distinct subsets, often in cahoots with state functionaries, create distortions of 'civil' practice (as in Margie Orford's *Gallows Hill* and Andrew Brown's *Refuge*). For writers in the postapartheid period, the easier-to-define moral order of anti-apartheid or struggle literature has disappeared, and they are compelled to work out a new way of seeing things. Here, the boundaries of right and wrong, of good and bad, have shifted and need to be redefined. Disorder, rule-breaking and malfeasance have saturated the private and public spheres to such an extent that virtuous conduct and wrongdoing are frequently blurred. Addressing this is no easy task, and the postapartheid fictional terrain dramatises a reconfigured contest over law and order in which the borderlines of legitimate and illegitimate are frequently under erasure. So pervasive is crime that neither the state nor any civil grouping has a monopoly over violence or legitimacy. The terrain is one of moral ambiguity, where newly validated cultural 'difference' becomes complicit in a gory inversion of the rule of law.

Postcolonial law and (dis)order

Rita Barnard draws attention to the manner in which the postapartheid state has brought with it 'new patterns of inclusion and exclusion, new meanings of citizenship, and new dimensions of sovereignty and power' (Barnard, 'Tsotsis' 561–562; see also Steinberg, 'Crime'). One aspect of this newer set-up, according to Barnard, is that 'minimal government, under pressure from a frightened citizenry (redefined as consumers and victims), can readily turn into its authoritarian opposite' ('Tsotsis' 565). For Jean and John Comaroff, the former colonial state evinces a particular preoccupation with the law, amounting at times to a fetishisation of legality. The preoccupation with law and legality, write the Comaroffs, runs deeper than 'purely a concern with crime' (*Law and Disorder* 32). This is an important consideration, since 'crime' in South African discourse is a problematic signifier, capturing very incompletely a more generalised scene of social instability. It has to do, the Comaroffs argue, 'with the very constitution of the postcolonial polity', since the 'modernist nation-state appears to be undergoing an epochal move away from the ideal of an imagined community founded on the fiction, often violently sustained, of cultural homogeneity, toward a nervous, xenophobically tainted sense of heterogeneity and heterodoxy' (32). The rise of neoliberalism, the authors continue, 'has heightened all this, with its impact on population movements, on the migration of work and workers, on the dispersion of cultural practices, on the return of the colonial oppressed to haunt the cosmopoles that once ruled them and wrote their histories' (33). Such effects 'are felt especially in former colonies, which were erected from the first on difference' (33).

Now, difference strikes back at the former colonies: '[P]ostcolonials are citizens for whom polymorphous, labile identities coexist in uneasy ensembles of political subjectivity'; such citizens tend not to attach their sense of destiny to the nation, but rather to 'an ethnic, cultural, language, religious, or some other group', despite the fact that subjects such as these do not necessarily reject their national identity (33). What are often labelled as communal loyalties (Abahlali baseMjondolo[15] for example, or migrants from other parts of Africa who have been the subject of xenophobic attacks) 'are frequently blamed for the kinds of violence, nepotism, and corruption said to saturate these societies, as if cultures of heterodoxy bear within them the seeds of criminality, difference, disorder' (33).

It is worth backtracking to give a more complete account of how the Comaroffs reach the rather startling conclusion that cultures of heterodoxy produce criminality and disorder as correlates of difference. How has it come about that the role of cultural difference, such a critical factor in the history of many postcolonies, could have shifted so drastically from a perceived virtue to something resembling a matrix for criminality?

The first step is to sketch the context in which such a keen preoccupation with the law, legality and its abrogation in the postcolony might be found – most recently, postapartheid South Africa.

Drawing on a wide range of case studies and ethnographic scholar-ship, the Comaroffs find that 'law and disorder' are constitutive of a social base in which legality and criminality depend on and feed off each other in an enhanced, or accentuated, manner. 'Vastly lucrative returns … inhere in actively sustaining zones of ambiguity between the presence and absence of the law'; in this way, value is amassed 'by exploiting the new aporias of jurisdiction opened up by neoliberal conditions' (*Law and Disorder* 5). In this environment, one might add, law enforcement officers feel at liberty to collaborate with underworld agents, helping to sustain sex-slavery rings in Cape Town amid a cha-otic and often dysfunctional criminal justice system, as *Noseweek*'s 2009 report indicates ('Trapped in Pollsmoor' n.p.).

Central to the Comaroffs' discussion about the consequences of neoliberalism in the postcolony is not only what one might call prevailing conditions of 'lawlessness', but also the widespread media representation of such conditions as 'bad'. Media versions of a venal, predatory approach to the 'free market' take their lead from an older, more equitable liberal rationality. Egalitarian political theory in South Africa, as expressed in a progressive liberal-democratic Constitution, exists in a state of disjuncture with socio-economic practice. The con-junction of 'neo' and 'liberal' creates a paradoxical nexus in which it is possible both to be part of a (benignly) liberal dispensation in the more traditional sense of this term, and to be part of its subver-sion – whether in the form of a corrupt police commissioner, or as an entrapped subject, caught in what is an essentially inequitable order of things. The crime writer often takes up the position of the galled citizenry, observing dirty doings in a newly created 'democratic' order that seems to belie, in its (reported) behaviour, every tenet of its underlying (liberal-democratic) ethos. Further, in the more reflexive writers' work, there is an awareness that the citizen so entrapped in witnessing widespread neoliberal quashing of what might be termed classical liberalism[16] is, willy-nilly, part of – i.e. caught within – the same system.[17] This kind of tension between an idealised notion of fairness and actual justice is consistently invoked in public discourse, such that it is almost a leitmotif. The persistent cancellation of the ideal of justice by practices that are essentially unfair typifies the post-colonial law/disorder condition in a similar way to that in neoliberal environments – though the edge is perhaps a little sharper, and the grain rougher, in the postcolony.

Ironically, in such conditions the law is fetishised, 'even as, in most postcolonies, higher and higher walls are built to protect the propertied from lawlessness, even as the language of legality insinuates itself deeper and deeper into the realm of the illicit' (*Law and Disorder* 22). Law and lawlessness, assert the Comaroffs, 'are conditions of each other's possibility' (21). And so, too, are these two leitmotifs of the postcolony inextricably linked in fictive imaginaries: citing Rosalind Morris, they write, '[m]ass mediation gives law and disorder a "communicative force" that permits it to "traverse the social field"' (21). These arguments appear to support Margie Orford's opinion[18] that crime fiction allows ordinary citizens imaginatively to traverse zones of law, and of the erasure of such laws; these are zones that are not generally open to anyone other than policemen and journalists. The 'crime' story is thus a 'communicative force' in which bolted-in, apprehensive citizens of the neoliberal postcolony can 'get out' and 'see' what might actually be going on in the dark of night, and in the clear light of day, too, in the frequently bewildering, unreadable postapartheid topography (see also, in this regard, my discussion of a 'wound culture' in Chapter 6).

Morris comments on the phenomenon of mediated 'crime' in South Africa: 'Transmitted along a myriad vectors, in televisual serials, newspaper columns, radio broadcasts, and music lyrics, crime is the phantom that haunts the new nation's imaginary' (61). Crime is both an event in the real world and a mediated condition feeding other fears and insecurities: 'Macabre tales of heavily armed robbers and single-minded carjackers, of remorseless murderers, and – most remarked of all – pedophilic rapists feed a national press that is insatiable for news of personalized catastrophe with which to signify or prophesy political failure' (61). Similarly, Gary Kynoch ('Fear and Alienation') argues for a deep preoccupation with narratives of lawlessness amid mounting political threat among whites in postapartheid South Africa.

'Crime' as an allegory for the sociopolitical

Understanding, interpreting, describing and responding to 'crime' in the 'new' South Africa therefore appears to be an everyday allegory for the sociopolitical terrain in a broad sense, speaking urgently to anxieties about very real conditions of social disorder.[19] '[T]he causes of crime's transformation are...usually construed in political terms,' argues Morris. 'Crime marks the boundary of the polis as much as any other wilderness,' she adds (61). Within such a sociopolitical milieu, regardless of finer points of form, genre or the writer's intention, writers ineluctably go to the heart of the political with every new narrative in which detection is imagined as a set of explorations across the social terrain, and the cause of a crime is sought within a chain of events in a dysfunctional polity.

Of course, many shades of the palette will be evident as writers seek to depict an emerging order through the lens of what a community deems to be 'criminal', in line with Emile Durkheim's credo that society learns to know itself by coming to understand the nature of its own criminal shadow. For Durkheim, crime – and more to the point, how people respond to its occurrence – provides a basis for the emergence of a normative consensus. 'Crime brings together upright consciences and concentrates them,' Durkheim wrote (103), and this continues to hold true more than a century later. The problem for South African writers on the cusp of the millennium, however, has often been the very equivocality – and contestation – of the line between legality and criminality, both in the civil and in the public sphere. The condition of 'plot loss' for such writers is acute: not only has the sociopolitical dispensation changed fundamentally, making what in the very recent past was illegal and unethical suddenly legal and right – and vice versa – but world politics, too, has undergone a disorienting transformation. In the 1990s, leading into the new millennium and beyond, two formerly discrete zones ('home' and the 'outside' world) began to play into each other, such that new levels of uncertainty bedevilled the general relief at having achieving a democratic consensus. In the wake of globalisation and its dramatic 1990s upsurge, the rules were rewritten across the transformed face of the world, especially for nations that had long defined themselves in relation to the antagonisms of the cold war. In addition, as Misha Glenny argues in *McMafia*, crime rapidly became a global network, creating new transnational alliances facilitated by globalisation.

Deon Meyer takes precisely the disambiguation of the post-1990 condition as his implicit task, his subtext, in his novel *Heart of the Hunter*. Meyer's hero in this tale, the muscled modern warrior, Thobela 'Tiny' Mpayipheli, embodies the intricate complexity of the postapartheid dispensation in several ways. Not only was Mpayipheli

schooled in cold war conditions as an MK soldier trained in Eastern
Europe under communist conditions; not only was he, too, 'forgotten'
by the ruling party upon his return from exile; he was also 'shopped'
by his political masters in the South African political underground
to the eastern Europeans as a crack assassin, in return for political
favours. Then, to make matters worse, this Xhosa 'hunter-warrior' –
associated explicitly in the text with a long line of precolonial cham-
pions, including Phalo, Maqoma and Ngqika – is abandoned by the
eastern Europeans after the fall of the Berlin Wall. They had been using
him as an unusually sharp cold-war assassin. Importantly, Meyer's
multi-layered 'plot' in this novel is built precisely upon the ruins of
earlier socio-historical plots: (i) the ANC's alliance with the USSR
and the communist world, all of which imploded on the eve of liberation in South Africa; (ii) the promised economic 'new deal' in South
Africa in the wake of what was supposed to be socialism's moral victory on the world stage – a deal that failed to materialise; the committed foot soldier of the revolution comes home to nothing, neither glory
nor compensation; (iii) the setting up of a working-class leadership in
a socialist republic – yet another conspicuous failure of intention. All
of these building blocks for what was long projected as a 'good' and
ideologically virtuous new South Africa had been swept away. The
ability to function like a sovereign state, or a relatively independent
entity, at least, was being critically undermined by the late-capitalist
world order, with its lack of respect for borders, in terms of money
flows particularly. (Unsurprisingly, it was during this period that the
'market-friendly' macro-economic strategy Growth, Employment
and Redistribution [GEAR], which emphasised tighter fiscal policy
and the loosening of foreign exchange controls, was formulated.)
Michael Allen's searching political-economic enquiry, *Globalization,
Negotiation, and the Future of Transformation in South Africa*, concludes (181–192) that the South African postapartheid state found
itself between a rock and a very hard place indeed as global economic
pressures increasingly set the agenda, especially for countries in the
developing or 'emerging' world seeking to achieve economic growth.

In search of the 'virtuous' postapartheid citizen

Meanwhile, inside the 'fragile, infant democracy' (*Heart of the
Hunter* 234) that Meyer's novel maps, matters are correspondingly

complicated. Gone is the old struggle order of good revolutionaries pitted against bad (mostly white) politicians, or commendable communists going up against exploitative Western capitalists. Now, in many instances, the government is at war with itself as certain alliance partners push to the left of an unstable centre and others, formerly rock-solid alliance partners, lurch to the right. Indeed, the terms 'left' and 'right' become increasingly unstable as 'left' easily becomes associated with a form of national socialism or fascism, evident in the case of the Economic Freedom Fighters (EFF).[20] At the same time, as enacted in *Heart of the Hunter*, separately constituted intelligence agencies (combining the information regimes of the former liberation armies with those of the former South African Defence Force and South African Police) find themselves crossing swords. The collateral damage that results from such intergovernmental feuds includes 'good' people like the struggle hero Mpayipheli and Miriam, his new love.[21] The 'good', as in 'good people', and how to define this in the 'new South Africa', ideologically speaking, was fast becoming a paradoxical category. And it is this blind spot about what exactly constitutes a 'good citizen', or a 'reasonable person' in legal parlance, to which crime writers, nonfiction authors and political analysts have repeatedly turned.[22]

Imaginative writers at work in this period[23] seem especially keen to probe the problem of the 'virtuous' individual – and the limits or pressures brought to bear in defining such virtue – as a litmus test for the health of the body politic at large. Where does one draw the line between legitimate cultural difference – a polymorphous 'good' – and less virtuous strains of difference? In a fragile ensemble of citizens aiming at a new democratic consensus, 'bad' difference seems to introduce a form of perversity. JM Coetzee probed the limit conditions of democratic consensus in his character David Lurie in *Disgrace*, and Gordimer in her examination of the trigger-finger character, Duncan Lingard, in *The House Gun*. Damon Galgut, in *The Good Doctor*, describes two doctors trying to do the 'right thing' in a rural hospital, against all political odds, asking the reader to weigh up their efforts (see Titlestad, 'Allegories'). Mandla Langa, in *The Lost Colours of the Chameleon*, takes the delicate question of where to draw the line in political behaviour into a fictional African state, thereby broadening the postapartheid canvas to postcoloniality. Orford's investigator, Clare Hart, persistently attempts to expose a criminality that is hidden behind a variety of faux-virtuous insulations. In *Gallows Hill*, Hart says at one stage that '[t]he collision of history and politics is complicated in Cape Town' (60; but this is true also of Mpumalanga – where the action shifts later in the story – not to mention the rest of the country). 'History', in this novel, delivers the bones of long-dead slaves discovered in a mass grave; near the place where they are found, the site of a new commercial development on Cape Town's 'Gallows Hill' (a public hanging site in the colonial era), lie the bones of a murdered Cape Town anti-apartheid activist from the 1980s. As the earth unveils unholy, improperly buried skeletons, pointing to the politically sanctioned evils of earlier layers of history (colonial rule, then apartheid), so the action of the novel in the postapartheid period reveals a new stratum of political crooks: wheelers and dealers who would rather throw cement over the bones of the indecently buried, and take a paycheck, than heed conscience. Orford's novel takes one to the 'scene of the crime' in both a historical as well as a contemporaneous sense, and puts together an ensemble of citizens who contest, via their various vested interests, the question of value, of material enrichment and political advancement, on the one hand, and the remit of legal and ethical reckoning, on the other. Mzobe's *Young Blood*, to offer another example, offers a reverse-angle view, from behind the scenes of what is taken to be 'crime', showing the precarious fate of a 'good' young man in Umlazi, Durban. This is a space where, as critic Wamuwi Mbao puts it, 'the criminal and the respectable jostle at close quarters' ('Report Card' n.p.). Mzobe's hero, Sipho, is an essentially upstanding character whose blameless aspirations lead him into a 'bad' world, a zone in which loyalty, astuteness and similarly excellent qualities are moulded into 'crime' by a culture of disadvantage and acute need.

How to define a 'good' person in the 'new South Africa' is, likewise, urgently at issue in Meyer's novel. By creating a single primary focus of public attention – a riveting road chase – Meyer succeeds in focusing the attention of three sets of readership (his South African readers, his sizeable international audience, and the imagined general-public consumers of media in the world that the novel represents) upon a critical question: is Tiny Mpayipheli a bad guy or a good guy, a hero or a villain? Is he virtuous or villainous within the redefined terms of the new dispensation? How far do we allow for 'difference' in the parameters of the new constitutional democracy? A 'good citizen' is a category that is under erasure, as Chipkin demonstrates (100); so it is, too, in the 'infant democracy' depicted in Meyer's novel. It is a question on which the fate of the country hangs, because if postapartheid South Africa gets this definition wrong, or badly skewed towards renewed injustice and 'bad' difference, then the newborn dispensation might just emerge from transition as a beastly adult. The stakes are high.

The political importance of this moral fixing of the notion 'good citizen' cannot be overestimated. Such 'fixing' – in the sense of stabilising as well as correcting – implies a discursive re-territorialising of the new South Africa, underpinned by consensus. It is therefore no surprise that Meyer addresses the difficulties of ethical compass-setting. He achieves a high degree of narrative concentration by launching his protagonist Mpayipheli on a movie-style motorcycle chase from Cape Town to northern Botswana. By using a plot-heavy thriller model, Meyer succeeds in achieving what very often eludes more discursive fictional modes in South African writing: he revivifies the *drama* – in the form of a big-screen sense of plot and colourful characters – as he narrates the story of postapartheid political change.

A Frankenstein or a Robin Hood?

Meyer's Mpayipheli, figured perhaps a little romantically as being in touch with 'the voices of his ancestors – Phalo and Rharhabe, Ngqika and Maqoma, the great Xhosa chiefs, his bloodline, source, and refuge' (*Heart of the Hunter* 3) – reluctantly agrees to help a former struggle comrade, Johnny Kleintjes, who is being held hostage by unknown parties in Lusaka following an intelligence sting. Mpayipheli is tasked with delivering a mobile hard drive supposedly containing sensitive information to Lusaka, where a group of obscure transnational kidnappers are based; his aim is to secure a compatriot's freedom. Mpayipheli is reluctant to undertake the assignment – he has bought a plot of land in his ancestral Xhosaland (Eastern Cape), to which he hopes to return with his beloved Miriam and her son. He feels compelled to nurture and re-educate the boy as a man of the people. Mpayipheli is keen to close down the bad parts of his history, to live pure and straight, but the past hauls him in for one (seemingly) last settling of scores. He 'owes' his comrade Kleintjes an unspecified 'struggle' debt, and Mpayipheli is nothing if not a man of his word. He books a flight from Cape Town to the Zambian capital, thinking he will sort out the business quickly. Unknown to him, though, various warring South African intelligence agencies are trailing him – they also don't quite know *what's going on*, and they want the information that Mpayipheli is carrying so they can find out. When agents try to apprehend him at Cape Town International Airport, he reveals his extraordinary physical prowess by staging an unlikely escape, exiting the airport and eventually 'borrowing' a BMW 1200GS motorcycle from his place of work, a Motorrad dealership in the Cape Town CBD.

Mpayipheli, accustomed to riding a 200cc Honda Benly, finds himself having to adapt to the brutish power of the BMW, almost wiping himself out as he makes his way onto the N1, the road that leads north, to Botswana and Zimbabwe, and beyond that, Lusaka. He knows that the combined forces of the SA Police Service, the SA National Defence Force, various arms of the postapartheid intelligence services as well as an elite reaction unit will soon be hunting him down. They do this with helicopters, satellite surveillance, roadblocks, and an arsenal of arms fit to kill a battalion of soldiers, let alone a solo fugitive on a motorbike. When *Cape Times* reporter Allison Healy gets wind of the story, the stage is set for a media spectacle that concentrates the attention of significant portions of the new nation on a dramatic chase, and what it represents.

In line with the idea that reporters and detectives traverse social shadow-zones on behalf of the citizenry, and send back dispatches on 'what's going on out there', Healy's reporting, along with other media reports, pitted against statements by the state, signals a fierce public-sphere contestation over how best to understand and interpret the events on the ground regarding Mpayipheli. The big question is how to 'read' him and his actions – is he a Frankenstein of the struggle, as the government media communiqués suggest, or a Robin Hood, as many civil subjects begin to think during the course of the story? Before long, reporter Healy is not only updating her reports on a daily basis in the *Cape Times* as she forges ahead in her work of detection, she is also being interviewed on national TV about her discoveries. The Mpayipheli affair becomes a media fanfare, and a test case to boot: who is more truthful, and more 'good', in this sapling democracy – the government's agents or the individual that these agents are hunting down? The resolution of this question carries an enormous burden of meaning for the health and longevity of the democracy: if Mpayipheli does turn out to be a Robin Hood, then why is the state so intent on crushing him, and others like him? Can the new government be trusted? If Mpayipheli is essentially an upstanding citizen, then what is being hidden from sight, and why? What is on the hard drive he is carrying with him? And how important are the consequences of such hiding?

These questions were especially important in the first decade of the transition period, when South Africa still loomed large in the global imaginary as a singular case of constitutional, democratic success among developing nations, a political 'miracle'. As German scholar Jörn Rüsen pleaded at a Witwatersrand University colloquium in 1998 called 'Living Difference', '[i]t is imperative for us that you [the democratic transition] succeed!'[24] He was reminding sceptical South African delegates how much was at stake, not only for South Africa, but also for the very possibility of constitutional democracy in the postcolonies of the world. Among the colloquium discussants at that event was Nancy Fraser, who is wont to question the relevance of Habermas's theory of public-sphere deliberation, framed as it is within Westphalian-state or 'national' contexts, as well as Benedict Anderson's notion of *nationally* constituted 'imagined communities'. Fraser argues that these notions are no longer valid in a globalising, post- and transnational context (11–13). South Africa, one might argue, was caught amidships in this period, between the stern of an inchoate national identity and the bow of globalisation, the point at which the country was navigating the swells of oceanic global interconnectedness.

On the one hand, the very existence of broad media contestation in South Africa might have suggested to Meyer's readers that a democratic public sphere is – or was, at that time – on a sound footing; the novel is set in the early 2000s, several years before the looming threat of the Protection of State Information Bill, or 'Secrecy Bill'. Such public-sphere contestation might suggest that Fraser's sense of a sequestered national public sphere is premature in the case of South Africa. Meyer is one of the few crime writers who, at least in his earlier novels, of which *Heart of the Hunter* is a good example, evinces optimism about the new democracy and its prospects for robust health – though he is correspondingly hard on the old white renegades who continue to crawl out of the woodwork in new-era knavery. At the same time, however, the underlying forces in Meyer's story, the very factors precipitating 'plot loss' among the state's functionaries – namely the

CIA and transnational agents at work in the novel's 'sting', alongside a covert intelligence scam *inside* the South African security establishment – are mostly beyond the nation-state's control and even awareness. This suggests that Fraser's theory of nation-states losing the luxury of an efficacious, bounded public sphere might be half-right after all. In Meyer's novel, as in many demonstrable real-world incidents in postapartheid South Africa, the state itself is too often in the dark about what exactly is going on for comfort; this is especially so in strategic instances, both with regard to external undercurrents and internally, where its own operatives are often indisputably at war with one other, as each week's news stories tend to suggest. The state, like its citizens, seems to have lost the plot, and to save face it has to present a unified front. In the name of 'national security', it has no choice in this novel but to back the most politic option in the short term: hunt down Mpayipheli to eliminate the risk that the intelligence he is carrying will compromise the state's security, not to mention its increasingly precarious dignity. In order to do this, however, it must fight a war of public opinion, and in the process betray Mpayipheli, one of its former MK soldier-heroes, painting him as a psychopathic, out-of-control renegade.

The question of what exactly constitutes a virtuous South African citizen – and, by implication, how to discern 'bad' difference – is therefore a matter of supreme importance, both in the world of the novel and also in the real world, involving an exploration of contending values. 'Virtue' here would include the typical diagnostic preoccupation in postcolonies with the idea of what makes a good or legitimate *legal* subject, a preoccupation which, according to the Comaroffs, is 'growing in counterpoint to, and deeply entailed in, the rise of the felonious state, private indirect government, and endemic cultures of illegality' (*Law and Disorder* 20). This has 'come to feature prominently in popular discourses almost everywhere' (20), including, I suggest, crime fiction. Furthermore, as governance 'disperses itself and monopolies over coercion fragment, crime and policing provide a rich repertoire of idioms and allegories with which to address, imaginatively, the nature of sovereignty, justice, and social order' (20). In the process, the kind of ambiguity about right and wrong, noted earlier as typical of various postcolonies and developing nations, grows ever larger. As if to demonstrate this very point, Meyer's character Janina Mentz, head of an elite intelligence unit among several other warring intelligence structures in the postapartheid government, tells her protégé Tiger Mazibuko that 'the world ha[s] become an evil place, residents and countries not knowing who [is] friend or foe, wars that [can] no longer be fought with armies but at the front of secret rooms, the mini-activities of abduction and occupation, suicide attacks and pipe bombs' (*Heart of the Hunter* 104).

'Intelligence' in a reconstituted public sphere

Taking this theme a step further, *Heart of the Hunter*'s focus on wars of intelligence (both strategic state information/espionage and 'sense-making' in an age of information overload) captures a crisis of old and new methods of warfare. The old methods included MK foot soldiers such as Mpayipheli conducting guerilla warfare, but such subjects now find themselves caught up in an information-age meta-war. In this newer kind of mêlée the old tricks of information and disinformation are elevated into a knowledge economy face-off, a data war of contending power-plays which claim human lives as collateral damage. By the end of Meyer's novel, one has come to understand that lives can plausibly be lost in a war of attrition around ownership and/ or control of information in and of itself, despite the fact that the data at the centre of the conflict might be quite worthless – or even false, as it turns out to be in *Heart of the Hunter*. And yet, at stake is the power to define what is 'right', what is legitimate (including what is *legally* right) in the name of the body politic. Therein lies the key to the knowledge/power equation. Everything, in a sense, depends on 'intelligence', a conflict which drives Meyer's novel relentlessly towards its bloody conclusion.

In the plot of *Heart of the Hunter*, government agents issue communiqués describing Mpayipheli as a deranged madman, based on the evidence of a high-ranking former MK 'hero' who makes this claim to escape a sexual harassment charge. Meanwhile, reporter Allison Healy portrays a very different version of Mpayipheli to her fictive (and Meyer's actual) readers: he was an old MK hero of great distinction, and he has repeatedly tried to avoid hurting people in the hunt-and-resistance story of the novel. Healy's version of Mpayipheli is, moreover, based on the testimony of a former comrade. In addition, the words of ordinary people, such as Mpayipheli's common-law wife, Miriam, and a streetwise shoeshine-man, suggest to Allison and her readers that Mpayipheli is indeed a man of the people rather than the villain the state wishes to make him appear in the eyes of the masses. Healy's 'Will the real Thobela Mpayipheli please stand up' (192) echoes the bigger question that forms the subtext of the novel. While virtue is strongly suggested in the character of Koos Kok, a 'Griqua troubadour' who helps Mpayipheli escape pursuit by police helicopters, the general public remains in doubt. The motor-cycle chase and its reported progress serve to emphasise that the line between law and (dis)order cannot be decisively demarcated. In addition, it reveals a political cartography that is both politically occulted and dangerously labile.

In the end, the novelistic 'resolution' is polyvalent and disorienting. Though Mpayipheli's common-law wife is killed as a result of a blunder by a state agent, he manages to save her son, Pakamile, whom he plans to take home to his ancestral plot of land in Xhosaland. This is his consolation after very nearly losing his own life at the hands of his former comrades. Public opinion about Mpayipheli's status as a heroic or a debased citizen remains ambiguous, however, as the 'new' South Africa dissolves into perversions of justice perpetrated especially against those who should be the heirs of the fruits of revolution.

Cultural difference is thus conceptualised as the locus for a redefined morality in the postapartheid imaginary – in the media, in commentary and in the powerful, popular genre of crime fiction. Together, these forms gesture towards a reconfigured sense of evil, one which coincides to some extent with a more general postcolonial condition in the wake of neoliberal hegemony across the globe. Whereas the denial of cultural difference (in colonial and neocolonial contexts) mobilised activism such as the struggle against apartheid for its revalidation and the restoration of putatively more symmetrical power relations, a widespread emergence of 'bad' difference has since become evident. The use of violence, too, has become morally ambiguous, as dramatised in the case of Mpayipheli in Meyer's *Heart of the Hunter* (and its sequel, *Devil's Peak*), as well as in works such as Orford's *Gallows Hill* and Mzobe's *Young Blood*. In *Devil's Peak*, Mpayipheli finds himself resorting to rough justice for paedophiles, using his assegai as a weapon, after he realises that the South African criminal justice system – and therefore the state – is incapable of protecting its most vulnerable citizens from abuse. And yet this form of kangaroo-style justice is shown to be an ultimately unsatisfactory measure, especially when Mpayipheli misidentifies two of the perpetrators and thereby becomes a murderer himself, rather than a virtuous avenger. Such are the moral intricacies of the new order. If the state does not have 'a monopoly on the legitimate use of force', then there is an urgent need for intensive investigation. The turn to crime fiction in South Africa should therefore be regarded not so much as an escapist, formulaic lapse in taste than as a form of social hermeneutics: in an ethically muddled topography, acts of detection identify, describe and explore the phenomenon of 'bad' difference. Alternatively, such detection investigates the *management* of difference, that is, the disingenuousness and deceit surrounding such management as the locus where the new order either coheres or falls apart. In the process, the basis of 'virtuous' citizenship within the postapartheid context is being extensively rewritten.

3

Freedom on a frontier? The double
bind of (white) postapartheid South
African literature

Around the turn of the twentieth century the early phase of 'transition' morphed into a sociopolitical category variously described as
'post-transition' (Frenkel and MacKenzie, 1–2), 'post-anti-apartheid'
(Kruger, 'Black Atlantics' 35) and 'post-postapartheid' (Chapman,
'Conjectures' 15). Kruger's neologism 'post-anti-apartheid' signifies
a period beyond apartheid, where the writing subject is, at last, delivered from the oppositional stance signified by 'anti' – no longer compelled to counter the material effects of the ideology of apartheid,
whether by means of plotting, or overall sentiment, be this moral,
ethical or political. This sense of remission from the prison house of
the past is key to the way the term 'postapartheid' has broadly come
to be understood: as a deliverance from the constraints – the shack-
les – of endlessly opposing legislated racism that relied on a succes-
sion of states of emergency and a culture of political assassination and
torture. Eventually, such oppositional struggle writing had become so
repetitive, and so dreary, that Albie Sachs made his call for a provisional ban on the notion of culture as a 'weapon of the struggle' in his
1991 ANC working paper, 'Preparing Ourselves for Freedom'.

Indeed, if there is one common thread in published research on
postapartheid South African writing, it is the sense that the country's
writing, resisting classification as a result of its 'unresolved heterogeneity',[1] has now become even more diverse, as befits its newfound liberty, its deliverance from what one might term the closure of apartheid
logocentrism. In keeping with this new script about the literature of
postapartheid, Frenkel and MacKenzie propose that 'scores of writers

[in the years 1999–2009] have produced works of extraordinary range and diversity' (1). These writers have 'heeded Albie Sachs's call to free themselves from the 'ghettos of the apartheid imagination', with 'new South African literature accordingly [reflecting] a wide range of concerns and styles' (1). This literature is 'unfettered to the past, but may still consider it in new ways' or 'ignore it altogether' (2).

Without contradicting Frenkel and MacKenzie,[2] I wish to suggest a line of reasoning that departs from the theme of being 'freed from the past'. In my view, a significant section of postapartheid literature finds itself less liberated from the past than engaged in the persistent re-emergence of this past. Frenkel offers the figure of the palimpsest to explain how post-transitional writing allows for 'a reading of the new in a way in which the layers of the past are still reflected through it' (25). I argue for an even stronger emphasis, and contend that in the hands of Kevin Bloom, Antjie Krog and Jonny Steinberg, the three writers who form the main focus of this chapter, postapartheid literature is inescapably bound to the time of before. A compulsive reiteration of certain South African literary tropes is evident in their work, particularly those of the frontier and the journey of discovery. Further, I argue that much postapartheid literature written in detection mode is distinguished by strong rather than weak or merely vestigial continuity with the past. Such ateleologial (re)cycling – decidedly against the grain of a widely alleged rupture with the past – runs counter to theses that postapartheid literature is mostly novel, or substantially different from earlier South African writing. However, it is also true that the very reprocessing I hope to uncover gives rise to features of authorial voice that are characteristic of a postapartheid generation of writing, for reasons I elaborate below. The argument about continuity or discontinuity between apartheid and postapartheid in South African literature, I suggest, needs stronger conceptual treatment of how past and present are disjunctively conjoined;[3] the time of now-and-going-forward and the time of history, or what-has-been, are, I propose, mixed in a way that suggests the conception of a split temporality – altering from a bad 'before' (apartheid) to a better 'after' (postapartheid) – is perhaps overworked. It might indeed be more accurate to describe what occurs 'in' postapartheid as a reconfigured temporality in which Hal Foster's 'future-anterior', or the 'will-have-been', persistently surfaces. This is consistent, to a large extent, with Grant Farred's sense of a doubled temporality (see Chapter 1), in which the supposed 'epochal progress' of postapartheid 'quickly showed itself to be less a march toward an ideal political future – let alone present – than a new democracy living in a double temporality' ('Not-Yet Counterpartisan' 592–593).[4] Foster's proposition is invoked by Ashraf Jamal in a critique of certain conceptions of South African literature. Jamal writes:

> My reason for this emphasis [on the future-anterior] rests on the assumption that South African literature in English has elected to sanctify and memorialize its intent, producing a literature informed by a messianic, liberatory, or reactive drive, hence a struggle literature (which precedes liberation from apartheid) and a post-apartheid literature (which establishes a democratic state of play). These phases, however, are hallucinatory projections, or candid attempts to generate a cultural transparency: see where we have come from; see where we now are; see where we are going. The logic is overdetermined, teleological, and in effect diminishes our ability to grasp that which is impermanent, hybrid... ('Bullet through the Church' 11)

Jamal identifies what he perceives to be a major fault in conceptions of South African writing: a fixation with going somewhere, of getting from a dead-heavy past to a re-envisioned future. Instead, Jamal proposes that the South African literary imaginary contains 'a latent sensation that South Africa as a country suffers *the unease of never having begun*' (16, Jamal's emphasis). Following Raymond Williams, Jamal argues that if nineteenth-century realism stems from the presumption of a 'knowable community, such a hermetic logic fails to apply to a heterogeneous outpost such as South Africa' (17).

It is with a similar sense of unknowability amid a scene of unresolved heterogeneity in South African culture at large that the texts I examine in this chapter, Bloom's *Ways of Staying*, Krog's *Begging to be Black* and Steinberg's *Midlands*, take on their burden of (re)discovery, as if nothing can be taken as known, again, and as always. Indeed a felt anxiety, again and renewed, about 'never [quite] having begun' lies at the heart of the affective charge in such texts. Now, however, the *notion* of postapartheid, and the popular, widely shared social imperative of a desired teleology, a clean break from the past, raises the stakes considerably. The writing of Bloom, Krog and Steinberg, though sharp and unsentimental, is, consequently, suffused with concern about the clear failure of postapartheid's grand narrative. This, despite the efforts of the Truth and Reconciliation Commission to set the story of the new South Africa on the right track. As Shane Graham comments in his book on the TRC and the South African literature that followed in its wake, the Commission ultimately succeeded in setting up a perceived 'contrapuntal dialogue' that enables a 'reconceptualization of such fundamental spatio-temporal constructs as the dichotomies between public and private, past and present' (*South African Literature* 33). Here, indeed, is a necessary form of 'plot loss', a corrective to the always-looming teleology inherent in the very signifier 'post-', whether this be understood as 'post-transitional' or 'post-apartheid'. Periodicity in its more commonly understood sense, as in the named phases of time marked as 'transitional', 'post-transitional', and so on, thus runs into a mash-up of temporalities in which the time of before intrudes on the present.[5] In using the term 'mash-up', I draw on both the literal meaning of a collision of forces implicit in the verb 'mash' and on the composite term's use in music and video as 'blend, bootleg and bastard pop/rock' in a song or composition created by blending two or more pre-recorded songs (Wikipedia). The 'bastard' blend of styles and versions, in this description, exhibits a violently reintegrated (mashed) character whose pulpiness defies pre-imagined, distinct shapes.

In *Ways of Staying*, *Begging to be Black* and *Midlands*, the felt torsion of oneself becoming implicated in such destabilising mash-ups, and of seeing others undergoing a similar grinding or crushing, is almost obsessively focused on a single, if contested, signifier – that ultimate South African scare word: 'crime'. Not only is 'crime' an everyday matter, integral to the daily newsfeed – with which it is complicit in the constitution of a 'wound culture'[6] – but it also has the potential to wreck the progress, the socially and economically necessary teleology, of the 'rainbow nation'. The spectre of 'crime' is, indeed, the joker in the pack for South Africa's negotiated settlement, creating as it does uncomfortable connections with the apartheid past, both in everyday life and in the realm that more immediately concerns us here, namely the felt imaginaries discernible in 'transitional' or 'post-transitional' writing.

Given the extraordinary saturation of the signifier 'crime' in postapartheid South Africa, a brief examination of social discourse in relation to this resonant (though problematic) term is necessary. The bogey of 'crime' has possibly been one of the most prevalent facts of life in South Africa over the past twenty years or so, as scholars such as Steinberg, Altbeker, Gary Kynoch and others have shown. Any street survey in Johannesburg, Durban or Cape Town that asks what the country's biggest 'problems' are will likely yield the answer 'crime', followed by that other 'c'-word, 'corruption'. This chimes with perceptions of criminal corruption elsewhere, as argued above in relation to conditions in which 'felonious' states are able to thrive in the world's postcolonies, which now include postapartheid South Africa.

The images of a 'spectre' and a 'bogey' are used because, although a statistical consensus about the incidence of crime in postapartheid South Africa remains elusive, the fear of crime has escalated, particularly but by no means exclusively among white South Africans. As commentator Sisonke Msimang writes,

> [i]t is only possible to be haunted by the death of a stranger when you are convinced that he could have been you or one of yours. Perhaps this is why South Africans are obsessed with crime. It looms large because although it disproportionately affects poor black people, it also affects enough middle-class people for it to have become a 'national question'. ('Caught' n.p.)

Crime, with or without the scare quotes, has over the past two decades replaced 'apartheid' as one of the country's most conspicuous, and contested, terms. Steinberg argues that white fears of crime as a form of retribution have been endemic but greatly exaggerated in the postapartheid period, although he nevertheless acknowledges the high incidence of criminal violence in the country as a whole ('Crime' 25–27). Altbeker similarly notes the exceptionally high rates of crime, but casts doubt on the popular myth that South Africa is the world's 'crime capital' ('Puzzling Statistics' 8). Echoing Steinberg, Altbeker adds, however, that the country's murder rates are 'far higher than those of the industrialized world' (8). Assessments such as these, which acknowledge an unusually high crime rate – 'near the top of the world rankings', Altbeker concedes (98) – nevertheless cast doubt on what one might call 'urban legends' about crime; as such, they are fairly typical.[7] Research findings in this area understandably seek to distance themselves from what the Comaroffs describe as 'mytho-stats' ('Figuring Crime' 215).

Benjamin Disraeli's 'lies, damned lies, and statistics' are certainly at issue in the many plot twists conjured up by disgruntled whites in the 'new South Africa' deal. The frequent invocation of crime statistics is perceived by many as a 'white whine', or an updated version of the persistent 'black peril' metanarrative in colonial and neocolonial South Africa.[8] Reading this narrative of fearfulness sympathetically, Kynoch comments that '[t]he crime epidemic is the most visceral reminder for whites of their diminishing status and protestations against crime provide an outlet for articulating anxieties about the new order without openly resorting to racist attacks' (2013, 439). Altbeker, in turn, argues that 'fear of crime has sometimes become a conveniently "apolitical" vehicle through which a disenfranchised elite can mourn its loss of power without sounding nostalgic for an unjust past' (*Country at War* 64). Kynoch concurs, though he points out that '[h]igh crime rates have been a feature of life in many black townships and informal settlements for the past hundred years or more' (2012, 3). He notes that this is a history that has been charted in a significant number of scholarly works, in which an urban African population is victimised by police and criminals in what are often politicised conflicts (2012, 3).[9] Steinberg also makes this point, arguing that the flip side of whites being let off so lightly post-1994 – 'no expropriation, no nationalisation, not even a tax increase' – was that 'a criminal culture whose appetite for commodities and violence was legendary in the townships arrived in the [white] suburbs' ('Crime' 26). Crime, according to Steinberg, began to haunt white South Africans such that around dinner tables

> a very different story about South Africa's transition began to circulate, and, while the finer details varied, the heart of the tale did not: it was about somebody who had been held up at gunpoint, another who had been shot, another who had been kidnapped in her own car. The anecdotes of guns and blood spread like an airborne disease, becoming something of a contagion. By the end of the millennium, much of white South Africa had died a thousand deaths in their own homes, around their own dinner tables ... Many whites believed that Mandela's discourse of reconciliation was rendered irrelevant by a far deeper, congenital

hostility to the presence of whites at the end of the continent, and that this hostility found expression in violent crime. (26)

Steinberg convincingly demonstrates that this 'diagnosis of crime' was 'spectacularly wrong' (27).[10] Providing evidence, he argues that in fact white South Africans were far less likely to be killed in their own homes than their black counterparts, who continued to bear the brunt of crime in the postapartheid period (27). And yet even Steinberg's finely balanced account makes the familiar gesture of offering a qualifier about crime being epidemic in South Africa, regardless of race:

> Levels of middle-class victimisation, both black and white, are high enough for just about the entire middle class to have experienced violent crime at close quarters. It is no exaggeration to say that almost every South African, whether poor or rich, has either had a gun shoved in her face, or has witnessed the trauma of a loved one who has had a gun shoved in her face. (27–28)

One may draw two conclusions from this: first, whatever actual crime levels may be, and regardless of the distribution of this 'epidemic' among the sectors of South African society, discourse about crime – especially emanating from whites – accelerated significantly in the transition period, thereby justifying the use of terms such as 'mythostats'. Second, taking into account this tendency to amplification, it remains clear that social violence in South Africa in the transition period (as in previous periods), manifested in the form of criminal behaviour, was in fact 'epidemic' by comparison with most other emerging economies.[11] Paradoxically, then, this also means that although, from a critical or scholarly point of view, one should not give undue credence to the exaggerations of white discourse about crime, this discourse nevertheless provides evidence of a state of being that is itself noteworthy. Steinberg, who goes so far as to call this a 'white phenomenology of crime' (28), continues:

> For a milieu in which the idea of mortality has always been hitched exclusively to the elderly and the frail, the constant threat of lethal violence is akin to an earthquake. The profundity of the fear of crime is deep enough to go all the way down, to the existential itself, to the cornerstones of one's relation to the

world...'Crime' has nestled inside the most exquisitely intimate and private domains of white experience. It has taken its place among the categories through which people experience the fundamentals of their existence. (28)

If one adds to this amped-up sense of existential fragility the fact that white South Africans in general inhabit the country on the 'shakiest of pretexts' (Steinberg citing JM Coetzee in *Youth*), then one gets a sense of the abysmal dislocation that is integral to the experience of such South Africans. Coetzee's young Cape Town protagonist in *Youth* implicitly knows that he 'must be a simpleton, in need of protection, if he imagines he can get by on the basis of straight looks and honourable dealings when the ground beneath his feet is soaked with blood and the vast backward depth of history rings with shouts of anger' (*Youth* 17).

In the discussion that follows, I deal with three nonfiction narratives of postapartheid conditions by white writers (Bloom, Krog and Steinberg) as a way of investigating changing modes of address in the broad category of 'postapartheid' writing. In making claims on this basis, I look at one of several seams – white creative nonfiction in what I call detection mode – in the greater patchwork of postapartheid literary culture. While one is loath to reintroduce categorisation in terms of race, the latter remains a stubbornly persistent feature, both implicit and explicit, in postapartheid modes of expression. The critic should be aware, however, that, as with literary culture during apartheid, totalising claims on the basis of a limited number of writers – especially in terms of race – are sure to founder. At best, the critic details diverse and divergent acts of writing under a nominal but ultimately (and necessarily) obscure totality in which particular renderings are both distinctive as parts, and also definitive in their own right. In this case, I am particularly interested in Steinberg's notion of a 'white phenomenology of crime', and how white writers of the generation after Gordimer and Coetzee may be said to express this. It is a state of affairs that has loomed large since 1994, and it seems appropriate to ask whether and how it reconnects with or disconnects from the *longue durée* of the colonial, neocolonial-segregationist, and apartheid past. Naturally, a view of black writing in which crime and corruption emerge as major themes[12] inevitably results in a differently inflected version of postapartheid writing that disrupts any coherent sense of literary totality. Part and whole – and indeed the relationship between the two – remain as vexed a conjunction as ever in South African writing.

Ways of Staying

It is precisely the white 'soft spot' in the postapartheid imaginary described above – an accelerating sense of personal threat over and above an abiding sense of not belonging – that both Bloom's and Steinberg's texts deal with. It is a sore area that Bloom targets in his 2009 nonfiction work, *Ways of Staying* – the title being a play on Zakes Mda's 1995 novel, *Ways of Dying*.[13] Bloom's book is noteworthy not only because it homes in on the condition of existential fragility identified by Coetzee and Steinberg, but also because it eludes the category of 'white whinger'. The book grew out of an event that shook Bloom's life to its core – the apparently senseless murder of his cousin, fashion designer Richard Bloom, aged twenty-seven, along with his partner Brett Goldin, who was twenty-eight at the time. According to the account by Antony Sher, who researched the incident for a documentary, Goldin and Bloom were carjacked as they approached their vehicles after a party on Cape Town's Atlantic seaboard. The year was 2006, a good twelve years into democracy. Their abducters were a band of young men high on crystal meth (or 'tik', as it is known in the Cape) looking for a car to steal. Sher takes up the story:

> The group held them up at gunpoint, stole one of their cars, stripped and bound them, and forced them into the boot. They then drove to a motorway a few miles away, and onto a traffic island. Perhaps they were intending to abandon Brett and Richard alive and make their getaway, but the car got stuck in sand. After a long, frenzied struggle to free it, during which their naked victims were forced to help, they shot them dead. Either the mixture of frustration and intoxication led to the murderous act, or – as the men later claimed in their confessions – their victims cried out and had to be silenced. ('Tidal Wave' n.p.)

Sher's subsequent comment distinguishes his sense of horror from the more routine kind of white discourse about crime. The story is chilling, Sher continues, 'because it isn't about racism or sex, or anything other than chance' ('Tidal Wave' n.p.). The timing of Goldin and Bloom's departure from the party 'just happened to coincide with the group driving past'. The targets could have been '[a]ny of the other guests…someone in the next street, it could have been you or me'. The renowned Shakespearean-actor-turned-writer concludes that his 'birthplace seemed changed in a way that I didn't like. Nowhere felt safe anymore' ('Tidal Wave' n.p.).

Such a feeling of unhomeliness, with the added seasoning of a real, and often visceral, fear for one's life, created a sense among many South Africans that the new dispensation had lost its way, at least as far as their own safety was concerned. Certainly, constitutional guarantees, specifically the right to 'be free from all forms of violence from either public or private sources' (section 12[1][c]), seemed remote, particularly for victims of what came to be called 'random violence' (also the title of a crime novel by Jassie Mackenzie). It is therefore no surprise that Bloom's *Ways of Staying*, written partly during a fellowship at the University of the Witwatersrand's Institute for Social and Economic Research (WISER), struck a chord. The book made the shortlists of both the Sunday Times Alan Paton and University of Johannesburg literary prizes, garnered enthusiastic reviews, and was taken up in 2010 by Portobello Books in London. It won an unusual amount of transnational media exposure, though its uncommonly favourable reception should not be attributed merely to Bloom's sense of timing. The writing, a subgenre of creative nonfiction, is sharp and probing. A compassionate enquiry into the lives of others, its style is reminiscent of that of Bloom's mentor and friend, Rian Malan. Surprisingly, in view of the circumstances that gave rise to the book, Bloom effectively writes *against* inward-looking white talk. He uses the occasion of his cousin's randomly brutal murder, and the personal as well as family shock it occasioned, as a kind of defamiliarising medium, a heuristic opportunity to approach 'the as-yet unanswered question of what I now feel towards my own country' (14). This sentiment is key because it reveals the felt sense, common in late-transition (or postapartheid) years, of having become a stranger in one's own time and place, dislocated from a familiar sense of home.

Bloom's narrative is cast in an interrogative-conjectural mood, taking the reader along as he explores the city of Johannesburg and the country at large, as if for the first time. This act of narrative journeying through and across the country and its cities, again, and anew, as if the country has changed – or not changed – such that fresh journeys of reconnaissance are necessary, is a leitmotif of much post-apartheid writing.[14] Early on in *Ways of Staying* Bloom writes: '[T]he change in my attitude to South Africa has revealed itself gradually, like a jigsaw puzzle materializing piece by piece at the edges. I see a picture emerging, but I can't yet say what it is' (14). The attitudinal shift that gradually occurs is a result of estrangement: the postapartheid country Bloom had believed in no longer seems to exist. His response is to set out on a quest to rediscover the 'new', or newly strange, South Africa, via acts of journalistic detection for the (then) *Maverick* magazine, and ultimately for his own book.

These journeys, or inbound travel (both geographical and personal-ideological), are in sharp contradistinction to the (mostly white) 'pack for Perth' response to estrangement. They are important not just in Bloom's case, but in a more general sense for postapartheid writing. In *Ways of Staying*, Bloom extends rather than contracts his intersubjective range of communication. He meets, talks to and takes notes on black South Africans who are transients in Johannesburg and who live in derelict buildings in the old central business district, now a filthy urban slum. Bloom also makes contact with African migrants holding out in various derelict parts of the 'golden city', who are at the mercy of both xenophobia and a struggling economy.[15] In this way, Bloom seeks a wider base for his reassessment of what it means to live in the country in which his own growing up coincided with the rainbow nation's coming of age, but which now seemed to be undoing itself in violent spasms. Bloom's readers journey with him into an 'unknown' hinterland, with the text replaying a centuries-old motif in South African literature. Now, however, the quest is to find 'ways of staying' rather than ways of leaving. This is in contrast with numerous others who chose not to stay, such as explorer Bartholomew Diaz and first Dutch governor Jan van Riebeeck; poets Thomas Pringle and Roy Campbell, both of whom returned to Europe; and Christopher Hope, Breyten Breytenbach and JM Coetzee, all of whom eventually headed for distant hills. Bloom asks: Is there a way in, rather than out? What will it take?

In the postapartheid period, Bloom occupies the far end of the imperial-colonial-neocolonial quest in southern Africa. This ongoing mission – for land and money, but also, just as critically, for knowledge and information – has come full circle from the 'heroic' journeyings of explorer David Livingstone and missionary Robert Moffat.[16] Its latest iteration is Bloom's expedition, as he, too, sets out to discover whether the habitat is a good one, or at least livable. In an ironic sense, this historical circularity underlines Coetzee's claim that whites are in the country on the 'shakiest of pretexts'. Whether or not one agrees with Coetzee's stance, white writers reaffirm such shakiness in each new chronicle of dislocation, and in accounts of restless wandering to secure a purchase on the land. This moment in postapartheid writing marks, paradoxically, a disjunctive continuity with pre-transitional writing: it is a literature of compulsive (re)-iteration, a literature seemingly always, and repeatedly, at the frontier of not-knowing, on the brink. It forms an arc, from Sol T Plaatje's *Mhudi* and Thomas Mofolo's *Chaka* (with their sense of imminent conflict across frontiers), through the 'Jim-comes-to-Joburg' novels such as Peter Abrahams's *Mine Boy* and Alan Paton's *Cry, the Beloved Country*, to Gordimer's *A World of Strangers* and Coetzee's *Dusklands*. In a sense, these are narratives about people who are deaf to each other as they traverse the same country. What is profoundly different, though, as suggested above, is that the white writer in the late-twentieth and early-twenty-first centuries seeks a range of reciprocity seldom sought, or found, before. This is, consequently, an attempt to discover the rapport that is denied in Coetzee's *Foe*, in Gordimer's *July's People*, in Eben Venter's *Trencherman*, in Etienne van Heerden's *30 Nights in Amsterdam* and in Marlene van Niekerk's *Agaat*.

Despite compulsive cycling, however, the postapartheid narrative has had some important breakthroughs. In the manner of certain antecedents – Livingstone's imperial survey *Missionary Travels and Researches in South Africa*; Olive Schreiner's remote view of black subjects on the 'African farm' in *The Story of an African Farm*; and Herman Charles Bosman's ironic, refracted stories about 'kaffirs' (for example, 'Makapan's Caves') – Bloom's narrative juxtaposes the experience of the (mostly black) poor with that of those on the other (mostly white) side of the fence. But Bloom goes much further in searching for a way out of the impasse: he seeks a commonality among his countrymen, and, to some extent, finds it. *Ways of Staying* narrates (in reporter's-notebook, fact-based mode) gruesome attacks by blacks against whites, murders and rapes whose seemingly gratuitous cruelty may cause the reader to infer that this is the revenge for a history of violent dominion. Bloom boldly asks, apropos a radio news bulletin heard while travelling in his car: 'Is the focus on [the murders of David Rattray, Brett Goldin and Richard Bloom] symbolic of a national undercurrent, their front-page status a function of resurgent white fears? Or might we be affirming by our fascination that such murders are inevitable, a necessary tax on history?' (20). However, Bloom goes on to report on black experience of dislocation and violence, too, showing how urban subjects live on a knifepoint of survival, and giving Agamben's term 'bare life' immediacy and specificity in the process.[17] His extensive recounting of the story, for example, of Tony and Claudia Muderhwa, a migrant couple from the Democratic Republic of Congo, probes the more objective and widespread conditions of 'plot loss' and contingency in the 'new' South Africa. At all levels, the people are eating dirt, Bloom's book effectively says, although only some have the luxury of 'leaving', especially for 'better' places. The irony is not lost on Bloom that while some of his own cousins have emigrated to Australia, the migrants seeking shelter in Jozi (Johannesburg) want nothing so badly as to *not* be thrown out of the country. In the end, Bloom's white protagonist – a narrative presentation of himself – decides to hang in there, so to speak, and stay.

If South African literature seems always to present a horizon of unknowing, irresistibly reworking a foundational trope in which the frontier dissolves and then reappears, then the ruptures in such a continuity might be found in the manner in which points of connection and disconnection implicit in the frontier trope are refigured in the moment of writing. The frontier as a figure, discursively overlaying any number of physical and imagined sites, is nothing if not a mirage, a phantasmal site of projected integration, repulsion and catastrophe. It is that ever-looming horizon, the imagined limit, where the game might change forever if one is not vigilant. It is, in addition, a figuration of the stakes involved in personal, familial and national life that may or may not involve transnational considerations. In practical terms, it becomes a daily exercise in weighing up personal safety and danger, political rule and misrule, and freedom and its opposite. It helps to answer, though always provisionally, the question: would I have a fair chance if I left my private space and entered that of the 'country', merging my identity with an imagined domain? And so, enquiry and detection are crucial aspects of the civic imagining[18] that is fundamental to ordinary life in postapartheid South Africa; for citizens, it involves the continual figuring out of the meaning of their

birthplace (itself a contested notion), and for migrants, of their desti-
nation country. For all, however, the act of detection is one of urgent
and ongoing reimagining, because this place – whether mediated or
actually experienced, whether seen and felt or merely imagined –
must be faced repeatedly, on each new day. We are here. We are staying. We want to be here. And we want to know the deep truth about
the country, now, again. How can these subjects – whether citizens or
'aliens' – find out, for real? The frontier – the place where the limit
condition is either experienced or imagined – is in a state of continuous revision or *refiguration* (as in Willem Anker's prize-winning
Afrikaans novel *Buys*). Though this may always be the case, there is,
nevertheless, a special urgency in conditions that are 'transitional',
and particularly so in the case of South Africa.[19] Here, the frontier is
always shifting, from moment to moment, as, in the instant of projection, reality is encountered. When assailed by anxiety concerning their
survival, human subjects, whether citizens or 'aliens' in a bordered
terrain, want nothing more than to be in a state of preparedness. In
particular, citizens in unstable postcolonial polities where law and disorder feed off each other tend to demand information concerning
the 'contact zone', and they will eagerly consume both factually presented and imaginatively reworked data – from the lurid headlines of
the *Daily Sun*[20] to the fact-based fictions of crime writers. In short,
the market for proxy detection is a big one – or at least big enough to
meet the writer's urge to go 'out there' and find out what the hell is
'really' going on.

Simply put, this quest is the business of a large chunk of current South African writing that deals with a social predicament in
which tropes from the time of before intrude jaggedly into the 'transformed' present, which is always on the cusp, or 'yet to begin'. This is
a moving present, then, a shifting frontier of time that refuses to yield
to a promised future of secular redemption, liberated from the bad
old days of frontier conflict and its awful aftermath. And while the
impulse to detect might be straightforward enough, the complexities
of detection are not. How does one 'write' the country, now, again,
write it up, so to speak, now that everything – and nothing – has
changed, and there seems to have been a retreat to a past that refuses
to be past? Two basic options for a writer are, of course, fiction or
nonfiction, although these categories, in local literary production,
at least, bleed into each other in ways that sound an alarm about

making distinctions. Fiction writers may (and often do) use factual, researched data to make educated guesses, rendered in imaginative form.[21] Nonfiction writers also use this data to set up narrative simulacra of the 'real',[22] but such simulacra are, of course, themselves reimagined, being narrative constructions of 'fact'.[23] Of course, different writers will be either more or less licentious with the combinations of invention and imagination, more or less liable to surrender to the seduction of formal closure demanded by genre when the facts may resist such closure. But in all of these cases there is a certain catharsis: a relief derived from discovering, at last, what is going on; or what amounts to the purgation of pity and fear in witnessing dreadful events, even when they are exaggerated or 'played up' by the writer. The reader of fiction may indeed welcome 'playing up', just for the hell of it, for the release, and so crime writers happily oblige. This is true as much of Henning Mankell, or Jo Nesbø, or Lee Child, as it is of local crime writers such as Angela Makholwa and Deon Meyer.

There is, furthermore, an edge to the nonfiction accounts, and to many of the factually loaded fictional accounts, too, a restless seeking for clues and traces deriving from what, in a different context, Carlo Ginzburg calls the 'conjectural paradigm' (105) of detection, based on a more general 'evidential paradigm' (96). Ginzburg traces the evidential paradigm and its clue-based conjectures to its sources in Sir Arthur Conan Doyle's Sherlock Holmes series, as well as late-nineteenth-century art criticism (98). This is an inductive approach: from small particulars and stories, it works to construct the bigger picture from micro-details, traces and imprints. Moreover, it maintains a hard-nosed scepticism about alibis and all forms of tall stories – which it counters with a 'God is in the details' approach.[24]

Begging to be Black

Antjie Krog's anguished meditations on the possibility of virtuous action in hopelessly compromised circumstances in *Country of My Skull*, and taken up in a different register in *A Change of Tongue*, find full expression in *Begging to be Black*. The latter is a nonfiction blending of the life and times of Basotho King Moshoeshoe amid colonial wars, on the one hand, and reluctant 'implication' (by political association) in a 1992 murder in Kroonstad, on the other. Like Njabulo Ndebele, another writer-intellectual who frequently ruminates on ethical matters in conditions of conflict and warring loyalties,[25] Krog offers reflections on the predicaments of transition in a book that is in large part the product of a fellowship in Berlin. At its heart is a reckoning of events that took place the previous decade, in the early 1990s: some of Krog's ANC-aligned political allies in Kroonstad, where she was then living and working as a high school teacher, killed an Inkatha-associated head of a local gang, a man who went by the name of 'the Wheetie'. Inevitably, there are suggestions in Krog's story of the bad faith of the National Party under FW de Klerk, which participated in negotiations to bring about democracy while at the same time engaging in behind-the-scenes 'third force' violence to weaken its chief negotiating partner (the ANC). It did this by forging alliances between Zulu-based Inkatha, a movement it historically favoured, and rogue units in the South African Police (SAP).[26] After the Wheetie's murder, his killers asked Krog to dispose of a red T-shirt worn by the Wheetie's killer, and they also hid the murder weapon on Krog's Kroonstad property, an act that had the potential of implicating her in the murder. (She was not aware of the presence of the gun on her stoep, and one of the men involved in the killing later removed it.) All of this caused Krog much anguish regarding her legal as opposed to her ethical responsibilities as an ANC loyalist. It was a predicament that forced her to face up to the consequences of taking a stand in a situation beset with contradictions. In such conditions, for Krog as much as for other writers, only truth-seeking narrative is adequate to the task of squaring things off. And so she resorts to a nonfictional mode, with its potential to prise open ethical dilemmas – fully aware, nevertheless, of its limitations, acknowledging: 'I…know that when I reach the end of this tale, completely worn out, I will still be asking: What would have been the right thing to do? – and the terror, the real terror of moral bewilderment, is lost among the words' (*Begging* 5). The carrying though, in writing, of such 'moral bewilderment', and the 'real terror' that flows from this, is Krog's hallmark as a postapartheid writer. The assumption of this burden, especially in the disorienting circumstances of plot loss, finds its more telling expression in nonfictional reassessments, as in Krog's major post-TRC writings, Ndebele's nonfiction within a fictional frame in *The Cry of Winnie Mandela*, along with numerous other works of nonfiction mentioned and discussed elsewhere in this book.

Krog must answer to her son, who bluntly asks, '[D]id you do any-thing wrong?' (*Begging* 43). Krog replies: 'No.' But she interpolates, in an aside to the reader: 'I sound more convinced than I really am.' Then she continues: 'Or let me put it this way: I haven't done anything wrong, but whether I did the right thing is difficult for me to work out' (44). In an earlier generation, Gordimer might have fictionalised such a situation, the ambiguity and equivocation, but here, now, in the time of transition, the pressures are too intense. The story demands factual unlayering, inspection and reconsideration, and there is neither the space nor the leisure that fiction requires. Soon after the Wheetie's murder, there is a reprisal: Hankan Petrus and Reggie – one of the former's accomplices – stand up in the school where Krog works to denounce a teacher supposedly involved in the reprisal. Krog reflects: 'I sit there, too astonished to utter a word' (46). Later that day, she remains in the grip of disorientation:

> For the umpteenth night I sit rigid in the bed with questions whirling in my head. To what extent is my position not moral at all, but simply privileged middle class? Am I against murder because I can afford to be? I'm white; I'm barricaded by money against anything that threatens my life. If I get a death threat, I go to the police. I even choose a policeman to suit my needs, because I was at school with them. Reggie can't. He has to defend himself within a hostile context where comrade and cousin, murder and protection have no separate meanings any more. But, again, it is post 1990. In what way is Reggie, with his extended house, his upholstered furniture and his BMW not middle class – perhaps not in education, but certainly in aspiration? Is Reggie not also better connected to powerful institutions than I am? Is it then the access to things like power and class that determines whether something is moral? (46)

Krog continues in this vein, probing and pushing, refusing easy ali-bis, tall stories, unexamined precepts, and resisting self-delusion. 'But isn't the respect for life something basic?' she asks herself, sitting up in bed (and presumably writing, writing, writing, as she declines sleep). 'Isn't it the oldest principle, the first major decision that a society takes?' she ponders. 'But, because of our fractured past, we as South Africans have never formed a coherent enough whole to decide what principles we agree on. It was okay to kill blacks, but not whites. It was okay to steal from whites, but not from blacks' (46). And so she goes on, what she says being difficult and therefore absolutely necessary for her fellow citizens to read.

Krog's meditations on the life of Moshoeshoe render visible similar fractures of belief, fissures relating to principle:

> Much has been written about the fact that Moshoeshoe died without being baptized. Some say that he died with one foot in the traditional world and the other in the Christian world; others say that, once again, he had slyly outmaneuvered everybody. But perhaps Moshoeshoe died as he had lived: To the end misunderstood and admired for his remarkably consistent striving to get people to live reconciled...In fact, it seems that most of what Moshoeshoe had been saying was misunderstood within the framework of French missionary beliefs, British imperialism and Afrikaner land hunger. (227)

Whether or not one agrees with Krog here on historical grounds, to engage in counter-argument would involve more than mere opinion, mere *talk*; it would require a similar excavation of layer upon layer in the contentious colonial archive. In the course of her fellowship at the Wissenschaftskolleg zu Berlin in 2007/8, Krog extends her explorations, crossing borders and citing, for example, Hannah Arendt during a collegial conversation at the Berlin college dinner table:

> 'I'm reading Hannah Arendt at the moment [says Krog to one of her interlocutors]. She discards precisely the desire to monumentalize the Nazi crimes and says that it was the way in which ordinary citizens abandoned decency that made those crimes possible. This, however, implies that there is a common agreement about what decency is...The problem in South Africa is that we have no common benchmark of what we regard as decency, and we do not carry the emphasis you have here on individual moral responsibility.' (247)

Here and elsewhere in the book, Krog deepens the 'long conversation'[27] about the South African predicament. Hers is an interlocution that revolves around the unresolved heterogeneity of irreconcilable subject positions, competing cultural positionalities, and the inability to speak a common language, in both the broad and the narrow sense of the term. In 2013, Krog described what she termed the 'two ontologies' at work in (postapartheid) South Africa:

> To talk ethics, you have to talk to someone. You have to engage with someone about exactly what the ethics are about. I thought I knew. I grew up thinking I knew. Since 1990 I've been at a loss. I feel I'm in a country that has a fractured morality; a country that is deeply confused about what its ethics could and should be, even what ethics is. We don't know what we're saying. We don't know what words we use in our own languages when we use the expression 'human rights'. What is the Zulu for that? What exactly is the Afrikaans for that? How do we contextualize that specific term? If you're a writer or a poet, in what language do you utter these ethical thoughts that you have? Things have been written and performed in this country that are severely critical of current events in the country, but they are in Afrikaans, or they are in Zulu, and you don't know how it helps us and influences us all to reach this ethical 'agreement'. Because we don't translate…We have a discussion *about* translation, but translation is not respected, it's not a job…no one cares about what people in indigenous languages are saying.[28]

For all its occasional hyperbole and hand-wringing, there is much to be reckoned with in this impassioned intervention. The sense of schism, of a loss of bearings, expressed here and elsewhere in Krog's nonfictional works, remains a major issue. And yet – as Breyten Breytenbach cautioned in reply[29] – one should be wary of smoothing out 'textures of diversity', and be on the alert for essentialisms in any core 'ethical agreement' set up to counter what Krog sees as a 'dual ontology'. Such are the issues that underlie – indeed bedevil – all art forms in the (seemingly permanent, forever unfinished) transitional situation, whether these be prose, poetry, or performance art such as Brett Bailey's highly controversial 'Exhibit B', which resulted in global protests in 2015. Attempts to assay the lie of the land are as hard to read now as ever before, having become even more bewildering as the 'rainbow' has faded.

Midlands

Ascertaining the lie of the land is exactly what Jonny Steinberg is up to in his first big nonfiction book, *Midlands*, a work that heralded the younger-generation postapartheid brand of writers who have made it their task to find out what exactly is going on in several spheres of the 'new' country's life. In *Midlands*, Steinberg's subject is the ugly reality of farm murders. *Midlands* deserves attention because it sets the tone of much postapartheid nonfiction, establishing the basis for a rigorous, inductive, evidential mode of approach. Such writing exudes an unsettling unease, a sense that the country finds itself in the position of 'never [quite] having begun', in spite of its hopeful postapartheid script. *Midlands* enjoyed a successful reception – it snatched up the Alan Paton Award, an event that saw Steinberg's status elevated almost instantly to that of key postapartheid writer – and Steinberg has strengthened his reputation with each successive book. *Midlands* is styled as novelistic, conversational nonfiction, in a register that is both sharply analytical and mindful of its reader's historical position: it settles on a quality of interlocution that privileges fact and evidence, and eschews all forms of embellishment. It is a voice and an interlocution that is as persistent as a jackhammer in getting to the bottom of the conditions that underlie a single farm murder and, inductively, the possible conditions behind murder functioning as a form of language in the 'new' South Africa.

Midlands is also something of a travelogue, transporting the reader into the 'heart of the country' – the lush interior of KwaZulu-Natal, seat of historic antagonisms between white and black – in order to expose the actual texture of conditions. It is a mission to acquire a form of knowledge that is outside of the scope of fiction, and whose details demand clear-eyed scrutiny: the point is to scratch below the surface of 'stories' because there are too many stories already. As Twidle reports in his 2012 article '"In a Country Where You Couldn't Make This Shit Up?" Literary Non-Fiction in South Africa', there was consensus among book-fair panellists Rian Malan, Altbeker and Steinberg that 'a plethora of emergent non-fiction narratives in South Africa...seemed to provide the most compelling and challenging medium for the serious writer at present' (6). The urgent task for such authors, then, is to gather evidence of below-the-radar conditions, to secure 'on the ground' intelligence and to record the details that emerge; the imperative is, quite simply, to report back. The writer's mission, it appears, is no longer to *imagine* a different (and ultimately better) future, or to show characters who try to do that but stumble in the process (as in the cases of Michael K in Coetzee's *Life & Times of Michael K*, Elisabeth van den Sandt in Gordimer's *The Late Bourgeois World* or Joseph Malan in Brink's *Looking on Darkness*), but to get to the bottom of a bewilderingly mashed-up present. While Krog works mostly from memory about intersubjective encounters in *Begging to be Black*, Bloom and Steinberg undertake their fieldwork with a high degree of self-reflexivity, making every effort to avoid bias in their recasting of stories told to them in good faith by informants. This taxing labour includes sifting, writing, and in the process reckoning with one's own relation to the information gathered. The urgency of the situation precludes make-believe. It is the age of what David Shields calls 'reality hunger',[30] and there is a keen appetite for data that demythologises, an abiding scepticism, and an acuity that is characteristic of journalism rather than conventional literary modes.

Such twenty-first-century 'travelogues', unlike those of previous centuries, refuse presumptions of prior knowledge, particularly where this relates to race, ethnicity, class or gender. Bloom and Steinberg re-trope the journey of discovery in hard-nosed detection mode; their writing functions as an exercise in social forensics, at once producing and responding to a reinvigorated appetite in the reading market.[31] *Midlands* exemplifies the best of postapartheid writing in the nonfiction mode, offering a perspective on authorial concerns in the knowledge-gathering journeys of detection. The quest is, however, as much inward as outward: suspending the teleological mythography of 'rainbowism', it seeks to understand not rupture, but reversion – reversion to a frontier condition, where murder is a signifier of anxiety, which now, however, relates to failed 'new' beginnings, 're-starts', and a disorienting loss of plot. It is a journey that no longer takes geography (place) as a terra incognita upon which to impose the beneficence of 'field science' (as Livingstone did, for example) in accordance with the classifying paradigms of naturalist enquiry.[32] Instead, it switches from a confidently deductive to a nervily inductive mode, seeking out details first, and making more general conclusions with appropriate caution.

Nevertheless, just a few paragraphs into *Midlands*, the reader is directly confronted with one of the oldest tropes in South African writing, the frontier: '[Peter] Mitchell was killed, not just figuratively, but quite literally, on the southern midlands' racial frontier, the dust road on which he died a boundary between the white-owned commercial farmlands to the west and the derelict common land of a dying black peasantry to the east' (viii–ix). Mitchell's murderers, who had shot the 28-year-old scion of a settler family on his father's farm, did so 'in order to push the boundary back', writes Steinberg (ix). This was a campaign the killers' 'forebears had begun in the closing years of the nineteenth century, and which their great-grandchildren believed it their destiny, as the generation to witness apartheid's demise, to finish' (ix). But Steinberg soon realises that his initial plan to write a book about multiple farm murders was unworkable. He would either have to write the full story of this one murder or abandon the project altogether, so complicated did its details and implications appear:

> I initially thought I was to write about an event from the recent past, but it soon became clear to me that much of the story lay in the immediate future, and I would do well to hang around and record it. This was a silent frontier battle, the combatants groping hungrily for the whispers and lies that drifted in from the other side. It was clear from the start that Peter Mitchell would not be the only one to die on that border, that I had arrived at the beginning of a deadly endgame. And I knew that the story of his and subsequent deaths would illuminate a great deal about the early days of post-apartheid South Africa. (ix)

The nonfiction account promises to yield insights, but here it offers little vision of a time and place beyond the threshold of the transition. Steinberg's account seems merely to take one back/forward into the future-anterior – to the brink again. This is a surprisingly persistent feature of many forms of 'post'-apartheid writing, offering the reader a future-anterior, or a will-have-been feeling, when a 'going forward' scenario is distinctly backward-looking, seeming to repeat, indeed to accelerate, past forms of conflict. So what, if anything, is different, or new, in a book such as *Midlands*?

What distinguishes works such as *Midlands*, *Begging to be Black* and *Ways of Staying* is the occasion for writing, and the manner of approaching, a very old topic. A revised register is required for this new occasion, which, at the most basic level, is the advent of postapartheid and a curiosity about the question, and real nature, of the 'transition'. Does it exist? If so, what does it mean? Has it led to anything beyond the 'threshold' implicit in its meaning? Are the very notions of a 'limit' and a 'beyond' a mere fiction? The immediate pretext for writing such as *Midlands* is the reported surge in what have come to be known as 'farm murders'. On the surface at least, such murders appear to be a form of retribution for the ills of apartheid, frequently involving acts of cruelty that seem entirely gratuitous. Steinberg writes:

> [T]he motive for the vast majority of attacks appears to be robbery; the perpetrators flee the scene of the crime with guns, cars and money. And yet, so many attacks are accompanied by seemingly gratuitous violence, the violence itself performed with such ceremony and drama, that the infliction of painful death appears to be the primary motive. 'Farm murders', as South Africans have come to call them, occupy a strange and ambiguous space; they tamper with the boundary between acquisitive crime and racial hatred...Now [soon after Mandela's inauguration], the dispatches from farming districts appeared to be telling us something all too real. Perhaps the goodwill of the Mandela period was illusory? Perhaps there were a host of unsettled scores we had brushed under the carpet? Maybe, for once, the countryside was way ahead of us, bringing a grim portent of life after the honeymoon. (vii)

Steinberg sets out to discover what lies behind the phenomenon of farm murders, which seem to have become a lurid 'new South Africa' spectacle, countering the optimistic vision of transition, the 'transformation' of South African society. He had become dissatisfied with the sketchiness of what he was able to write, and the limits to what he was able to find out, while working as a crime reporter for the Johannesburg newspaper *Business Day*. Having secured funding, and a desk at the Centre for the Study of Violence and Reconciliation in Johannesburg, he left his job at *Business Day*, and began a series of forays into the 'country', both in the sense of the rural hinterland, and in the broader sense of the sociopolitical and geographical entity that is postapartheid South Africa.

Steinberg's long and exhaustive investigation concentrates the reader's attention on his voice as narrator. Over the course of a compelling, rigorous and exhaustive narration, Steinberg's analytical, sceptical voice sets a distinct tone. There is a sense of impatience in it, a refusal to indulge his interviewees, the white farmers especially, and yet this voice is considerate of its reader, whom it addresses directly in the second person as 'you' ('you will remember'; 'I will tell you this story a little later'). It is also self-reflexive in its putting together of the bits and pieces of the narrative, its sharing with the reader the difficulties of where and how to position various segments of the overall puzzle that is the murder. Steinberg effectively narrates his acts of detection, adopting a new kind of mood, and doing so with a new kind of reader in mind. This 'new South Africa' reader is well informed about politics and economic history, tired of the spent falsehoods of the past, hungry for untainted information and impatient for real social change. It is a putative reader that belongs to a generation of urban South Africans who came of age politically in the explosive 1980s. Many, like Steinberg himself, had joined the United Democratic Front (UDF) or one of the popular civic movements ('civics') in the struggle against apartheid.[33] Steinberg's is a probing yet respectful voice, wary of self-justificatory mythmaking, always alert to half-answers and evasions, clearly dubious of self-serving political rationalisations, whether from the white or the black side of the political fence.

The white or the black side? The political fence? Surely such phrases are, or should be, redundant in the postapartheid age? The fact that this is *not* the case, as Steinberg shows over the course of his vivid, generally dispiriting encounters, partly explains the businesslike brusqueness in the investigator-narrator's voice: like a surgeon's scalpel, it probes and cuts away. To switch metaphors, it is as if the stakes are suddenly very high – for the isiZulu-speaking black citizens as well as the white South Africans in Steinberg's story. It is as though postapartheid has not changed the game, but merely accelerated the moves, shifted the positions on the board, altered the roles of players, and upped the reward money while failing to pay out equal start-up amounts. Suddenly, it is all or nothing, and now that the political game is on, the payout is power, whether monetary or political, or, as is more often the case, mere survival.[34] Once-pliable partners suddenly play dirty; players often change sides without declaring their motives; the rule book has been rewritten in the language of fairness, but enforcement of the rules is weak, with some players complaining that where 'enforcement' does occur, it is often openly partisan or racially biased. And so, private reckonings such as the murder at the centre of *Midlands* seek to balance competing interests, confirming the hypothesis that law and disorder in the postcolony are parasitically codependent. A discourse of prevarication prevails, as both sides of a reconfigured 'racial frontier' keep their cards close to their chests in the quest to win this new and dangerous game.

Can such a condition truly be called a 'transition' to democracy? Perhaps so, though only in a postcolonial style, where the 'post' is less temporal than conceptual, paradoxical and recursive, as it plays out (or 'acts out') anew on the old terrain of the frontier. Political power has changed hands, but economic might emphatically has not, apart from rare but conspicuous black-elite enrichment. White people in the Midlands area, where Steinberg's investigation takes place, remain sturdily wealthy; they continue to own the land and its riches. Black people are either unemployed (the great majority), wage earners on white farms (a fortunate few) or small-time entrepreneurs with political connections (a tiny handful, making up a ragged – and vulnerable – local elite). The condition of postapartheid, in Steinberg's analysis, is felt, not in any newly enfranchised euphoria or material advancement, but in the urgency of frustration about a seemingly elusive economic freedom for the majority of the population, about 'never [quite] having begun'. These are people who, on the whole, remain trapped in centuries-old poverty, despite having an ANC president and a bill of rights. So, on the black side of the racial frontier, indignation and hostility are running hotter than ever before in the country's history – leading, indeed, to the farm murder in Steinberg's story – while on the white side there is a level of fear and insecurity about the rule of law that supersedes earlier versions of a 'black peril', which no longer looms, but threatens to engulf. All parties appear to feel a lot worse than they did before – they are, jointly and severally, deeply unsettled, but with a new sense of entitlement, each in their own way seeking to rely on the provisions of an immaculately conceived but waywardly (and inefficiently) enforced regime of fair play. Well-nigh unenforceable, its chief outcome is an ever-accelerating sense of desperation on all sides.

This situation may explain why the farm murders Steinberg sets out to investigate have a 'bite to their horror that is absent from the horror of most murders' (5). '[W]hite farmers,' Steinberg avers, 'were not killed under apartheid. Not like this, at any rate. They were killed by jealous spouses, by disturbed neighbours and by crazed children. But never like this' (5). Under apartheid, he writes, people on farms had to lock their doors when they went away on holiday: 'But murder? Never. No black man entered the vast commercial farmlands to kill a member of a powerful white family. And on the handful of occasions when a crazy black man did kill a white, the police would comb the countryside with their fists and their electric shocks and they would get a confession' (6).

Such policing is no longer the norm: the local murder and robbery unit in Steinberg's spotlight is both under-resourced and demoralised. White detectives, such as *Midlands*'s Louis Wessels, belonged to squads that were 'shattered by the [supposed] demise of apartheid' because '[t]he cause that animated the unit's work – already somewhat misty – was defeated, and vanished from the face of the earth' (81), although many would argue that it did not vanish but morphed into less visible and camouflaged forms. Furthermore, democratic South Africa 'was a rough country to police' (81). There were many towns assigned to individuals such as Wessels, where a detective sent to interview a suspect 'is not sure whether he will come out alive' (81). And so, why bother to investigate? Steinberg writes: 'So much mortal danger, so much fear – in the service of a political order from which men like Wessels are so thoroughly estranged' (81). Steinberg's analysis of the state of policing in democratic South Africa (73–90) is sobering: it is a centralised 'monster of an institution' (78), the second-largest in the world, and it is 'chaotic and ungovernable' (78). Just as police units in KwaZulu-Natal under apartheid were often highly compromised, with white policemen openly furthering the agendas of Mangosuthu Buthelezi's apartheid-linked Inkatha Freedom Party, so is contemporary policing mired in local politics, which itself has criminal connections. Steinberg shows how, in the rivalry following the Mitchell murder, the black parties, up against their white accusers, regard the local murder and robbery squad (a separate, mostly white-led unit) with deep suspicion. Blacks regard the unit as being on the 'white side' ('I know these policemen are yours,' says a member of the Cube family), while whites see the (entirely black) local police station as being on the 'black side' (87). In Steinberg's narrative, the Mitchell family comes to view the new, equitable, constitutional dispensation as nothing more than 'an edifice behind which the criminals, the savages and the killers of this country took refuge' (88).

For whites, such barricading is not confined to the matter of policing. Reflecting on the discourse of Colin Waugh, one of Steinberg's key interlocutors, the author notes that '[Waugh] had blurred the distinction between racial difference and a military frontier' (16–17). But that is not all. 'Later,' Steinberg writes, 'when I tried to enter Izita in my white skin, I discovered that [Waugh's] "opposition" had done the same' (17). Here, then, is another instance of 'bad' difference,[35] only now it is the inverse of the essentialism underpinning 'self-determination' in apartheid's 'separate but equal' racial ideology; here one sees how the discourse of pluralism and heterogeneity, which lies at the heart of South Africa's constitutional democracy, is dishonoured. It is mangled in the hands not only of those who interpret and administer the law, but also of those who are subject to it. Bias, antagonism, misperception, and misrecognition of difference – all age-old South African frontier characteristics – are here recast and resituated within the new game. Paradoxically, this occurs against the background of a new, hard-won constitutional democracy. What have really changed are the odds, as well as the relative weighting of factors such as lawmaking and the enforcement of laws. For Elias Sithole, a struggle stalwart whom Steinberg encounters during his search for clues, politics is corrupt to the core. Sithole sets out his view of things as follows:

> And so what is the ANC now, that noble organisation in the name of which people died horrible deaths? The ANC in Izita is run by a bunch of small-time, crooked businessmen who couldn't give a damn about their constituencies. They want to make money, and to keep making it they need power, and that is why they get involved in politics. Politics has become the playground of the corrupt. It is no more than that. He shook his head in disgust. (121)

It is Sithole's view that young people have been afflicted by a new scourge. 'Something terrible' has happened to the once-revered revolutionary subgroup, 'the youth'.[36] They continue to think of themselves as soldiers, he says, 'but there is no war to fight' and '[s]oldiers without a war are bandits' (122). He defines a bandit as 'somebody who has retained the revolutionary's disrespect for the law' but has no ennobling ultimate goal (122); the bandit 'just sweeps, just smashes' (122) without putting anything in its place. The bandit, Sithole says with manifest distaste, 'calls himself an entrepreneur' (122). One might add that, in so doing, such 'entrepreneurs' instrumentalise disorder, confirming Mbembe's interpretation of conditions in postapartheid South Africa as atomised, instrumentalised chaos (Mbembe, 'Our Lust for Lost Segregation'). For ordinary people in the Sarahdale/ Izita region, Steinberg suggests, the postapartheid frontier situation has developed into an 'endgame': 'The truth is that things had spiralled out of control. Mitchell and his enemies were caught up in an endgame, one neither had bargained for, one that was bound to end with the spilling of more blood on the border between Izita and the Sarahdale farms' (75). As the narrative progresses, Steinberg perceives a stark underlying logic in the complex events he unravels:

> I realised then that what was going on between Mitchell and his tenants was quite simple, really. They had tried to push him off his farm and rob him of his vocation, and now the idea of farming that land the way he had done before his son died contained the most meaning he was ever going to squeeze out of his life. I also realised that his tenants would never leave him in peace. Whenever he dipped a cow, mended a fence or planted a seed, he would be getting his revenge. They would haunt him in the taking of his every pleasure. (184)

The narrative quest is to find out what is actually going on, behind the facade of the transition. The enquiry as to where in fact the 'transit' in 'transition' has taken the constitutional democracy results, with nauseating repetitiveness, in the discovery of a toxic endgame. In Sithole's view, the combination of hope and disappointment is plain:

> In the 1980s there was hope. Change was around the corner. The ugly things would soon be leaving. Then democracy came. Mandela's government. Then another election. Mbeki's government. And the white farmers still run the countryside. Things are getting worse, in fact. The farmers are building these game reserves and taking over miles of land they have never used before. They don't trust the police any longer so they create their own private police forces. These men in their uniforms stand on

the hilltops watching your every move with their binoculars and their night-vision glasses, defending the law of their land.

There is nowhere to escape to. You can't go to the cities because there is no work there. You will starve to death. You are a prisoner in the white man's countryside, and now there is no prospect of anything different. It is you against him for the rest of time. So when he marches onto your land and tells you he is going to interview your future son-in-law and decide whether he can live in your house, you take matters into your own hands, because nobody else is going to. (245–246)

In response, Steinberg asks: 'You kill his son?' Sithole replies: 'Yes. It has come to that' (246).

Here, then, is a mortal counterpoint to any sense of a seamless 'transition' to a 'postapartheid' South Africa. Instead, this is an 'endgame' whose finality suggests, paradoxically, a return to a prior state – to the frontier, 'post-apartheid South Africa's racial frontier' (x), as Steinberg puts it. He repeats the phrase 'racial frontier' a further five times in his book, an ineluctable reminder that, far from having moved 'beyond', we are still in this deadly game, and that this is now endgame time. Steinberg's term ironically reaffirms, and recycles, another long-standing trope in South African literature – especially in white writing – namely apocalypse or end times.[37] It is therefore clear that any suggestion that South African literature is 'post-' transition, 'post-transitional' or 'post-postapartheid' should be regarded with caution. If inductively based reports such as those offered by Bloom, Krog and Steinberg are at all credible, then postapartheid's material conditions contradict the promise of any such forward-looking temporalities: they call into question the scripts of (even faltering) progress in the here and now. Instead, and again, we have the spectre of never (quite) having begun the journey to another, better place.

4

The transitional calm before the postapartheid storm

The previous chapter opened with a consideration of discourse about crime, and the manner in which public discussion about wrongdoing has contributed to the disorienting nature of the postapartheid period. The argument explored a 'white phenomenology of crime', as perceived by Steinberg, and moved on to a consideration of Bloom's *Ways of Staying*, where it found, instead of a contraction into a psychological laager, a breakout impulse, a widening of the authorial lens, the effect of which is to suggest a more widespread sense of contingency. Similarly, in Krog's *Begging to be Black*, the greater reach of integration among races also results in increased states of fear and growing suspicion. The expanded range of intersubjective encounter, along with states of peril differently distributed to those in the past, distinguishes nonfiction narratives of detection in the postapartheid period from earlier chronicles of unbelonging, namely travelogues and journeys into the interior, despite the persistence, if not compulsion, of the trope of journeying. In spite of what I earlier typified as 'compulsive (re)iteration, a literature seemingly always, and repeatedly, at the frontier of not-knowing, on the brink', there are signs in this literature that the writer now understands more than ever before that his viewfinder must include the larger race, class and gender picture; in addition, his or her tone must be stripped of all forms of paternalism. There is a new impatience to move on, working in Ginzburg's 'conjectural paradigm' of detection, based on a more general evidential paradigm (as noted in Chapter 3). So, despite black and white writers alike finding the symptoms of democracy perverse, brimming with 'bad' difference, it is also true to say that the return, in the sociopolitical sphere, of 'frontier' conditions is rendered deeply problematic, and subjected to what one might call a more stringent, peculiarly postapartheid critique. This critique, unlike many past reckonings with apartheid, cannot settle the matter in struggle preconceptions. It is a critique, rather, that must define the material details that underpin ruptures in the feverishly imagined discourse of democratic South Africa. The devil is in such detail, since master-narratives no longer hold sway. And postapartheid writers, occupying an unsettled domain, more often than not appear sick to death of such metanarratives. Evidence, and a cool head, are central to their timely interlocutions with readers. This stands in contrast to the erratic recriminations that pose as argument on social media, especially in the wake of the #RhodesMustFall campaign in 2015. Despite literary culture in the postapartheid period increasingly intersecting with an all-pervading new media, especially in the consolidation of an emotive 'wound culture' (see Chapter 6), analytically detailed consideration remains a notable – if relatively rare – counterpoint, with authors such as Mbembe, Pumla Gobodo-Madikizela, Gevisser, Dlamini and Baderoon holding their tempers, so to speak, and prioritising cogent, inductive argument over rant – which has assumed an elevated status.

Accordingly, inductive, evidence-based detail – in the making of plot, style and story – is wielded as an alternative to the overdeterminations of race dualisms, whether in their pre-1994 or reanimated post-2010 forms. Such an evidential approach manifests as a liberating force – in fact, as the fundamental force of such writing. What was perhaps not foreseen in Ndebele's appeal for embracing the 'ordinary' in all its manifestations, nor in Albie Sachs's call for a celebration of life beyond the limits of struggle parameters, was the extent to which social perversity would mutate, and the liberation script disintegrate, and how writing would, perforce, find itself investigating, in both fictional and nonfictional form, the details of the derailment of the postapartheid deal. In so doing, however, literature (among other forms) is reasserting its primary function by locating and identifying sociopolitical perversity, all in the name of a freshly affirmed evidential social criticism, and a reimagined sense of (un)belonging.

'Spring is rebellious': The early-postapartheid script

As a complement to understanding this impulse in postapartheid writing, one needs to recall how earlier examples of transitional literature – and commentary – set up a script that would
later be rudely abandoned. This 'setting up' occurred within a
literary-critical community of scholars who played a key role in
constructing the field that came to be known as 'SA Lit'.[1] Various
pronouncements in the early 1990s, by among others the venerable
triad of Ndebele, Sachs and Brink, played a strong role in ushering
in a wave of optimistic anticipation about renewed possibilities and
transformed literary landscapes. Brink has been much cited on this
score, saying things such as 'more than ever before … literature has
to make space for the private vision, the personal imagination, the
individual small, still voice' (Brink, 'To Re-Imagine' 1). He quali-
fied this, however, by denying a return to 'earlier forms of individ-
ualism', and favouring instead 'the articulation of a personal space
informed by an experience of suffering and witnessing with others';
for Brink in 1993, writing in the *Weekly Mail & Guardian Review of
Books*, the writer's task is a 'rewriting, a reimagination of history',
and 'to grapple, exuberantly and adventurously, with the limits of
the possible' ('To Re-Imagine' 1). This strikes a chord – with a
distinctly ludic note – of hopefulness about imaginative liberation
in early-transition discourse; also with Ndebele's oft-cited plea to
narrate the 'ordinary'; and with Sachs's injunction that 'weapon of
the struggle' versions of culture should be suspended to allow for
a respite from the kind of art in which 'all that is funny or curious
or genuinely tragic in the world' has been 'extruded' ('Preparing
Ourselves' 187). For Sachs, this would help assure that 'ambiguity and contradiction' would not be 'completely shut out' (187).
Attwell and Harlow (3–4), reflecting on early-transition literature,
characterise what they call the fields of 'South African literature
since 1990' as engaging with 'the experiential, ethical and political ambiguities of transition'; the 'liberalism of the new order',
they write, 'is more accommodating than a revolutionary culture
could ever be, to the re-invention of tradition, to irony, to play'.
The notion of 'play' – the ludic, or the grotesquerie of carnival –
is key: it incorporates a sense of freedom from the fixed agendas
of the past, and proposes an artistic space in which it is possible

playfully and fearlessly to reimagine both the past and the present, not to mention the 'future *im*perfect', in Loren Kruger's proleptic phrase ('Black Atlantics' 35). In the early 1990s, this sense of exhilaration inherent in possibilities for a greater ludic dimension found expression in two collections of essays whose very titles, *Spring is Rebellious* (edited by Ingrid de Kok and Karen Press) and *Exchanges* (edited by Duncan Brown and Bruno van Dyk), betray their anticipation of release, of a loosening from the claustrophobic grip of realist, socially 'responsible' and relentlessly 'serious' literature, moribund in its state of stalemate. Both collections are ensembles of responses to Sachs's call, containing optimistic gambits by writers, critics, 'cultural workers' and art practitioners. On the whole, the contributors embrace a new era of artistic autonomy, and their tone is buoyant, anticipating a kind of ludic licence that had been largely repressed until 1990, when Nelson Mandela was released and liberation movements unbanned.

Even while this intoxicating ferment was being stoked up, a playwright by the name of Zakes Mda was putting the finishing touches to a first novel that would become a cause célèbre, in the early-transition period, of precisely such a sea-change. That novel, initially published in 1991 by Oxford University Press Southern Africa, was *Ways of Dying*,[2] and its critical reception reveals much about the early consensus, or script – a majority position, perhaps – on how postapartheid literature should be imagined. It is important to look at the nature of this first-wave optimism so that the second-wave critique of the causes of its (supposed) collapse might be read in context.

For Rita Barnard ('On Laughter' 278–279), *Ways of Dying* 'looks hopefully toward the postapartheid future' while also taking 'a backward glance: not only to the apartheid years but also to the history of other African nations, where juridical independence was rapidly succeeded by disillusionment'. Barnard sees Mda's first novel, despite its clear focus on death, as 'essentially an optimistic work' (279). Such a perception is concordant with Mda's own statement, captured in a YouTube video, in which he says the following:

> It was very important for me that the story, even though it's about death, should be an upbeat story, and it should be optimistic; at the end we see that, actually, this is not the kind of situation that's going to last forever; these are just the pangs of birth of a new

society. Sooner or later, things will change. It was important for
me to show that.[3]

The idea that 'sooner or later, things will change' is nothing if not a
declaration of faith, and little more than optimism. There was scant
basis for such faith in the early 1990s. Economic conditions then, in
the almost-democratic South Africa, were sharply skewed, mostly
along racial lines, with a thin slice of haves and a massive majority of
have-nots. The optimism of the moment was, nevertheless, heady, and
few were immune to it. Barnard's position on Mda's novel is representative of much critical opinion at the time, at least in its endorsement of the novel's transformation of deadly conditions into a spirit
of creative idealism. Barnard usefully captures the critical consensus
about Mda's novel as a 'narrative desire...to transform fighting children into playful ones: to replace a sober militancy with gaiety and
laughter' ('On Laughter' 280). The militancy recalled in the novel
should not be underplayed, though, taking on the shape of 'necklacing' as a means of mob justice in the 1980s, when *impimpi*s – people
fingered as collaborators with the regime – were burned alive; youthful township mobs placed flaming car tyres around suspects' necks,
chanting as they watched their victims collapse and die. In *Ways of
Dying*, the character Noria's six-year-old son perishes in this manner. Arguably the most decisive gesture in the novel's action, and certainly one of the main reasons behind its extraordinary uptake in both
critical reception and university curricula, is that communal engagement is recast, transformed from this kind of ultra-violent activity
into artistic, creative engagement. Barnard ('On Laughter' 282) is
quick to align such regenerative transformation – what she calls a
new 'prosaics' – with the positions taken by Sachs and Ndebele. She
concludes (deferring to Loren Kruger's phrase) that Mda's work is
'post-anti-apartheid' both in content and in its 'multilayered, fantastic
plot'; it breaches the 'generic constraints that the culture of resistance, with its demand for realist immediacy, had for years placed on
the black writer' (280). So, the early-post-anti-apartheid novel, in this
formula, is not only post-realist and 'fantastic',[4] it also 'breaches
generic constraints', or breaks form. Although it is tempting, when
describing postapartheid literature, to overlook the frequent 'breach-
ing of generic constraints' in pre-1990 literature,[5] it is true that imaginative literature after 1990 does indeed show a pronounced inclination

to break the earlier dominance of social realism, whether it does so playfully or not.

Barnard distances herself from the less sanguine position of Grant Farred, who finds Mda's novel problematic because it allegedly privileges performance above materiality: 'Preoccupied with the staging of spectacle(s), the novel evacuates itself of historical meaning,' writes Farred ('Mourning' 204) in an uncompromising critique. Farred's opinion chimes with those of materialist critics of the transition such as Patrick Bond (*Elite Transition*), Neil Lazarus and John Saul, all of whom are impatient with what they see as mere gestures of celebratory togetherness. For them, such postures are premature. They are, moreover, belied by the adoption of macro-economic policies that have led to material conditions which threaten social cohesion – let alone promote regeneration – except in a late-capitalist market of goods and services, and the 'freedom' to buy commodities as 'equally' as anyone else. However, Barnard, like many Mda critics (see Bell and Jacobs; Fincham), prefers to find value in Mda's aesthetic of a 'redeemed form of laughter: one that may serve as an inoculation against the laughter of helpless passivity or cruelty that resounds in situations of oppression' ('On Laughter' 296). Relying on a sense of the carnivalesque derived from a reading of Bakhtin, Barnard sees the reader of Mda's novel as being 'confronted with the monstrous fertility of the creative imagination' ('On Laughter' 299), which, rather than producing the pity, sadness or guilt often evoked by descriptions of poverty, invites us to see 'the ingenuity born from destitution, the human capacities that may eventually bring about its transformation' (299).

In retrospect, the implicit stand-off between Barnard and Farred helps one to demarcate some of the outer lines on the 'field' of postapartheid literary culture. One such boundaryline, set down by Barnard and other Mda enthusiasts, signifies that the ludic imperative is robust. In criticism, the literature-as-play move is frequently made under the literary authority of *Ways of Dying* and works by other writers in which realism is suspended, or ruptured, or in which various forms of playfulness are foregrounded, and the hard politics of deprivation are less accentuated. Other authors who can be invoked on similar grounds include Mongane Wally Serote, whose long poem *Come and Hope with Me* (see Seema) is a lyrical appeal for the reconstruction of a broken land; Chris van Wyk, whose *The Year of the Tapeworm* pokes fun at authority figures and undercuts conventional social realism (see Moslund 'Beyond Realism'); Marlene van Niekerk, whose daring novel *Triomf* mixes uproarious antics in language, philosophy and action with comic exuberance in its plot; Ashraf Jamal, whose *Love Themes for the Wilderness* seeks to throw off fixities of identity in favour of affirmatively free-flowing subjectivities (see Stobie); Ivan Vladislavić, whose novel *The Folly* was taken up as a work in which whimsical imaginative leaps and modal shifts supersede mimetic dread (see Wentzel); André Brink, one of the early-transition 'magical realists'; and Achmat Dangor, of whom Loren Kruger says the following in her discussion of post-anti-apartheid texts of the 'transitional 1990s':

> Certainly, In *Kafka's Curse*, as in *Waiting for Leila* and the *Z Town Trilogy*, Dangor takes on politics and collective narratives, but he does so not in the sense of adopting them or defending them single-mindedly, in the manner of the classic anti-apartheid narrative, but rather in the sense of tackling them, parrying them, or even of fending them off. In so doing, he offers readers schooled by the strategic dichotomies of anti-apartheid discourse a language for exploring – if not, as yet, completely encompassing – post-anti-apartheid stories. ('Black Atlantics' 45)

Exploration and play were both, of course, major themes in the 1990s and early 2000s for South African critics, especially those who were inclined in their critical-theoretical practice towards liminality and aporia rather than foundational 'truths', especially when these were seen to reproduce hoary old structures of perception undergirding – in the form of ideology – discriminatory social structures. Critics who published notable critical monographs in this vein are Ashraf Jamal (*Predicaments of Culture in South Africa*) and Louise Bethlehem (*Skin Tight*). Jamal's book carries an impassioned critical plea for greater mobility and fluidity of cultural and critical expression in an affirmative rather than a claustrophobic register, while Bethlehem seeks a form of criticism that is alert to representational slippage, casting doubt on all manner of inherited cultural certitudes. Michael Titlestad's *Making the Changes* (on jazz 'discourse' in South Africa) is likewise driven by theories of improvisational expression and the torsions of inventive play in South African literary and musical discourse.

A dog chained to its own vomit?

Jamal in particular deserves consideration because his work outlines a strong position that remains a provocation in South African literary and cultural studies. The following interchange between writer Russel Brownlee and Jamal, looking back from the vantage of 2006, usefully condenses Jamal's core argument in *Predicaments of Culture*:

> [Brownlee]: Your latest book-length publication, *Predicaments of Culture in South Africa*, takes a critical look at the state of artistic freedom in this country. You suggest that despite political liberation, the defining characteristic of our cultural [imaginary] remains the ghetto – and by ghetto you mean the propensity for people to associate themselves with groups holding set positions from which they attempt to establish a new orthodoxy. In short, South African cultural production is not yet free. How do you see this lack of freedom in a practical sense – how does it actually manifest and inhibit the output of writers, artists and critics?
>
> [Jamal]: As you well know, it is very easy merely to criticise a perceived limitation. In my case, and in defence of my position regarding South African arts and culture, I've noticed a persistent failure of the imagination and an absurd overrating of the talents of particular individuals. I should certainly add that I've also been party to this absurd misperception. If I reflect now on my craven adoration for the writing of JM Coetzee I simply wish to weep. Undoubtedly he has a remarkable stylistic gift – that is, if you value a style that is both resonant and arid. However, his graft of human experience is appallingly bleak and rather naïve because of its bleakness. Similarly, that other bloated sacred cow in South African culture, William Kentridge … again, remarkably intelligent, but precious little spirit, or vitality. It is as though South African culture, through the works of figures such as these, appears dead on arrival; as though all that was possible was the mirroring of our sorry morbidity. (Jamal and Brownlee n.p.)

This passage is typical of Jamal's irreverent public voice, which he maintains despite the significant reputational risks of pointedly taking swipes at cows as sacred as Coetzee and Kentridge, and holding 'South African arts and culture' collectively responsible for a state of 'sorry morbidity'. Jamal's key intervention is less a hard or rational argument, at base, than a plea for a change of spirit, a decisive turn in the *affective disposition* in which all acts of culture, for him, are enveloped. For Jamal, what is missing in the first instance is a certain kind of courage:

> What I'm getting at is that I've very rarely encountered the ability or the courage to grasp the unthinkable; to shift the axis away from the tedium of polarisation, as though our minds and imaginations were transfixed by the Manichean dialectic and precious little else. I never feel that Coetzee, or Kentridge, or even Fugard has in fact lived. (Jamal and Brownlee n.p.)

Not only do celebrated writers appear never to have 'lived', that is, lived affirmatively, with the courage to see beyond self-created 'ghettoes' of the mind, but there is a general 'pathology' in the culture arising from what Jamal perceives as a 'failure of imagination':

> Why, then, are [Coetzee, Kentridge, Fugard] so remarkably successful? Precisely because they have cashed in on a pathology that is domestic and international. When Coetzee says that South Africa is as irresistible as it is unlovable he, precisely, re-enacts the procedure of fascination and loathing which largely characterises the continued psychic state of our fellow citizens. Still, just because he is accurate does not mean that the position is meritorious. My counter-view is that South Africa is as resistible as it is loveable. By this I mean that only by conceptualising the country in this way will we counter our pathological inheritance. But then, perverts that we are, we prefer to rot in our fallibility and our weakness. Which of course means that freedom is the last thing that anyone wants! (Jamal and Brownlee n.p.)

Jamal's challenge to artists does not sound too different from Breyten Breytenbach's invocation of the importance of creativity in his 2008 essay 'Mandela's Smile': 'For the mind has to be allowed to dance, even with death, if we want to stay it from reverting to despair and narcissistic self-love. To survive, we must assume the responsibility of imagining the world *differently*' (46; Breytenbach's emphasis). He continues:

> Writing as the production of textured consciousness is the mediating metaphor between fact and fiction. It is in the movement

of the heart-mind and the thinking awareness of physical and/
or cultural displacement that creativity is born – as sequences of
perception bringing about new combinations of past and present,
projecting future shapes and thus helping to shape the future. We
are hardwired to see *intention* in the world, and thus predisposed
to the art of learning by intervention. We become by making. We
realize ourselves through acts of transformation. And these journeys bring with them implications of accountability. By imitating
the forms of creativity we apprehend the contents of *meaning*;
in the enactment of ethics we learn about the prescription and
the limitations of the will to have being emerge: together these
constitute the freedom way. ('Mandela's Smile' 46, emphases in
the original)

This call, invoking Mandela's legacy of reconciliation, of 'smiling'
even at his detractors, finds little resonance in Breytenbach's contemporary, JM Coetzee, who made his statement about the country being
unlovable in his Jerusalem Prize acceptance speech in 1987, and in
many ways confirmed the dire import of this message in *Disgrace*, his
swansong to South Africa before relocating to Australia in 2002. It is
significant that in the Jerusalem speech, Coetzee, like Jamal, proceeds
from the premise of a failure of love. Opening with the statement that
'[i]n a society of masters and slaves, no one is free' (*Doubling the Point*
96), Coetzee adds that what lies 'at the heart of the unfreedom of the
hereditary masters of South Africa is a failure of love' (97) because
their 'excessive talk, about how they love South Africa has consistently been directed toward *the land*' (Coetzee's emphasis) rather
than its people. The love, or 'fraternity', that the white master-class
seeks, Coetzee argues, is not to be had, because it 'ineluctably comes
in a package with liberty and equality' (97). It is on this basis that
Coetzee then makes his oft-quoted statement about the 'deformed
and stunted' state of South Africa:

> The deformed and stunted relations between human beings that
> were created under colonialism and exacerbated under what is
> loosely called apartheid have their psychic representation in a
> deformed and stunted inner life. All expressions of that inner life,
> no matter how intense, no matter how pierced with exultation or
> despair, suffer from the same stuntedness and deformity ... South

> African literature is a literature in bondage, as it reveals in even its highest moments, shot through as they are with feelings of homelessness and yearnings for a nameless liberation. It is a less than fully human literature, unnaturally occupied with power and the torsions of power, unable to move from elementary relations of contestation, domination, and subjugation to the vast and complex human world that lies beyond them. (98)

For Coetzee, material conditions and interpersonal relations ('torsions of power'; 'relations of contestation, domination, and subjugation') rather than attitudes or states of mind are primarily responsible for the 'deformed and stunted' relations he observes; this is also implied in the passive statement 'were created under colonialism and exacerbated under…apartheid'. By the elliptical, passive phrase 'were created', he surely means that the stunted relations he refers to were *produced* by the force of what historians have come to call racial capitalism, by the ensuing asymmetrical distribution of land and resources. He can only mean, further, that such conditions came about through violent means, through coercion rather than consensus, bullets rather than ballots. One must deduce that, for Coetzee, a 'deformed and stunted inner life' is a *result* of such a history, a history that cannot be rescinded, edited or substantially revised. Unlike Cervantes in *Don Quixote*, Coetzee continues, the South African writer cannot 'quit a world of pathological attachments' (98) – despite dearly wishing to do so – and so cannot enter the 'realm of faery' as Cervantes does; this is because the 'power of the world his body lives in to impose itself on him and ultimately on his imagination' (99) is irresistible:

> The crudity of life in South Africa, the naked force of its appeals, not only at the physical level but at the moral level too, its callousness and its brutalities, its hungers and its rages, its greed and its lies, make it as irresistible as it is unlovable. (99)

After citing Nietzsche's line that 'we have art so that we shall not die of the truth', Coetzee concludes with another frequently invoked – and reverberant – line: 'In South Africa there is now too much truth for art to hold, truth by the bucketful, truth that overwhelms and swamps every act of the imagination' (99). We have no choice, as writers in South Africa, Coetzee was saying in 1987, just three years before the

onset of the transition, than to succumb to the pathological determin-
ism of a 'deformed and stunted inner life' as a result of 'deformed
and stunted relations', because the material conditions – 'truth by the
bucketful' – precede and determine the pathology. These conditions
produce the pathology in the sense that they are its origin and cause.

Jamal, however, views the 'ghettoes' of the mind as themselves
determinative, insisting that Coetzee's line, that the country is as
'irresistible as it is unlovable', functions as a kind of mind-clamp.
South Africa as a country, Jamal avers, is both resistible *and* lovable,
thereby unclamping not only thought but also feeling. You *can* resist
the 'crudity…the naked force of its appeals', its callousness, brutali-
ties, hungers and rages. You *can* say no to being determined by such
conditions, and *choose* to see differently; as a result, for Jamal, the
country can and must be lovable rather than unlovable. The respective theoretical positions may be framed as, on the one hand, a view
in which (unchangeable) materiality precedes (pliable) feeling or
affect – Coetzee's stance; and, on the other, an insistence that attitude
or will is not necessarily subject to material conditions. In fact, Jamal's
argument holds that a dogged insistence on a certain viewpoint actually predetermines material conditions, like a dog chained to its vomit
(as Jamal is wont to say, recalling Samuel Beckett's 'habit is the ballast
that chains the dog to his vomit', in his 1930 essay 'Proust'). Further,
Jamal finds that at least one of Coetzee's novels does in fact prove his
point, namely *Life & Times of Michael K*:

> Coetzee's *Life & Times of Michael K* is the only visionary and rad-
> ically political work to have emerged from South Africa (in the
> English language at least). That it remains his only work of great
> significance is telling. The reason why it is a great work is that it
> creates a character who is a squatter in systems who escapes detec-
> tion, a condemned man who remains strangely free, uttering little,
> understanding even less, disclosing nothing, his passage through
> life inscrutable. He is a creature who is neither friend nor foe,
> who neither flees nor engages the world, the embodiment of that
> most austere of conditions: *distance* – not the calibrated distance
> between things but distance itself. In other words, Michael K is the
> closest we get to what that brilliant and much maligned thinker,
> Homi Bhabha, calls the hybrid moment. Clearly it is a moment
> that bypasses the Manichean dialectic, and for that crucial reason

it opens up another method of thinking... Its vital plea is to remind us that to love is to think, and that it is lovelessness that is the negation of thought, and hence of life itself. (Jamal and Brownlee n.p.)

Regardless of Jamal's sweeping statements ('his only work of great significance'; 'the only visionary and radically political work [in English] to have emerged from South Africa'), the larger point is worth taking seriously. Jamal is effectively asking why it should not be possible for South Africans, and especially artists, to emulate Michael K. Surely the capacity of Michael K to escape camps and ghettoes of both the mind and geography – an art of escape, and an insistence on freedom that is profoundly figured in Coetzee's novel – should also be a possibility for a larger South African culture? Jamal, in effect, is suggesting that Coetzee's own narrative art (in *Life & Times*, at least) negates and overrules what Jamal regards as the pathological pessimism of the Jerusalem Prize speech.

In addition, Jamal contradictorily couches his faith in what he calls the 'hybrid moment' – Bhabha-esque and poststructuralist – in anti-rationalist terms: 'love'. (For poststructuralists, appeals to emotion are often thought to be just one step behind the bogey of essentialism.) This leads irresistibly to a glancing consideration of how Jamal's call intersects with a movement that would come into vogue soon after this interview, namely the 'Affective Turn'.

An elegiac South African moment in the Affective Turn?

Jamal's emphatic statements – 'to love is to think', and 'it is lovelessness that is the negation of thought, and hence of life itself' – bring him much closer to a movement in critical theory that was gaining ground at the time he was in conversation with Brownlee (2006), though it is one that Jamal does not explicitly invoke: the Affective Turn.[6] How far removed, one may well ask, is what Jamal is quoted as saying, above, from the following statement by Rita Felski in her influential article 'Suspicious Minds'?

Suspicious reading inscribes itself in the psyche as a particular mode of thought and feeling, a mind-set equipped with distinct qualities: distance rather than closeness; guardedness rather than openness; aggression rather than submission; superiority rather than reverence; attentiveness rather than distraction; exposure

rather than tact. It constitutes an orientation in the phenome-
nological sense; a matrix of feelings, attitudes, and beliefs that
expresses itself in a particular manner of turning toward its object,
of leaning toward or recoiling away from a text, of engaging in
close – yet also critical and therefore distanced – reading. Like
any repeated practice, it eases into the state of second nature; no
longer an alien or obtrusive activity, but an internalized, habitual,
and self-evident aspect of one's identity as a reader. (222)

While Felski is primarily concerned with a dispositional inclination
in the act of 'critically' reading literary texts, her position inevitably
relates also to the broader ambit of critical theory. As Felski herself
argues, '[t]he critic fashions a sequence of cause and effect that correlates textual clues with underlying systems of political inequality
or oppression' (224). Cultural anthropologist Michael Hardt, in his
essay 'For Love or Money', goes even further, arguing that, despite
Hannah Arendt's dictum that love is inimical to politics, it is possible
to argue for 'a love that is properly political':

> But what if we were able to identify or invent another love, a
> love that is properly political? Such a political concept of love
> would have to be characterized by at least three qualities. First, it
> would have to extend across social scales and create bonds that
> are at once intimate and social, destroying conventional divisions
> between public and private. Second, it would have to operate in a
> field of multiplicity and function through not unification but the
> encounter and interaction of differences. Finally, a political love
> must transform us, that is, it must designate a becoming such that
> in love, in our encounter with others we constantly become differ-
> ent. Love is thus always a risk in which we abandon some of our
> attachments to this world in the hope of creating another, better
> one. I consider these qualities the primary pillars of a research
> agenda for discovering today a political concept of love. (678)

Lauren Berlant, in direct response to Hardt, expresses the following
sense of what a 'properly political' form of love might be:

> A properly transformational political concept would provide the
> courage to take the leap into a project of better relationality that

would give us patience with the 'without guarantees' part of love's various temporalities; a properly transformational political concept would open spaces for really dealing with the discomfort of the radical contingency that a genuine democracy – like any attachment – would demand; a properly transformational political concept would release courage and creativity about how to make resources for living available to all objects in their thatness. ('Properly Political' 690)

Without venturing into the highly contested terrain that is theories of affect, particularly in literary studies,[7] it is worth noting the resonance between Jamal's discourse of 'courage' and Berlant's use of the same term. Jamal's perception of the lack of courage to 'grasp the unthinkable, to shift the axis away from the tedium of polarisation', and his sense of 'our minds and imaginations ... transfixed by the Manichean dialectic', speaks powerfully to Berlant's '[releasing of] courage and creativity' for the project of '[opening] spaces for really dealing with the discomfort of the radical contingency that a genuine democracy – like any attachment – would demand' (690). This 'discomfort' relates specifically to the embrace of difference – cultural and class difference, primarily – though without polarisation (the Manichean dialectic) or normalisation in the name of a specious unity.[8]

It appears, however, that the courage so hopefully envisaged by early-transition writers and critics, as outlined above, has either entirely evaporated or is widely perceived to have failed. Such a conclusion is inescapable in a work such as Steinberg's *Midlands*; in Marlene van Niekerk's 2010 play *Die Kortstondige Raklewe van Anastasia W*; or in any number of late-postapartheid works.[9] Looking at moments of writing such as these, it is difficult not to conclude that, as refracted in many post-2000 works, 'bad' difference has prevailed over more benign forms of difference, especially as this is expressed in the ideal form of the Constitution, and as the myth of the 'rainbow nation'. Correspondingly, it is hard not to conclude that 'bad' affect has won out over 'good' affect, as demonstrated in Van Niekerk's discordant play[10] and Mhlongo's dark novel *Way Back Home*. But the fact of such palpable postapartheid disillusionment does not lessen the poignancy of the appeal for, and belief in, the courageous approach to the politics of the period that was held out in near-visionary terms by the likes of Jamal, Sachs and the many 'cultural workers' of the time. Moreover, Jamal's position helps to define a broader movement in which early-transition writers set up a horizon of expectation that must now stand as a *fin de siècle* historical moment for South Africa, generating a sense of expectation as the country stood on the cusp of a new century.

Such a view accords with Paulina Grzeda's notion about the spate of magical realist fiction that appeared in the early-transition period. Grzeda positions South African magical realist texts 'at the intersection between literature of celebration and literature of disillusionment', emerging out of what she calls the 'short-lived co-existence' of these two trends in South African literary history (158–159).[11] Grzeda speculates as to why certain writers abandoned magical realism, but leaves the question open. As I see it, the unsparing economic deal in both the Mandela and the Mbeki administrations – taken to even greater heights of instrumentalism under Zuma – dampened any sense of 'magic' in South Africa's same-as-the-rest brand of democracy, placing a premium on writing that focused on the (still) ugly real, or literature that retreated into interiority. Grzeda cites Lazarus's critique of the ANC's embrace of neoliberalism and 'globalist thinking' ('The South African Ideology' 613–614), pointing to a resultant shift in focus from the public sphere (what she calls 'the national and the political') to 'the private, more intimate sphere of self-reflection, favouring intro-spective literature' (172). This would accord with neoliberalism's hyper-individualist ethos and its withdrawal from politics,[12] which is coincident with an all-absorbing mindset of individualised con-sumption. Gone are the early-transition ambitions of, in Grzeda's words, '[m]erging postmodern and neo-realist narrative techniques, conjoining black and white writing traditions in South Africa, blend-ing African-derived belief-systems with Western modes of thought and perception, blurring boundaries between fact and fiction, and eroding divisions between the past and the present'; no longer is there a perceived need for magical realism 'to be a narrative of rec-onciliation par excellence' (171).

Thabo Tsehloane's notion of an end-of-history mentality in the South African body politic seems genuinely to have taken hold (80), as black postapartheid writers such as K Sello Duiker and Niq Mhlongo 'express...political and social anxieties through an ambivalent desire for a utopia they can neither access nor dismiss' (Tsehloane 81). To switch metaphors, the plot has run off the rails, derailed by corruption and maladministration. The big South African stories are done. What remains is atomised narratives of politically neutered subjects disabused of the notion that writers or indeed critics can effect change. 'There is,' writes Tsehloane, 'a "struggle fatigue" or "hope fatigue" about imagining further possibilities of change' (80). Citing Francis Fukuyama's 'end of history' argument, Tsehloane continues:

> The post-apartheid state thus projects itself as the 'end of history' which cannot be transcended. It perceives itself as a perfect society and state beyond which no kind of a different future is possible. The apt reflection of this adulatory self-representation is captured by the saying (claimed to have been said by the African National Congress president after an election victory) that 'the ANC will rule until Jesus Christ comes again'.[13] The subtext is that the liberation from apartheid and the consequent coming to power of the ANC are indicative of this 'end of history' beyond which no political event is imaginable. Consequently, it has not been easy to imagine a different future to the present, despite a deeply and intensely felt dissatisfaction with the present. (80–81)

Tsehloane sees K Sello Duiker's *The Quiet Violence of Dreams* and Niq Mhlongo's *After Tears* as follows:

> The dissatisfaction with the present makes it imperative ... yet it is impossible to imagine the coming into fruition of this alternative future. As an embodiment of these anxieties the narratives have been ambivalent and equivocal about the new dispensation, hence the marked absence in the post-liberation literary discourse of both honeymoon literature and literature of disillusionment. (81)

Although there is much in postapartheid literary culture to suggest that a 'literature of disillusionment' does indeed continue to exist, even in the texts that Tsehloane discusses, his larger argument is on point: 'These narratives ... embody an attempt to satisfy a yearning for a different society while remaining conscious of this hope as futile' (81). It is within such a state of confounding indeterminacy that the diagnostic turn finds purchase; the quest for detection is the driving force in the fictional and nonfictional forms examined in the next chapter.

5

Biopsies on the body of the 'new' South Africa

If Tsehloane's 'end of history' thesis about postapartheid literary culture is at all accurate, in the sense that writers embody in their works a 'yearning for a different society' but see such a hope as 'futile' (81), then the task of detection seems ever more urgent: what went wrong, and how was the early-transition plot, with its tropes of springtime and rainbows, of reconciliation and renaissance, so conclusively lost? Postapartheid South African writing in the 2000s enters what might be described as a forensic phase, following on from the Truth and Reconciliation Commission; however, there is no single line of development in the various tropes and modes of diagnosis. Whether phantasmagorically or factually spun, in neo-noir thrillers or nonfiction accounts of a sick social 'underbelly', the tales in the later postapartheid phase have forfeited any innocence they may have laid claim to in the earlier, prelapsarian phase. A broader look at this collective act of diagnosis, a kind of collective biopsy on the ailing body of the 'new' South Africa, therefore seems apposite.

Neo-Noir 1: Roger Smith's *Wake Up Dead* and *Mixed Blood*

One of the most potent fictional treatments of a social condition perceived to be in an advanced stage of ill health is to be found in the work of thriller-writer Roger Smith, particularly his densely (over)-plotted first two books, *Mixed Blood* (2009) and *Wake Up Dead* (2010). Despite its Byzantine plot, *Mixed Blood* is a strong thriller debut. It examines the devastation wrought by apartheid upon the people of

Cape Town – especially the large 'coloured' sector – and works it into a neo-noir style; noir itself is both a style in which excruciation is narrated with cool, worldly aplomb, and a mode in which, according to Foster Hirsch, 'middle-class citizens [are] unexpectedly invaded by or lured into crime' (13).[1] Indeed, Smith's method is to create, in even in the most prosaic elements of literary style, settings that are saturated with the imminence of catastrophe and death, stricken with signs of disease and invasively contagious. And, as per the noir formula, the middle class, not to mention the extremely well-to-do, get sucked into a criminal culture despite their best efforts to remain separate from it. It is as if the actual material world of postapartheid conspires in the spreading of a murderous contagion. In the opening line of *Mixed Blood*, protagonist Jack Burn stands on the deck of his opulent Atlantic-seaboard home, 'watching the sun drown itself in the ocean' (12); in *Wake Up Dead*, night comes 'like an animal stalking the day' (235); the sun '[turns] the ocean into broken glass on the horizon' (50); and one of the deadliest characters watches the 'sun choke itself dead on the smog' (235). If this is what one expects from hardboiled writing, then the style seems peculiarly adequate to a country with a seething netherworld untouched by any democratic 'miracle', and a middle class stricken with fear. Smith thus finds special purchase for what might otherwise be generic noir in a Cape Town whose regular criminal ledger is often equal to the worst that hardboiled crime thrillers can offer. Likewise, Smith strikes both a generic and a naturalistic chord in setting his stories in the actual intersection, the crossing of paths, of Cape Flats meth-addicts-on-the-make, dire desperadoes, and the bloated fat cats on Cape Town's 'candy castle'[2] Atlantic seaboard. Like that of Cape Town's leading noir stylist, Mike Nicol, Smith's fiction profits from the adjacency of two disjoint but proximate worlds, bringing them into a violent articulation which not only seems sociopolitically inevitable, given their history, but also serves the stylistic purposes of noir thriller writing. Such adequation[3] involving two otherwise disparate spheres (genre 'stock' derived largely from mid-twentieth-century America, on the one hand, and neocolonial social detritus in the global south, on the other) is, I would argue, one of the more remarkable features of postapartheid writing in fictional detection mode following postapartheid's 'end of history'.

In some senses, it is a timely coincidence, this unexpected 'fit' between stock noir and an ever more bruising 'rainbow nation' hangover. It is a fit that seems roundly to beat its modal predecessor in narrative fiction – liberal-humanist social realism – in the job of adequating, in formal, stylistic terms, a sense of anomie within a setting of advanced urban degradation and the decay of hope. Take, for example, the description of the minor character Carmen Fortune and her baby in *Mixed Blood*. The infant lies in his crib with 'withered limbs' as she feeds him, food 'dribbling from his mouth' (20). We learn that the baby was born three months premature, 'blind and deformed, with massive brain damage' (20). The circumstances behind this situation are unlikely to surprise any social worker or police officer acquainted with conditions on the Cape Flats:

> Nobody knew how or why he'd survived. Except Carmen. She knew God had cursed her. Made sure that every time she looked at her son she remembered all the tik she had smoked while she carried him inside her. He was a constant reminder of the hell that waited for her one day. (20)

Adopting a hardboiled style of narration at this point removes the possibility of patronising condescension – a constant risk in liberal-humanist fiction; however, it also allows for a surprisingly accurate register of self-consciousness in the free indirect narration of Carmen's consciousness and self-conception. That is to say, for her to see her own child as a 'constant reminder of the hell that waited for her' serves as a register both of noir style (entertaining in the dark manner typical of hardboiled writing) and also of trenchant characterisation (on the mark in registering sociopolitical conditions in fictional form). Carmen's further musings are similarly resonant:

> If it wasn't for the grant the state paid every month for Sheldon, she would put a pillow over his face and no one could blame her. But her useless bastard husband, Rikki, smoked away whatever money he scammed or stole. What the fuck, she was already in hell. Could it, honest to God, get worse? (20)

The 'useless bastard husband' Rikki (Ricardo Fortune), meanwhile, is acting as an agent of both the noir formula (in accordance with conventions of the genre) and the postapartheid scenario (validated by criminological research) in terms of which the well-heeled ineluctably get sucked into the septic tank of crime just below the surface of bourgeois life. Rikki and his meth-smoking mate, Faried (Adams), have gone to 'deal with' Faried's girlfriend, who was 'selling her ass in Sea Point when she was supposed to be visiting her mommy in hospital' (16). Faried, we are told, didn't mind that 'she was hooking again, but he'd absolutely minded that she wasn't giving him any of the money', and so he 'wanted to catch the bitch on the job' (16). Faried and Rikki search for the girlfriend, Bonita, without success, and then decide on an alternative course of action: smoking a tik-pipe and invading one of the wealthy homes on the slopes of Signal Hill. Here, they encounter the American émigré Jack Burn, who – most unfortunately for Faried and Rikki – is himself a violence-prone refugee from justice in the US, and an ex-Marine who did service in the Iraq War. Acting in self-defence, Burn kills both men with a carving knife when they barge into his home just moments before he is about to serve dinner to his pregnant wife and son.

The scene is set for what, in essence, is a head-on smash between two social classes in a fearful social asymmetry. It is a collision with the very underclass that the elite on the more moneyed end of the Cape Town social spectrum spend their lives denying and/or ignoring, as if their wealth has nothing to do with the sprawling slums of the Cape Flats and their adjacent shacklands. But the return of the repressed manifests itself in the regular arrival of the oppressed on wealthy doorsteps, and the implication of all parties in what inescapably degenerates into a criminal mêlée. It is this moral co-implication – a kind of codependency between victims and perpetrators – that makes Smith a particularly interesting postapartheid thriller writer. In *Wake Up Dead*, a similar invasion of an Atlantic-seaboard suburb by Cape Flats desperadoes occurs in the form of a carjacking. This time, the bloated big-shot, who is injured by a bullet in the thigh while resisting the attackers, gets finished off by his own (abused) American wife: she seizes the opportunity to get away with murder after the attackers flee in the hijacked car, leaving behind a 'smoking gun' in their getaway. (The wife takes her chance and uses the gun to finish her husband off, pretending it was the work of the invaders.) The rest of the novel plays out the drama of the wife's play with murder, and her mounting degradation, despite her best efforts to stay 'clean'. In *Mixed Blood*, Jack Burn likewise thinks he can get rid of the bodies of the attackers he has killed and escape responsibility for the killings – as a fugitive from American justice, he cannot risk calling the police and pleading self-defence. But in both novels the moment of criminal intersection between classes that are separated in a spatial and material sense also serves as 'a precipitation of shape and meaning, some simulacrum of understanding of how meaning can be construed over and through time' (Brooks 35). Smith's detailed plotting, involving more twists and turns than one would reasonably expect from a standard noir thriller, might in consequence be seen as more than just overeager imagination or amateurishly written narrative. Indeed, Smith's style is unusually accomplished, with visually and figuratively rich capsule characterisations of individuals that are striking both as social types and as fallible individuals, though the exaggerated offensiveness of many of his characters occasionally stretches the reader's credulity. Still, the characters are drawn into entertainingly twisted scenarios, and the wayward and increasingly unpredictable nature of the convoluted coils of plot may be read as a peculiarly late-postapartheid response to contingency. The latter signifies plot loss in several interconnected spheres of the body politic – principally social, economic and moral. I have argued that the two most starkly available responses to such contingency are underplotting and overplotting (see Chapter 1): on the one hand, one finds 'serious', discourse-heavy novels with minimal 'plot' that attempt to work things through via character and events that are thematically rather than mimetically invested, and on the other, overplotted stories that are replete with 'proofs' or instances of waywardness. Exemplifying the latter, the densely woven plotting in Smith's writing merits closer scrutiny.

Staying with *Mixed Blood*, I shall briefly condense the rudiments of this novel's plot, and then, rather than examine the many lines of development along multiple character lines, chart the course of one character's destiny through the action of the novel. This may turn out to be meaningful in a scenario in which plot is, in a sense, 'fate', inasmuch as plot is the narrative equivalent of human action in situations of high stakes and chronic uncertainty. In such scenarios, action is resonant with moral choice and ethical inclination, revealing the interplay of socially determinative conditioning, motive and choice. Plotting the story in this novel, in a form of critical re-description, is an apt manner by which to chart the characterological range, as well as the contextually embedded nature of options available, under the contingencies of postapartheid. For Brooks, plot is 'the active interpretive work of discourse on story' (27), and it is perhaps not too far-fetched to suggest that in detection mode under late-postapartheid conditions, novelistic discourse naturally turns to emplotment as a way of interpreting – that is, ordering and weighing – what may otherwise appear to be a random aggregation of events.

The character we shall follow is the pungently named Billy Mongrel. When the two meth-heads Rikki and Faried invade ex-Marine Jack Burn's house, coming to grief in the process, Mongrel is an unobserved witness who sees the two youths help each other climb up the house's deck, but he is not privy to Burn's act of slaying the duo in self-defence once they get inside the house. Mongrel, along with his beloved security-dog Bessie, work for a security company that is guarding a neighbouring house under construction. Looking down from his position on the building site, Mongrel can see by their clothing and insignia that Rikki and Faried are 'Americans' – members of the biggest gang on the Cape Flats – and therefore his natural enemies. He is a 'blood Mongrel', a member of the 28s prison gang, although he is trying to stay out of prison now, at roughly forty years old, after beginning his prison 'career' at the age of fourteen. Mongrel's witnessing of the strange non-reappearance of the invading meth-heads plays a key role in the story, especially in the plot's co-implication of various characters that act as types in a corrosive postapartheid ensemble.

The other character who converges with Mongrel on the site of Burn's house is a corrupt Cape Town cop nicknamed Gatsby. This man is an obese loner who consumes as many 'gatsbys' as he is able to during the working week; these take-away meals he buys in Cape Town are described as 'a football sized French loaf stuffed with chunks of steak, eggs, melted cheese, and fries, all drenched in mayonnaise and industrial-strength chili' (*Mixed Blood* 43). Gatsby is not only obese, with halitosis and bad body odour, he is also routinely corrupt, like many real-world policemen in South Africa, taking protection money from gangsters to supplement his inadequate salary. He enjoys killing people, despite being a charismatic Christian, and he has become expert at covering his tracks. Often, he must kill to keep other policemen off his trail and out of his Cape Flats gangland sphere of control. Essentially, he is a mafia-middleman with a police badge. As such, he is emblematic of the bleeding of law and disorder, with his behaviour reinforcing waywardness, or plot loss, on the ground.

Gatsby is owed protection money by the very Rikki who invaded Burn's house, and he goes on the hunt for Rikki, eventually finding his way to the abandoned red BMW in Sea Point used by Rikki and Faried, and now standing idle outside the Burn home. After Gatsby questions residents up and down the street, his policeman's intuition, spurred by Burn's nervous answers, makes him suspicious about the ex-Marine. As the plot unfolds, he comes to learn of Burn's fugitive status, as well as his misdeeds in the US, giving Gatsby a basis on which to extort money from the American. This happens at a critical moment for Gatsby, because an anti-corruption agent from the ministry of police, a man named Disaster Zondi, is closing in on him for the murder of a young Cape Flats boy, someone who had something he shouldn't have, motivating Gatsby to shoot him at point-blank range. Under apartheid, Zondi was a militant whom Gatsby at one point tortured. Gatsby's real-world surname, Barnard, may be a deliberate reference to Ferdi Barnard, a member of the notorious 1980s apartheid security police unit the Civil Cooperation Bureau (CCB). Ferdi Barnard, as dramatised in Jacques Pauw's nonfiction work *Little Ice Cream Boy*, was convicted of murdering anti-apartheid activist David Webster, and so the name adds a further layer to the play of reference in *Mixed Blood*.

Just as Gatsby's extortion of Burn is about to bear fruit for the corrupt cop, Mongrel intervenes. He wants revenge against Gatsby because the policeman killed his dog, Bessie, after an earlier run-in between the corrupt cop and Mongrel. Briefly, both Mongrel and Gatsby were keeping watch on the American in Sea Point, and when their paths crossed, the fact that they are natural enemies – in terms of race and class, primarily – eventuated in conflict. More to the point, though, is the fact of multiple co-implication in crime within a society that feeds off and finds profit in a stench-filled, over-rich zone that straddles law and (dis)order. Not one character orbiting the Burn house – from the meth-kids to Gatsby, Mongrel, Burn's lawyer, and the Cape Flats hoods dependent on Gatsby to keep their dealings safe – can survive in any but a criminal culture, to which they are inured as fish are to water. Indeed, the handful of innocent characters in this unusually violent novel, principally Burn's wife, his son, Matt, and the baby born in the closing stages of the story, appear to be fish out of (a huge, murky expanse of) water, in a widespread culture of criminality.

Let us return to Mongrel, and more specifically to his characterisation and the manner of his emplotment.[4] Early in the story we learn that he 'had been in and out of jail since he was fourteen' (14). His last term was a sixteen-year stretch, and now, in early middle age ('he wasn't sure, but he guessed he was turning forty'), he is determined to stay out of Pollsmoor prison:

> So that's why he was pulling the night shift on a building site as a watchman. The pay was a joke, but with his [disfigured] face and the crude prison tattoos carved into his gaunt brown body he was lucky to get a job. They gave him a rubber baton and a black uniform that was too big. And they gave him a dog, Bessie. A mongrel like him, part Rottweiler, part German shepherd. She was old, and she slept most of the time, but she was the only thing that Bennie Mongrel had ever loved (14).

Here, as in the case of *Wake Up Dead* and the character of Piper – the prison-gang leader who falls in love with a young man, a prison 'wife' called Disco de Lilly – love flowers amid perversity, like a rare green shoot emerging from toxic waste. However, this love unerringly leads to killing and score settling. So, when Gatsby attempts extortion, thinking he has the upper hand on Burn, Mongrel enters the fray to avenge his dog and his hurt pride. Gatsby, meanwhile, has kidnapped Burn's son, Matt, and when, following a money drop-off, Mongrel and Burn eventually trap the morally sick police inspector, Mongrel ties him to a chair and proceeds to torture him by slowly cutting up his body, in small strips, with a sharp blade. The torture has a dual function: extracting information on the whereabouts of Burn's son, and revenge for Gatsby's killing of Mongrel's dog. By this point in the narrative, in a manner reminiscent of Quentin Tarantino, the plot has drawn the reader into a state of complicity with the violence: having witnessed Gatsby extort and kill several other characters in the novel, few readers will be immune to the gratification of revenge, of seeing a form of justice being enacted against this thoroughly obscene character. He is the epitome of everything that was – and remains – twisted about South African race relations; he is a torturer, a swindler, a racist, a killer and a monstrous bully acting under the protection of the law. He is also a convincing character for readers who have any knowledge or experience of apartheid – or, indeed, postapartheid South Africa.

For Gatsby represents everything that is hateful about a patriarchal, militarised culture with its mendacious veneer of parliamentary democracy: this was once the case under the minority National Party regime, which seems to be replicated in the postapartheid dispensation, with the increasing influence of a corrupt, militarised state under which ordinary (and mostly poor) people suffer.[5] Gatsby and his kind continue to flourish beyond 1994 and into the new millennium, which explains the sense of relief when he is brought down, despite this occurring in an extrajudicial manner. As a reader, to pretend not to be co-implicated in the orgy of criminality in postapartheid South Africa, as this is represented in Smith's novel, is frankly disingenuous. When Gatsby finally dies in flames with a tyre around his neck in the mean streets of Paradise Park, the Cape Flats area whose hoodlums and drug dealers he has exploited to his own benefit, it is difficult not to feel that he thoroughly deserves his fate. This is especially so in view of the fact that his antagonist, Disaster Zondi, is one of the rare Smith characters who is not only likeable but also on the right side of the law. Still, though the reader might root for him, his all-too-lawful methods of dealing with Gatsby were never going to cut the ice. Unlawfulness is the medium in which events gather their meaning and find their systemic place under postapartheid street conditions.

And this, indeed, is what every other line of plotting in the novel will reveal: a trajectory of complicity with a criminally saturated culture in which, for the weak and poor – let alone the rich – to remain 'innocent' is all but impossible.[6] As any scientific survey of the wealth gap[7] would suggest, the disparity in levels of income in the Cape Town of *Mixed Blood* and *Wake Up Dead* is such that the wealthy are threatened by the looming tides of lawlessness – and want – that wash up against their high walls. As we have seen in earlier discussions, fear and anxiety dominate middle-class discourse, creating a phenomenology of crime in which citizens from all social strata are enmeshed.

Neo-Noir 2: Angela Makholwa's *Black Widow Society*

One of the notable things about Angela Makholwa's blend of laconic chick-lit and remorseless neo-noir in *Black Widow Society* is the almost casual manner in which co-implication in a culture of stealing and murder is a given, or taken as normal. The novel is set in the post-Polokwane era – that is, after Jacob Zuma's 2007 victory, at the ANC

National Conference in Polokwane, over the incumbent ANC leader and then president of South Africa Thabo Mbeki. *Black Widow Society* is a crime story that posits as quite *un*remarkable a set of social dealings in which all parties share a social language of revenge killing. This includes the reader, who cannot but be complicit in the story's pathologisation of social relations, and gender relations in particular. Of course, one might read against the grain, with a sense of revulsion, but the genre 'pact' with the more general reader (as in Roger Smith's novels) is one of keeping company with the offbeat and (almost comically) depraved characters who set the plot in motion. As in the case of Smith, such innovative writing breaks the mould of 'SA Lit', with its ethical conundrums, its clear contestations and its grand moral parables. Rather, much post-transition literature arises from a 'normalised' popular culture in which matters are routinely murkier, in South Africa as elsewhere, offering rich material for crime-story plotting.

Here, the neo-noir femme fatale is no longer, as in traditional noir, a 'symptom of male fears about feminism' but an 'affirmation of the difference between the genders' (Martin 93), illustrating 'the challenge the contemporary woman now poses to the masculine domain at work…at home…and in bed' (93). Indeed, Martin's description seems mild when it comes to Makholwa's strain of clinical retribution, in which a secret organisation, the Black Widow Society (BWS), arranges 'hits' on abusive husbands and then cleans up on their life insurance policies. What is unusual about such blood letting in Makholwa's case, apart from its effortlessness, is the nature of its morality-tale framing. This bears some examination.

The novel opens with a depiction of several marriage relationships involving 'new South Africa' couples (mostly black, and solidly middle to upper class) in which unrepentant husbands chronically abuse, mistreat and cheat on their wives. One such a wife is Tallulah Ntuli, a businesswoman who goes on to become a founder of the BWS. She is found locked out of her comfortable home in Diepkloof Extension, Soweto, after being ejected by husband Mphikeleli (a prominent surgeon and political activist) because she had not cooked him dinner. In a second framing story, the character Thami arrives at her 'palatial golf estate home' and 'offload[s] her Apple Mac and her Gucci bag onto the kitchen counter' (4) before catching spouse Lloyd on his cellphone, sweet-talking a woman who turns out to be Thami's longtime bête noir. Lloyd is 'in' with the Jacob Zuma camp, and he has been rewarded with the post of director general of foreign affairs, but Thami, who comes from a respected family whose 'political struggle credentials had certainly gone a long way in propelling [Lloyd's] career forward' (27), has cold comfort: 'she had become an irritation' to Lloyd, who seemingly 'wished to just swat her away like a fly' (5). She is annoyed at his apparently futile immersion in his work: 'Did they feel they had such a firm hold on the events that were occurring on the South African political scene that they'd take themselves so seriously?'(5). The very idea of such delusionary behaviour exhausts her: 'Nobody could help the downward spiral of the country's politics at this time so why did Lloyd and his cronies even bother?' (5). Notable here is the embedding within the book's characters of a shift in political morality: the patriarchal venality of the Zuma administration is mentioned merely in passing, as if it is hardly novel or noteworthy. Meanwhile, the broader political terrain is abandoned in favour of a more immediate mission: to right gender wrongs. If the high-stakes social game of influence and patronage is unsurprising – indeed unexceptional – in its bully-boy tactics, then the smartest thing to do is to outplay it on its own terms by instrumentalising its pathological means in order to achieve justice – or at least retribution – in a delimited domain. In short, cut one's losses and do the best for one's own – or one's group – interests, given the circumstances. Here, the specific means of redress comprises severe punishment, a way of getting even for heinous wrongs against women, and providing a 'final solution' for the social illness the perpetrators would otherwise carry forth into future generations.

The catch, of course, is that the attainment of such a rebalancing in the gender scales, an entirely worthy end, especially under South African conditions, comes at the price of complicity in murder. This, however, is not treated as a big issue in the novel. *Black Widow Society* is shown to operate in a world where '[p]olitical connections, struggle credentials, daughters, sons, nieces, nephews of exiled politicians washed up and renewed [*sic*] to emerge as BEE entrepreneurs or "tenderpreneurs"' (11). That is where conventional politics has brought matters, without any damage to male malfeasance. In fact, if anything, patriarchal malefaction has increased. And so, as Tallulah opens a meeting of the society, she surveys the scene, reflecting to herself: 'Many of the women in this room had come to the society broken, weak, vulnerable, and without confidence. Today, some of these whom she had met years ago were now strong, solid and in control of their destinies' (18). 'Sisters,' she announces,

> '[f]or many years, others like us endured pain, trauma, and torture at the hands of unappreciative dogs who badgered and bludgeoned us. Pelted us with vitriolic words and violent beatings until one day, we finally stopped and listened. We listened to what our souls told us. Yes. Yes. We listened to what our souls told us.' (19)

Having invoked what one might call the natural justice of what people's 'souls' tell them is right amid a sea of public misdemeanour, Tallulah continues:

> 'We are here purely because of the ties that bind us. We have a moral duty to ourselves and each other to protect what we've lost, that innocence we recognise whenever we glimpse those who have not had to endure our baptism of fire.' (19)

The secret society's modus operandi, the reader learns, is to use a professional hit-man, one Mzwakhe Khuzwayo, to eliminate and dispose of the 'unappreciative dogs' who have earned their sorry fate by making women's lives a misery. After knocking the 'dogs' off, the BWS then cashes in on the victim's life insurance policies. Of course, this is all good fun, within the parameters of chick-lit genre writing. The wicked glee that readers are likely to take in such an entertaining fictional conceit is, however, soon rendered somewhat messy when things start veering off the rails. As Tallulah makes her plea, a senior member of the BWS interrupts her, pulling her out of the meeting with the news that one of their associates has been murdered. As things turn out, Nokuthula Gumede, who has been shot dead in her home in a 'robbery', has in fact been 'taken out' in a hit organised by her husband, China Gumede. The catch, however, is that the BWS had, that very day, 'eliminated' China Gumede himself in one of its own operations. Tallulah ascertains that the murdering philanderer is indeed dead, bundled up in the boot of Mzwakhe's car ('That's the beauty of a Passat...there's enough space for two in there,' Mzwakhe quips, 21), upon which Tallulah remarks: 'Nx! Imagine a husband killing his own wife – the mother of his children? You really have to wonder what kind of society we're living in.' The reader is told that she says this 'without the slightest hint of irony' (22).

The story continues in similar vein until Mzwakhe turns the tables on the BWS, and a bloodbath ensues in which several members are shot and killed at one of their meetings. While the plot is unexceptional, following a predictable pattern once the framing devices have been set up, the novel's focus on moral relativity is of great interest. The implied narrator guiding the reader in her telling of the story seems neither to condemn nor approve of the actions of the BWS, or indeed of the various deeds that give rise to the widows' revenge in the first place. Readers are left to form their own opinion, and to react as they may amid a mêlée that is sketched in almost comic-book style, with a certain laconic distance from scenes of crime, as if this is the only way to gain a form of objectivity about, or a cool distance from, such social conditions. If anything, it is this sense of sophisticated knowingness about the lay of the land which defines both the Smith and the Makholwa novels. It is as if both these authors are saying, yes, we're aware that the rainbow nation has gone belly-up, but for heaven's sake, get used to it! Let's have some fun, anyway, with the low life, and drop the postures, the high seriousness, of earlier generations. Makholwa herself gives voice to such a sense in an interview:

> I think the frustration for me with much of apartheid-era literature is that it was grounded in race...The feedback I get from many readers is: 'I never used to read South African fiction'... The South African books I read were the classics like *Cry, the Beloved Country* and I loved them, but I guess they framed South African fiction for me, which was race, race – all the time. I was, like, 'what about the other stuff?' I guess there were other people out there thinking like me. (Gedye n.p.)

Makholwa represents a generation of writers who take the pulse of a pathological public realm, and describe its excesses in 'entertaining' or more palatable forms for readers who, like them, have lost their innocence about rotten political set-ups but want to move on anyway.

Biopsies via nonfiction 1: Steinberg's *Thin Blue*

The more serious vein of writing does, however, persist, especially in nonfiction, a genre that typically diagnoses the body politic in a more clinical manner. The pathologies are far too pressing to leave to genre stylists alone, or indeed to the practitioners of 'literary' fiction. In nonfictional forms, the approach is unambiguous and direct in answering the question: what exactly is going on here, on the ground, and under our noses? In this regard, Jonny Steinberg's *Thin Blue: The Unwritten Rules of Policing South Africa* is essential reading for anyone who is interested in how the culture of 'ungovernability' under apartheid – a successful strategy against oppressive, police-state conditions – morphed into a crisis of policing following the political transition to democracy. Steinberg's argument is that, thirteen years into democracy (2007, at the time of writing *Thin Blue*), 'South Africa's general population [had] yet to give its consent to being policed' (22). In addition, as Steinberg amply demonstrates in his descriptions of police patrols in Johannesburg's Alexandra township, patrols that he accompanied as an observer, 'the line separating police officers from the scores of private enforcers and protectors who litter South Africa is uncomfortably blurred' (22; see also Glenny 183–207). As Steinberg argues, the detested South African Police (SAP), apartheid's enforcers, were driven out of many townships in the wake of the 1976 Soweto uprising, and they were 'evicted from the rest', as he puts it, 'less than a decade later during the insurrectionary period of the mid-1980s' (22). Following these momentous events, policing in any normal sense was never going to be an easy proposition: 'In the vacuum left by the police, anti-apartheid politics and the politics of self-protection often became indistinguishable' (22). And it was to this scene, where 'security was bought, sold and bartered, and also exchanged for solidarity and friendship' (23), that the supposedly reformed and restructured South African Police Service (SAPS) returned in the transition years of the early 1990s. 'My contention,' Steinberg asserts, 'is that they never found sufficient moral authority to rise above the logic of this terrain, nor to refashion it, and that they thus had to negotiate their way into it and join its other players' (23). This conclusion, substantiated with empirical evidence in a scholarly mode, chimes with the depiction of the loathed, malodorous cop in *Mixed Blood*, Rudi 'Gatsby' Barnard, and with his twisted dealings as a law enforcer. Conventional police corruption, by no means confined to South Africa, found even greater purchase in the transition period, as Steinberg and others argue.[8] Corrupt policemen competed with extra-legal players in protection rackets in South Africa's endemically 'ungovernable' territories – its townships and shacklands, its hijacked buildings in decayed inner cities,[9] all temporary zones inhabited by transients, both foreigners and nationals. As Steinberg contends in *Thin Blue*, even for 'good' cops in the SAPS, engaging in corrupt dealings frequently equates to being in a position to maintain a middle-class lifestyle in once-forbidden suburbs:

> [P]olice officers find themselves somewhere near the tail end of a frantic, unseemly dash to join the new black middle class. The middle class is a very expensive zone to occupy right now: what with pricey schools and homes in the suburbs, being middle class is far, far dearer than it has ever been before in South African history. (22)

This, however, does not deter the very modestly remunerated police officers in the SAPS:

> The police are among a large category of township people who aspire very much to find a place in this class, who do not earn quite enough to get there, and who thus live beyond their means. They are, as a consequence, widely reputed in township life to be among a new breed of scavengers, prone to corruption and to the most expedient and instrumental attitudes to their own vocation. By virtue of their class position and their social aspirations, they are denuded of the authority required to do their work. (23–24)

If one adds to this Steinberg's conclusion, expressed in *Midlands*, that police headquarters in Pretoria is a centralised 'monster of an institution' (78), the second-largest in the world, and that it is 'chaotic and ungovernable' (78, as noted above, in Chapter 3), wholly out of touch with the actual conditions of law enforcement, then one might be forgiven for lending at least some credence to the otherwise seemingly wild and improbable scenes in the work of South African 'krimi' authors such as Smith, Makholwa, Orford and others. Events and conditions that might otherwise be thought of as overtly *fictional* and generically exaggerated for the sake of thrills and spills, in fact constitute the banal reality of the mean streets of postapartheid South Africa. Writers such as Steinberg, Dlamini, Altbeker, Bloom, Pauw, Wiener, and other nonfiction scribes who eschew fictional illusion in favour of fact and observed reality, arguably have an easier ride in terms of riveting plotlines and reader credibility. Indeed, the week-end encounters so grippingly described by Steinberg in the streets of Alexandra, where police and township residents interact in bizarre stand-offs as they negotiate their respective bids for the upper hand, demonstrate that fiction – in the carnivalesque conditions that make up the postapartheid 'real' – may even be held to be at a disadvantage. Following this line of thought, *making up* for such a disadvantage may account for certain grotesque excesses of the krimi genre in South Africa – for plotlines evident, for example, in Mike Nicol's tales of careening-out-of-control private investigator Mace Bishop, whose jousts with government agents approximate the phantasmagoria of what Lyotard has termed the libidinal economy.[10] The latter is instantiated as much in Smith's homicidal plots, in which violence is invested with enormous – and lavish – desire and gratification, as it is in the eroticism of the love-hate duel winding its way through the interconnected plotlines of Nicol's Revenge Trilogy. Here, Mace and femme fatale Shemina February vie for ascendancy in a contest that began while both were working in military camps across South Africa's borders. Under apartheid, they were once struggle comrades. But now they are connected by a tension between desire and repulsion as neither is able to gain a firm hold on the new millennial grail – political legitimacy.

In the landscape of *actual* policing, as empirically observed and reported in Steinberg's *Thin Blue*, a similar joust or dance takes place. This involves subjects on different sides of the uncertain boundary designating the legitimate, or sanctioned as such by communities, which of course in postapartheid conditions does not always coincide with that which is strictly 'legal'. This explains the phenomenon, smartly described in *Thin Blue*, of 'performative' policing, such as the scene in which a large group of beer-drinking Mozambican migrants occupying a shack settlement in greater Alexandra 'allow' two vulnerable policemen on patrol to 'take them to task' for illegally consuming alcohol in public. Once the policemen see that the Mozambicans are openly drinking beer in the street, they cannot ignore this misdemeanour for fear of losing their authority and self-respect. But neither can they make multiple arrests, since the numerically superior group would not allow it, and the policemen would not risk this. So the two officers stop, get out of the patrol vehicle, and each confiscates a single bottle of beer from two individuals, pouring the contents out onto the street. A surly, tense stand-off endures for the few moments that the police engage in this restricted, ritualised display of authority. Then they get back into their vehicle and drive off. Steinberg comments:

> The officers did what they did to salvage some dignity. The crowd humoured them; they were prepared to watch two bottles of beer seep into the ground so that the police officers could go through the motions of saving face. Why was the crowd prepared to do that? A simple cost-benefit calculation, no doubt. If you beat up two cops, the police must retaliate. The following evening they will throw a cordon around the shacks and descend upon the Mozambicans in large numbers, backed up by air support and a phalanx of vans waiting to be filled with arrestees. Two lost bottles of beer is not worth that. (33)

Even though this appears to be a negotiation, one in which each side makes a move and then retreats, it is the Mozambicans who ultimately set the rules of engagement and influence the outcome:

> Of the two sides to this relationship, the police and the Mozambican community, it is the Mozambicans who ultimately decide to what extent they are policed. Here and now, they will lose two bottles of beer to the street, but not two people to the police station cells, in order to assist to recoup some of Inspector L's dwindling self-respect. That is today's threshold; no doubt it wobbles and shifts: the unwritten rules are drafted and redrafted. (33)

Steinberg's travels with policemen on patrol in townships in Gauteng reveal to him that the one place where the SAPS are secure – where their presence is welcome and they are *permitted* by the people to police them – is in the private space of the home, following domestic disputes:

> While most self-respecting police officers would deny it, they gravitate towards domestic conflict. Some of them might treat the women who come to them badly, imposing careless and destructive solutions upon the problems they are called to solve,

but the domestic sphere has become their natural home. It feels good to be there. It is a refuge from the street in which they are put upon, insulted, and threatened. It is the one sphere in which their authority is rarely questioned; they are there because their presence has been demanded. And it feels good because it is the only part of their work that allows them to express themselves as moral agents after a fashion. (129)

Outside of this limited domain, however, postapartheid police officers are at best participants in performances where they play a secondary role, and which they have not scripted; in this scenario, the sovereignty of the law is a theoretical notion, at most. While justice is deeply compromised by a criminal justice system unable to cope with overwhelming demands, the situation is exacerbated by the fact that impartial and rigorous investigation has itself degenerated into a dodgy 'business'. In his investigation into the work of detectives, Steinberg finds that most ordinary township people do not trust criminal investigators and will not share reliable information with them:

'The only people who talk to a detective,' Constable T replies, 'are his informers. Nobody else will talk to a detective.' If that is true, the consequences are very far-reaching indeed. If enough people begin to believe that investigating officers are shabby entrepreneurs, the belief becomes self-fulfilling. For if nobody is prepared to talk to a cop they don't know, then the only information that ever flows is exchanged for money, for allegiances, for loyalty. It is a game, every player is an informer of sorts, and who is to say who's working for whom? A murder investigator cannot be assumed to be the state's agent, here at the scene to solve a crime. One cannot be sure that the state has an agent attending to this matter at all. (127–128)

Biopsies via nonfiction 2: Altbeker's *A Country at War with Itself*

Steinberg's dispiriting conclusion, suggesting as it does a state without the ability to police its own territory, and without the requisite monopoly on (legitimate) violence, finds support in Altbeker's analysis of policing and crime in his 2007 study *A Country at War with*

Itself: South Africa's Crisis of Crime. Altbeker's study is a uniquely wide-ranging and even-handed assessment of the 'problem' of crime. The author worked as a security expert in the Ministry of Safety and Security for a two-year period in the mid-1990s. He contends that, despite the unreliability of most statistical measures, 'the unavoidable, irreducible reality is that every single piece of reliable data we have tells us that South Africa ranks at the very top of the world's league tables for violent crime' (12). Altbeker criticises the Mbeki administration for its persistent 'denialism' regarding the very existence of crime, let alone the fact that it is a 'problem', and argues that government 'tortured its crime stats to make them jump up and sing' (13). But he proposes that, rather than being its cause, this denialism is in fact symptomatic of an 'inability to roll back the crime wave' (13). Altbeker suggests that this is 'not because policy-makers are stupid, uninterested or ill-intentioned, but because our crime problems really are that intractable' (13). From Altbeker's insider knowledge of the ministry, he goes on to recount how a perception took hold, in the early-transition period, that the 'lunatics were running the asylum' (28). Not only was police recruitment being down- rather than upscaled, but

> the process [of reforming the country's police service] was almost entirely driven by the abstractions of policy rather than the operational questions of what it would take to provide decent policing. Papers were passed from one office at police headquarters to the next. They were read, parsed and criticized. Then they were sent back. It was like an enormous game of pass-the-parcel, and it only very occasionally involved anyone working outside the bureaucratic towers in the middle of Pretoria. What was going on in the street – that was for others to worry about. (28)

Furthermore, argues Altbeker, 'everything that came out of the policy process smacked of an unarticulated contempt for law enforcement and, by extension, for law enforcers' (28). Such disdain, moreover, was to some extent justified by the reality, of which the ministry was well aware, that 'useless policemen' were in many situations likely to exacerbate rather than remedy, or at the very least ameliorate, problems of social instability on the ground (29). For their part, ordinary policemen found themselves between a rock and a hard place: on the one hand, they intuited that their bosses had little confidence in them, and that policing was perceived to be one of the country's problems rather than an essential service (29); on the other hand, these same police officers were seeing things on the streets that were 'scaring the be-jesus out of them' (29). How was it possible, a policeman asked in the wake of Altbeker's 1997 departure from the ministry, that 'they tear up all the umbrellas just as a storm is breaking' (29).

The policymakers' chief focus was political rather than opera-tional. They disdained the notion of mere 'bandit-catching' (30), preferring instead the more ideologically amenable idea that an 'inte-grated programme of fundamental social re-ordering' would solve the issue of criminal wrongdoing (30). This, argues Altbeker, was an understandable reaction, reinforcing the notion of the 'essential goodness of the people' and assigning blame for the 'darker traits in the national character to the legacies of the hated policies of the past' (30). This idea also 'reinforced an instinctive left-of-centre politics which held that the socio-economic upliftment of the peo-ple would lead to the withering away of crime' (30). Nonetheless, crime in post-liberation South Africa 'quickly became a hot polit-ical problem', writes Altbeker, and the 'honeymoon ended': by the late 1990s, 'the apparent wisdom of government's conviction that crime had its roots in social problems … began to sound like a refusal to take responsibility'. For some, comments Altbeker, such an atti-tude seemed to parallel the callousness of US Secretary of Defense Donald Rumsfeld, who remarked, after the looting of Baghdad in 2003, that 'stuff happens' and 'freedom is messy' (31). In 1999, the appointment of Steve Tshwete as Minister of Safety and Security signalled a change. His 'signature tune', says Altbeker, 'was a call on police officers to treat criminals as a bulldog treats a bone' (31), and when Jackie Selebi was appointed national commissioner of the SAPS, 'the language and thinking of police strategists became more aggressive', with 'cordon-and-search operations in which whole city blocks were closed down, doors … kicked in and anyone suspi-cious … taken in for questioning' (31). Tougher legislation on bail conditions and jail sentences was pushed through. Still, a 'growing sensitivity and defensiveness in government's pronouncements on crime', and public dispute about crime statistics in which President

Mbeki also became involved, created an environment which Altbeker describes as 'paranoiac', skewing public debate and leaving many questions unanswered (33).

Seeking an answer to the question, '[w]hy do we have the most serious armed robbery crisis on the planet?', Altbeker suggests: 'Our basic problem…is that there is a terrifying amount of violent energy in our society. It has built up over decades and, like the electricity in a Johannesburg thunderstorm, it is discharged in acts of sudden and sometimes spectacular violence' (82). In a long-range analysis of the roots of this culture of criminality, beginning with slavery and subjugation and extending to the inherently violent migrant-labour patterns of racial capitalism, Altbeker contends:

> The gist of this account of the roots of crime is that the violence used in the shaping of modern South Africa has not dissipated; it lingers on as a kind of background radiation, deforming and dementing us even as the forms in which it is expressed have mutated. (97)

Altbeker proposes a four-part explanation: (i) postapartheid crime is unique not so much because of its volume, but on account of its 'extraordinary violence', including 'interpersonal violence' and an 'exponential growth' in robbery (33); (ii) South Africa's 'addiction to violence' is only partly explained by history and socio-economic conditions: the 'rest of the explanation lies in the way in which violence and criminality have themselves come to shape the context within which young men make decisions about how to behave' (33) – an argument that he later expands, contending that a 'violently criminal culture' characterises postapartheid South African conditions; (iii) the crime crisis cannot be solved via prevention, but through an enhanced capacity – not yet evident – to 'identify, prosecute and incarcerate criminals' (34); and (iv) 'moral regeneration' cannot be achieved through lectures by teachers and churches, and instead demands the 'rethinking of institution-building right across society', including a criminal justice system that 'comes down like a ton of bricks on people who commit violent crimes' (34). For all the astuteness of his prognostications, Altbeker's somewhat academic remedies are nowhere near being put in place.

The extent of the crisis is best described by verified South African crime statistics, which Altbeker presents chillingly:

> Fifty murder victims a day is about a busload of people. The 19,000 people murdered a year would be regarded as a big crowd at any of our cricket or soccer stadiums. And 220,000 deaths – the number of murders in the past ten years in South Africa – is four times larger than the death toll over a similar period of Americans in the Vietnam War, an experience that haunts that country's imagination to this day. Add to the 19,000 murders the half-million or so cases of assault, serious assault and attempted murder recorded by the police every year, the roughly 200,000 robberies and aggravated robberies, and the 55,000 rapes, to say nothing of the 300,000 burglaries and 85,000 stolen cars and, before we even think about the ocean of crimes that go unreported or unrecorded, it is clear that a substantial portion of South Africans are victims of at least one serious crime every year. It is almost no exaggeration to describe ourselves as a country at war with itself. (37–38)

Looking at these ciphers, it is clear that the country has come a long way from its 1990s 'spring is rebellious' moment, when scholars, activists, artists and 'cultural workers' seemed united in a spirit of *fin de siècle* optimism rather than despair. Sadly, Altbeker's finding of 'a country at war with itself' has an all-too-familiar resonance in the writing of other notable authors such as Loren Kruger, Achille Mbembe and Breyten Breytenbach.[11] The much anticipated moment was all too fleeting.

Biopsies via nonfiction 3: Wiener's *Killing Kebble*

In the marketing blurbs for Mandy Wiener's bestseller *Killing Kebble: An Underworld Exposed* (2012), there is a compound word – a cliché, to be sure, yet telling nevertheless – that keeps popping up: 'underbelly'. For the outspoken Johannesburg DJ Gareth Cliff, *Killing Kebble* is a 'story that will make you uncomfortable about just how rotten the criminal underbelly of Johannesburg really is'; former ANC member of parliament Andrew Feinstein, who blew the whistle on the ANC's biggest corruption scandal to date – the arms deal – and author of

After the Party: Corruption, the ANC and South Africa's Uncertain Future, says Wiener's book 'reveals the intertwining of business, politics and organized crime that is one of the greatest threats to our democracy', adding that it 'demonstrates the extent to which prosecutorial independence and the rule of law have been undermined by our political leaders and the resulting quagmire that is law enforcement in the country...in the process illuminating the dark underbelly of South Africa that is unknown to most of us'. In the updated edition of her book, Wiener herself refers to the social context of *Killing Kebble* as a 'seething underbelly'.[12]

This 'underbelly' is a term worth pondering for a moment. It suggests a foul, hidden rot, a treacherous morbidity underlying civilian life and the state. And yet such a notion is not peculiar to South Africa, for just about any democracy, including those of the USA, India and Australia, when probed, will reveal a 'dark side', or a corrupt 'underbelly' in what are purportedly clean political set-ups. A good proportion of all noir novels and movies rely on a similar, widely held assumption concerning the corruptibility of law enforcement and the fallibility of justice systems across the world. The imperfect detective who is often on the brink, tempted to do the wrong thing while trying to pursue the right path, is a standard trope in the morality tale of urban modernity that crime fiction frequently dramatises, even in Henning Mankell's seemingly serene Sweden and and Jo Nesbø's nominally normal Norway. Why, then, should the existence of this condition in a very young postcolony such as South Africa be met with such surprise, such a sense of the country's presumed exceptionalism? The answer, of course, is clearly evident to many observers and scholars of the South African democratic 'miracle':[13] it is precisely this mantra of the 'Mandela miracle' which raised expectations, both inside and outside the country in the wake of the 1994 democratic moment, far beyond what would turn out to be even remotely possible. Inside the country, expectations were understandably raised by the tsunami of optimism that followed the successful avoidance of bloody revolution. All of this is well documented. However, there is another factor, and that is South Africa's deep-seated sense of its own provincialism, its desire to be more than it actually is, or can ever possibly be, on the one hand, and its liminal awareness, on the other, that it will never quite be up there with countries in the 'big league'. Such ingrained provincialism is something that JM Coetzee found difficult to endure, and it is a good part of what he walked away from when he emigrated to Australia, as a reading of JC Kannemeyer's biography of Coetzee suggests. This provincialism, or 'cultural cringe', is an impossible longing among South Africans for their country to play more than the rather slight part on the world stage that, by any account, it does. South Africa's sense of its own exceptionalism was memorably critiqued by Mamdani,[14] who, in *Citizen and Subject*, argued that the self-image of South African scholars regarding their specialness was illusory, and that the country was merely part of a much larger African history, 'with specific differences' (27). Yet the myth of exceptionalism has been slow to die. Ordinary South Africans remain keen to claim even the most unflattering 'records', such as being the 'crime capital of the world', as we have seen. Such eagerness to be special, and the desire to prove and show it to the world, extends to the dubious notoriety of being the best in bad, or in vice. And there is a correspondingly perverse desire to *prove* just how 'good', or exceptional, the country's bad actually is. This desire for proof, and the need to *corroborate* what's 'really' going on amid obscured conditions under postapartheid, may, to some extent at least, account for the proven preference among South African book-buyers for nonfiction above fiction. While this may be a growing global trend, in South Africa the thirst for first-hand knowledge, or corroboration of presumed ills, and the need to discover just how bad the 'criminal underbelly' of the country really is, especially when it includes collusion with agents of the state, is very strong indeed, and sells plenty of books. Wiener's *Killing Kebble*, which, for many readers – mostly disgruntled whites, perhaps – hits a sweet spot of schadenfreude about postapartheid corruption, sold over 50 000 copies in its first print run. In a market where a work of fiction is deemed successful if it sells 4 000 copies, and print runs are often no more than 800 for new titles, such sales are spectacular.

However, what's 'really' going on in the South African underworld, to judge by Wiener's voluminous account, is that the 'underbelly', despite being 'seething', is a farcical, ragtag (tragi)comedy of errors; it bears very little resemblance to the professional hit-business as portrayed in certain South African crime fiction, for example Nicol's Revenge Trilogy. Such fictional works seem to err in attributing a sleek professionalism to the South African underworld, one which is lacking in reality. Still, they do not err in their *apparently* exaggerated portrayals of criminal wrongdoing involving collusion by agents of the state. To the contrary – that is, if we are to credit Wiener's exhaustively researched account – Nicol's *Payback*, *Killer Country* and *Black Heart* under- rather than overplay the extent to which postapartheid South Africa has become a violent Mafioso-style domain with proven links to politicians in power. This is, essentially, the subject matter of both Wiener's account and Nicol's trilogy, with Nicol stylising the scene, and giving it more elan – far more polish, more panache – than it seemingly deserves.

Wiener's account is massively detailed, a reporter's notebook spilling over with allegation and counter-allegation, version and alternative version. Based on several years of radio reporting for Eyewitness News in Johannesburg, the book comprises interviews, court records, statements, affidavits, oral testimony, phone records, emails, SMS messages, and the like. It follows every conceivable trail in the thicket of confusion surrounding the death of Johannesburg millionaire and former mining boss Brett Kebble. The salient facts are that Kebble, who was connected to key figures in the ANC, and generously funded (some would say 'bribed') the party, became ensnared in fraudulent financial transactions. He thereby came into conflict with other parties, to the extent that he felt compelled to employ 'protection' – shady 'security' operatives from the Johannesburg underworld, whom he allegedly requested, eventually, to stage his own murder. With a small army of 'heavies' ready to do his bidding, this staged killing – an assisted suicide, in essence – is shown to have become a comedy of errors. The 'hit-men' whom Kebble employed to kill him failed in two out of three attempts – on each occasion with Kebble's direct assistance – bungling the job quite amateurishly before eventually finding the resolve, and a car that did not overheat, to go through with the plan.

Taking up the story *in medias res*, we have the reported testimony of Clinton Nassif, whom Wiener describes as a character 'you'd not want to bump into in a dark alley in the middle of the night' (36). Of Lebanese extraction, Nassif grew up in the mean streets of the formerly white gangland of Mayfair, Johannesburg. Nassif was, by all accounts, the leader in Kebble's planned suicide. He owned a scrap-metal business, but his main activities were directed at providing the muscle for a Johannesburg security outfit. When Kebble, as head of Randgold & Exploration, became embroiled in corporate espionage involving DRDGOLD chairman Mark Wellesley-Wood, things got dirty. Kebble resorted to seeking help from Glenn Agliotti, a known 'mob' figure in Johannesburg. Agliotti, of course, was later proven to have been extensively engaged in corrupt dealings with the then national police chief, Jackie Selebi, who, and by all accounts, was likewise drawn into dealings with the dodgy Kebble empire. When Nassif instructed one of his lieutenants, former nightclub 'bouncer' Mikey Schultz, to shoot Kebble as part of the 'suicide' plan, Nassif 'assured Schultz that he would be protected by the National Police Commissioner Jackie Selebi' (170). Mikey Schultz testified in court as follows about what Nassif said:

> 'He said that if all goes as planned, Jackie Selebi will be in charge, the Police Commissioner will be in charge of the shooting. He said that Jackie Selebi was going to commission [Clint's men] to investigate and to assist with the investigation. He said by this we would at all times know exactly where the investigation was and, if there was any heat coming, we could derail the police,' Mikey testified. (170; square brackets in original text)

In the light of subsequent events, in which such control of the investigation by Selebi did not eventuate, it is hard to decide which is more naïve – Schultz's belief that this level of protection could in fact be guaranteed in a loose verbal arrangement, or Nassif's offering of such an undeliverable promise in the first place, especially in view of the predictable media spotlight following a suspicious murder involving a prominent mining magnate openly connected with government. In the event, several investigations were conducted: the official police probe was led by Captain Johan Diedericks; a separate team consisted of Judge Willem Heath, along with outspoken forensic scientist David Klatzow, and a pathologist, Jan Botha (this investigating team was privately appointed by the deceased's father, Roger Kebble); another probe was conducted by private investigator Piet Byleveld; the Scorpions also investigated Brett Kebble's affairs extensively over several years (134); and several journalists – among them Wiener – conducted their own investigations.

Within weeks of Roger Kebble's high-level private investigation being announced, Klatzow was taken off the team, Wiener writes, on the orders of Police Commissioner Selebi, who told Roger Kebble that if he persisted with a private investigation, the police would 'pull back' (207). Wiener speculates that Klatzow had perhaps 'scratched too close to the wound', discovering that Brett Kebble had taken out life insurance to the value of R30 million just months before his death, naming his wife as beneficiary. (The policies were duly paid out.[15]) Klatzow was one of the first to make public allegations that the killing was an assisted suicide (207–208); these were eventually corroborated by court evidence and found believable by Judge Frans Kgomo in the Kebble murder case against presumed kingpin Glenn Agliotti.

Allegations of top-level postapartheid political involvement in organised crime are legion, but in this case Mr Justice Kgomo went on record as follows:

> In my view this case is about hidden and/or sinister agendas perpetrated by shady characters as well as ostensibly crooked and/or greedy businesspersons. It is about corrupt civil servants as well as prominent politicians or politically connected people wining and dining with devils incarnate under cover of darkness. (383)

Judge Kgomo drew explicit parallels with Mario Puzo's *The Godfather* trilogy, to which, remarkably, he turned in delivering final judgment:

> I revisited the book [said Judge Kgomo, delivering judgment in the Agliotti murder trial in Johannesburg] after listening to the evidence that was led so far in this matter because it is my view that some of the trickery and shenanigans that were practised by the Cosa Nostra, that is the mafia in the Sicilian parlance as demonstrated in that book, was also practised in this particular family of the Kebbles. For example, what was happening within the Corleone family was not very unlike what was happening within the empire presided over by Brett Kebble. The evidence sketched out by Clinton Nassif about this empire was based on skimming money from the JCI group of companies, RandGold as well as others like Western Areas mines and then buying patronage with it from high-ranking police officials, prospective directors of public prosecution, politicians at the highest levels and all or any person in the position of authority from whom a favour may or could be obtained. (383–384)

It is not unknown for judges to cite literary authority such as Ralph Waldo Emerson or Niccolò Machiavelli, but Mario Puzo's *The Godfather* may not be the eminence one would wish to be associated with a rainbow South Africa, however faded its hues. However, crime fiction as the leitmotif for a stringent, evidence-based juridical analysis of events was what it had come down to when Judge Kgomo handed down his 2010 judgment. The judge drew elaborate parallels between the rank structures depicted in Puzo's novels and the authority structures in the Kebble-Stratton-Agliotti 'mafia': the *Don*, or Godfather, was Brett Kebble; the *Consigliere*, or right-hand man, was Kebble strategist and close confidante John Stratton; the *Caporegime* under the *Don* was Agliotti and the *Lower Caporegime* was Clinton Nassif; while the *Button Men* – operatives required to kill without asking questions – were Mikey Schultz, Nigel McGurk and Fiazal 'Kappie' Smith. Judge Kgomo elaborated on these structures, explaining in precise juridical analysis the mode of interaction between the various levels, and their respective regimes of authority (383–385).

Judge Kgomo was by no means off the mark: Brett Kebble had played an active role in several public feuds where political interference was clearly evident. The most bitter of these involved the country's first National Director of Public Prosecutions (NDPP). The director, Bulelani Ngcuka, suggested at a press briefing with black newspaper editors[16] in 2003 that Kebble was paying protection money to the ANC Youth League (124). A furious Kebble retaliated by threatening to sue Ngcuka for defamation, publicly accusing the director, as well as the minister of justice, Penuell Maduna, of pursuing a 'private agenda' (124). As Wiener explains, both Kebble and his father were facing fraud charges at the time, and it was in Kebble's interest to discredit the NDPP. This, Wiener alleges, was also one of Kebble's motives for supporting Jacob Zuma in the latter's own claims that the NDPP was being manipulated. Zuma was at the time facing an investigation for alleged corrupt activities with his financial adviser Schabir Shaik,[17] and Kebble appears to have thrown in his lot with the Zuma camp, hence his close ties with the ANC Youth League, who at the time were backing Zuma to oust Mbeki (who, two years later, would himself relieve Zuma of his position as deputy president). These allegations appear to make sense from another angle, too. Brett Kebble's bête noir, Mzi Khumalo, was said to be supporting the Mbeki camp – Kebble had in fact bankrolled Khumalo to buy a

Black Economic Empowerment stake in mining company JCI, but by now the situation had turned toxic (123–124).

The link between crime fiction and postapartheid politics seems far less fanciful than might first appear. The various activities of Schabir Shaik suggest the intersection of struggle politics and questionable business dealings involving senior government politicians. Not least among these dealings is the controversial arms deal. In Mike Nicol's *Payback*, a composite of the Schabir Shaik type makes his appearance as 'Mo Siq'. In *Killer Country*, a similar figure, Obed Choco, does the honours. In Nicol's novels, as well as in the actual social environment in which Judge Kgomo situates his *Godfather* analogy, the grey zone in which politics and organised crime intersect is ubiquitous. Criminal co-implication emerges as a major trend as much in the courts of South Africa as it does in postapartheid writing. And so, Durkheim's dictum inevitably springs to mind: one comes to understand what the right way might be, amid the noise of competing legitimacy claims, by discovering what is criminally wrong in any given society. Uncovering crimes, disclosing the criminal 'underbelly', has become a key task for contemporary South African writers – and unavoidably, the reader is in for some thrills and spills.

6

Referred pain, wound culture and pathology in postapartheid writing

The move from apartheid to postapartheid in the early to mid-1990s is momentous not only for the more obvious reasons, but also because it roughly coincides with globalisation and the rapid growth of digital media. The sprawl of the new media has coincided with new emphases in data consumption: visual salience, speed, brevity, and the predominance of surface over depth.[1] Actuality, often in seemingly raw and semi-processed form, rides high in this environment, whereas older forms of 'deep' literature, and expectations of close reading, fare less well. In addition, the relatively passive media consumers of earlier generations have morphed into interactive media agents: screen readers and content makers – 'writers' of an entirely new kind – who consume and also produce media in quantum loops (Surette 14).

As if to corroborate these trends, in which the 'real' and the actual are pushed, publishing in South Africa, especially in the postapartheid period, has seen nonfiction increasingly outsell genre as well as literary fiction. In addition, several high-calibre South African writers, among them Van Niekerk, Krog and Malan, have observed that postapartheid conditions are such that nonfiction appears to be a far more serviceable mode of writing than fiction, as noted earlier. This stands in contrast to the apartheid period, when realist fiction in the Gordimer 'history from the inside' mode, and metafictional fabulation with a focus on ethical agency, in the manner of JM Coetzee, were paramount. The conjunction of the new media, as a 'glocal' digital emporium and a dominant site of reading and writing, on the one hand, and a trend towards nonfiction, on the other, underlie a sea-change in South African writing (a necessarily larger category than 'literature').[2] These shifts in modes of writing and forms of address, and in audience, medium and reach, have produced a transformed space of literary production, one that is modelled to a lesser or greater extent on the continuous, looping 'content' (a blend of fact and commentary) of the new media. It is as if 'writing', including the ascendant category frequently referred to as creative or literary nonfiction, cannot but align itself with the energy, form and flow of the new media in the information age, of which it is an integral part. This is a site where practitioners have, to some degree, abandoned the academic cloisters and joined the 24/7 media wrap. They populate an informational 'reality show' that has profound implications for what cultural scholars such as Best and Marcus express in the phrase 'how we read now' (1).

Much of this can be explained in terms that call to mind the claims of the Affect movement in literary-cultural studies,[3] which also places more emphasis on what is perceivably and affectively 'out there' – what can be seen, touched and felt – than on the hidden subtleties and complexities of meaning within narrow (and 'deep') aesthetic forms. Like the post-2000 digital generation, Affect adherents tend also to value the visual, the surface, and therefore feelings associated with an immediate, tactile world. Linked to this, in literary-cultural studies, is the phenomenon characterised by Shields as 'reality hunger' in his book of the same title. For Shields and his sympathisers, this appetite for the real and the raw is encouraged by a newfound impatience with the illusions of fabrication. Reality hunger in the new media is accompanied by a calling for open access, free use (and abuse)[4] of sources, citizen scholarship – in fact any use of 'writing' (including copying) in the quest for a sharper take on the rough and unfinished data of 'the real'. The growing digital humanities campaign in academia (especially in the developed countries of the north, as well as Japan and Australia in the east) shares many of these imperatives – especially citizen scholarship, crowdsourcing research techniques, and visual salience.[5] Meanwhile, as large sectors of the global community, in developed as well as developing countries, become more atomised, and expanding populations diversify, new media performs a valuable 'discovery' function, given the global spread of a heterogeneity that is incommensurate and multitudinous. In this process, 'reality' becomes occulted, stranger by the day, and ever more compelling.

In Paul Virilio's notion of a 'dromosphere', a digitally conditioned sensorium ruled by the 'logic of speed', our horizons have simultaneously expanded and contracted, a matter that was of great concern to Marshall McLuhan, too.[6] In the dromosphere, trajectory is lost (Virilio, *Polar Inertia* 36–50; Ulmer). Moments of departure, and intervals or stages in between, disappear in a blur. What remains is an eternal sense of (belated) arrival, a claustrophobic 'now time' that never ends. The technologies of what Virilio calls 'telepresence' (*Open Sky* 131) facilitate a process in which place, too, is often uprooted, along with older philosophical understandings of being in the world.[7] More to the point, in a world of accelerated digital access to (the illusion of) everything 'out there' – what Gregory Ulmer terms 'electracy' (1) – fiction, i.e. made-up stories with stylistic or aesthetic pretensions, faces altogether new challenges.

In this environment, fabricated stories are a kind of *surplus* of affect, of invented characters and feelings and circumstances, which a certain class of people once needed to pass time. But today very few people have sufficient leisure, or the need to 'pass' time. Time is passing them, overtaking them – and with it data, at unnerving speed. In such circumstances, a growing number of people remain in the throng,[8] in the ever-receding, expanding space of 'now', partly because there is so much, always, to catch up on, so many facts and events that are, affectively, 'shocking', 'disgusting' or 'Like-able'. There is an ever-looming quota of sensation in the new-media sensorium, always and instantly available at one's fingertips. What is 'out there' demands noting, not least because it seems to threaten one's hold on, one's understanding of, a world projected as dangerous and empirically unknowable. Of course, many people continue to resist the lures of this simulacral sensorium, but it is becoming increasingly difficult to remain outside of it without sacrificing shared information, especially among professional associates and researchers.

In addition, the perceived need to remain alert to possibly dangerous conditions out there is especially acute in postapartheid South Africa, with its 'phenomenology of crime', as Steinberg ('Crime' 28) puts it. The catharsis of affect, once mostly found in aesthetic performativity, is arguably now felt just as often in the outrage and pain consequent upon viewing mediated spectacles, looping 'tales', intermediated by fellow digital consumers, of 'real' events that are marked as bad or revealing news about wrongdoing in the public sphere. Such outrage is urgent, and relevant, because perceived wrongdoing is seen to threaten the actual, real-time victim and the voyeuristic viewer, too. If it can happen to you, it can happen to me, especially if the conditions under which we live are similar. Here, then, is a form of referred pain; it is experienced within what Mark Seltzer calls a 'wound culture' embedded in a 'pathological public sphere' (Seltzer, *True Crime* 11 ff.). The elements delineated above – a leaning towards 'raw facts' within a 'media a priori' (*True Crime* 10–18) that brings about, in affect, a fever of anxious telepresence – are all suggestive of a terrain in which, for writers, true crime as a category assumes a prominent role. Here, written accounts feed into the often anxious and politically sceptical mood of new-media reading cultures, and so the recent work of writers on conditions in the everyday world of postapartheid life, such as that by Gevisser, Mzilikazi wa Afrika and Maria Phalime, find strong purchase.

Wound culture in a 'pathological' public sphere

In his work on 'wound culture' and the 'pathological public sphere', Mark Seltzer identifies 'addictive violence' as 'not merely a collective spectacle but one of the crucial sites where private desire and public space cross' in late modernity ('Wound Culture' 3). For Seltzer, the convening of the public 'around scenes of violence' (such as rushing to the scene of an accident, either an on-the-scene-event or a voyeuristically experienced multimedia happening) is constitutive of 'wound culture'. The latter is the 'public fascination with torn and opened persons, a collective gathering around shock, trauma, and the wound' (3). Seltzer's 1990 work culminated in his study *Serial Killers: Death and Life in America's Wound Culture* (1998), directing its immediate attention to conditions in the USA, particularly in the latter part of the twentieth century. Recall for a moment the rise, in that time, of confessional narratives that opened private wounding to public view. Shocking, intimate stories involving violence and/or sexual abuse emerged, such as Anne Heche's 2001 memoir *Call Me Crazy*. This period saw the rise, also, of men's narratives in which the subject discloses previously occluded masculinity issues.[9] It is noteworthy that the 'wounded attachments' that Wendy Brown describes ('Wounded') have saturated identity politics.[10] In postapartheid South Africa, the *fin de siècle* saw a different manifestation of 'wound culture' in the

Truth and Reconciliation Commission, during which the public witnessing of private wounding constituted a convening of the public around what were sometimes even rehearsed 'scenes of violence'.[11] In the process, the pathological public sphere of apartheid was laid bare. The trends set in train in the wake of the TRC remain robust in postapartheid writing, particularly autobiographical forms of witnessing,[12] both in reconstituting the past (such as Krog's *Begging to be Black*) and in coming to terms with a wayward present (Mzilikazi wa Afrika's *Nothing Left to Steal*). Seltzer seeks to explore the processes by which the public sphere is 'pathologised' in late modernity, as well as the conditions that underpin this process. For him, the scene of private wounding is taken up in communicative relays via a 'media a priori' such that it gathers a mass of public spectators. Seltzer talks of the 'doubling of act and observation' ('Murder/Media/Modernity' 14), citing the following example:

> In Los Angeles, among other places, the in-transit eyewitnessing of the everyday accident – what's called the 'spectator slowdown' – enters into the radio traffic report that runs (along with the cell phone) as a kind of soundtrack to the commuting between private and public spaces. In this way the reporting on the event becomes part of, and enters into, the event reported on. ('Murder/Media/Modernity' 14)[13]

Here, the public sphere might be described as there-but-for-the-grace-of-God-go-I onlookers at the bloody scene of a crime, an accident, a sexual assault or an 'incomprehensible' murder. At such mediated events, witnessing is at once voyeuristic and deferred. Critically, though, such witnessing enters into the reality of the event, becomes part of it, as the live radio traffic report contains both the event and its doubling in the act of mediated observation.

In South Africa, as elsewhere, such hypermediated events often have pronounced sociopolitical determinations, whether it is a killing, an accident, or a political service-delivery scandal resulting, for example, in electrocution by pirated wires in shackland conditions.[14] The 'scene of the crime' in such cases is not confined to the physical site of the event, but includes its doubling in the media, where onlookers feel the wounding of referred pain. The case of Andries Tatane is pertinent here: during a service-delivery protest in Ficksburg in the

Free State in 2011, he was beaten and shot with rubber bullets in full view of onlookers and the media. The video clips of his beating, shooting and death on the scene quickly went viral, sparking outrage and disgust with the conduct of the South African Police Service some seventeen years into democracy. Here, as elsewhere, the grief of the family (see, for example, CNN's coverage of the incident and its effect on Tatane's next of kin[15]) is redoubled and affectively witnessed by masses of individuals as part of the event itself. While in such cases (i.e. accidents, crimes, or the effects of incompetence and/ or corruption) the onlooker-citizen is affectively engaged on behalf of the victim(s), the citizen experiences a simultaneous, personal sense of injury – a more general effect of plot loss, assaulting any claim to personal security in a climate where cheek-by-jowl neighbours, fellow citizens, are subject to deadly conditions. In the wake of the events that arise from such conditions, social media memes proliferate, each more toxic than the last, so that this sense of personal injury accelerates and deepens, as the movement that has come to be known as Fallism, and the hashtag wars of 2015/16, so dramatically demonstrate (#RhodesMustFall, #FeesMustFall, #ZumaMustFall, #FuckWhitePeople, and the like).

Perceived neglect by those in power (whether these be self-absorbed politicians or distracted university vice-chancellors) is felt to be atrocious and shameful, eliciting a sense of disgust – personally felt – that is instantly communicated in a digital cascade, where genuine outrage is, one must add, often indistinguishable from virtue-signalling. The contact zone between the private and the public, the scene of the 'accident', then, is also the place where the actual and the professed are played off against each other, and 'political bullshit' is exposed. There is a keen appetite for such exposure, which involves the unmasking of people and institutions that are seen, or perceived, to be distorting the truth. Among new-media reader-writers, such deception is seen as hard to swallow after the propaganda and lies of apartheid. Consequently, citizens (including figures as influential as Ronnie Kasrils and Moeletsi Mbeki) feel a strong need to bear witness to the unveiling of what they perceive as massacres of truth, and it is no surprise, therefore, that the commentary of Max du Preez, Justice Malala, Sisonke Msimang, Richard Poplak and Raymond Suttner, among others, not to mention the cartoons of Zapiro, enjoy significant social media uptake. The reading or viewing of such commentaries, which blend reporting and opinion about what's happening on the ground, under the radar or behind the smokescreen, is largely an affective experience. In new-media upwellings, arising from what Mbembe calls the 'politics of impatience',[16] the sense of plot loss looks beyond the failures of government alone, embracing a more general 'decolonisation', and a radical dismantling of perceived, pervasive, white postapartheid hegemony.

Witnesses to media-saturated accidents – which culminate in 'torn and open bodies and torn and opened psyches'[17] (as in the Marikana event[18]) – engage with raw forms of 'reality' in ways that are both compulsive and time-consuming. Less time is therefore available for other modalities of reading and writing, and this may account to some extent for the swing in literary book production – and sales – towards 'true' crime, a 'factional' conjunction of the real with the fictional. In addition, the witnessing at the centre of such reading and writing is mostly *deferred* witnessing via media looping. The sense of wounding, with consequent *referred* pain, recalls what sociologists call 'moral panics': publicly mediated, or orchestrated, fears about social conditions, which frequently force politicians and bureaucrats to act in one way or another. 'Panics' of this nature often evoke a 'golden age' of strong moral discipline and social control that supposedly counteracted potential disorder in an overly idealised past (McRobbie and Thornton 561). In postapartheid South Africa, the 'golden age' that is often invoked is, of course, the brief Mandela regime of 1994–1998, with its message of reconciliation and commitment to 'a better life for all'.[19] As McRobbie and Thornton argue, the 'moral panic' theory, always strongly tied to the role of 'legacy' media (newspapers, broadcasting and television), belongs to an earlier age and needs conceptual updating under new-media conditions. 'Communication' under the new conditions, instead of being conceived as one plane in a triangle, with government and citizens making up the other two, is instead perceived as a space in which all parties are engulfed, and in which agentive roles have both multiplied and, paradoxically, diminished – more space to shout, with less effect. Seltzer's pathological public sphere, in which a wound culture operates under conditions in which a 'social tie on the model of *referred pain*' (*True Crime* 11, emphasis in original) is posited, seems one way of understanding the state of pronounced postapartheid 'panic' about plot loss.

The notion of a pathological public sphere under postapartheid conditions, as bodied forth in traditional as well as new media, suggests the idea of watchful citizens who are either bewildered and sceptical, or passive and disillusioned, using the scene-of-the-crime 'spectator slowdown' media event as a kind of catharsis for their own suppressed fears; many such citizens are genuinely incredulous in the face of the gap between what the ruling class professes and the (mass-mediated) evidence on the streets. This is the 'shock of contact', the 'excitation', that interests Seltzer. When, for example, one 'witnesses', via a Facebook or Twitter post, children in the Cape township of Gugulethu drowning in a marshland, possibly after being electrocuted by illegal connections, or the rape and disembowelment of a young woman,[20] or any number of similar atrocities in contemporary South Africa, then it is difficult *not* (i) to become affectively engaged; (ii) to see such events as instances of 'criminal' failure by government and/or the ruling classes to live up to the promise of 'a better life for all' after apartheid; and (iii) to experience this 'shock of contact' as a moment, and a space, in which the public and the private intersect in ways that are perceived to be critically important, demanding cultural and political attention.

The conjunction of event and media spectacle – 'atrocity exhibitions' within a wound culture, a 'cult of commiseration' (Seltzer, 'Murder/Media/Modernity' 13) – speaks to much in the hyped-up new-media/social-violence copula of postapartheid, in which the line between public and private, and between 'fact' and 'faction', becomes blurred. This results, to a certain extent, in what Seltzer calls the 'murder of reality' (32). However, what mitigates the somewhat deterministic assumption in Seltzer of a wholesale 'murder' of reality is the fact that violence and the relaying of violence via the media, includes, in an integral manner, a condition of reflexivity. Rather than being passive consumers, observers have agency, that is, discernment and the ability to reflect. It is in *this* space – the gap of reflective parrying, also about the 'murder of the real' – that critical diagnoses and important determinations about the state of things in the public sphere are made. This is where Michael Warner's publics and counterpublics, in all their diversity and atypicality, make their calls about the world.[21] The world of true crime (and modernity itself) is 'a self-observing world of observers' (Seltzer, 'Murder/Media/Modernity' 14). In the 'generalization and intensification of this reflexive situation', the event and its 'registration' combine to make a 'different reality, consisting of itself plus its registration and revelation' (Baecker in Seltzer, 'Murder/Media/

Modernity' 14). So, true crime is 'always taking exception to itself, always looking over its own shoulder, and by analogy, inviting viewers to do the same' ('Murder/Media/Modernity' 13). Here, then, is a form of autopoesis, of self- and world-making, in which the 'known world of true crime is the observed world – and the knowledge and observation of that' (14). Importantly, it is a condition in which '[f]orensic realism takes as given...the compulsion to observation and self-observation that is a precondition of modernity' (14). Further, 'forensic realism'[22] is 'conditional and counterfactual', and is 'itself observed as the real work of true crime'. This is a key point, as postapartheid writers of literary nonfiction often write against the grain of accepted 'facts' and public opinion, such as when Jacob Dlamini unsettles perceptions about 'askaris' (ANC members who were 'turned' by the apartheid security forces into collaborators), or when Antony Altbeker exposes the wrong-headedness of public opinion concerning a young man's guilt in a murder case involving his late girlfriend in Stellenbosch.[23]

Jeremy Green, too, in his study *Late Postmodernism: American Fiction at the Millennium* (2005), reminds us that much recent work on transformation in the public sphere, in the media age, especially by Foster, Seltzer and Warner, 'has explored the ways in which anonymous and dispersed publics seek representations of mass subjectivity in spectacles of disaster, atrocity, and violence – in images, precisely, of suffering bodies' (167). Warner, in 'The Mass Public and the Mass Subject', writes that '[t]he mass subject cannot have a body except the body it witnesses' (250). Warner is worth quoting at length:

> [I]nflicting and witnessing mass injury are two sides of the same dynamic in disaster discourse. Being of necessity anywhere else, the mass subject cannot have a body except the body it witnesses...The transitive pleasure of witnessing/injuring makes available our translation into the disembodied publicity of the mass subject. By injuring a mass body...we constitute ourselves as a noncorporeal mass witness...The same logic informs an astonishing number of mass publicity's genres, from the prophylaxes of horror, assassination, and terrorism to the organized prosthesis of sports. (250)

'Prophylaxes' of horror in what Warner calls 'disaster discourse', something he sees as germane to the mass subject, suggest that the 'mass public' in a pathological public sphere resorts to the contemplation (via witnessing) of 'horror' as a substitute for realising itself in public discourse, as Warner suggests (250). Furthermore, the prophylaxis of disaster discourse assists in dealing with referred pain, just as prostheses (a term Warner borrows from Lauren Berlant) stand in for the gratifications of violence as deferred through the spectacles of contact sports. (Berlant's work on prosthetic subjectivity – see, for example, *The Female Complaint* – is relevant here.)

For our more immediate topic, the postapartheid imaginary in current forms of writing, it seems feasible to propose that 'literary culture' in a broad sense is undergoing a slow but steady transformation: from a relatively elitist, mainly highbrow concern with (meta)-fictional excellence in deep forms that require rigorous 'unpacking', to imbrication within a mediated public sphere in which affect and surface, the raw and the real, loop recursively in open, public forms of witnessing and writing. In particular, this is an imaginary that is predominantly engaged in a wound culture, a 'cult of commiseration', in which the violated or 'opened' body, mediated in forms that range from social media to creative nonfiction and crime writing, comes increasingly to stand in for the body politic, serving the function of a prosthesis. Further, if true crime and a pathological public sphere are the axes of cultural intermediation, then they are also the foci for reflexivity about what is actually 'going on' in postapartheid South Africa: the plot may well have been lost, but exactly how this happened remains a haunting question.

Lost and Found in Johannesburg

A reading of Mark Gevisser's 2014 nonfiction work *Lost and Found in Johannesburg* resonates with many of the above notions. The book as a whole, in literary terms, is premised upon the play between cartography – in particular the various street-mappings of Johannesburg – and the reflexive gap[24] that forensic observation reveals about the actual territory represented by the maps, all of which is rendered in sharp reportage. The city maps that Gevisser investigates are beguiling and alluring to his boy-self as signifiers of the unexplored and the unknown, but they are overdetermined by their makers' presuppositions. And so, the city 'guides' – maps emphasising boundaries, thereby setting up barriers – point straight back at the cartographers and their ideological compulsions. The Gevisser child persona plays a game he calls 'Dispatcher', in which he routes random imaginary journeys across Johannesburg for his messenger, from one given point in the city to another. The adult author, and centre of consciousness in *Lost and Found*, now goes back to those maps, from the early Holmden's 'register' of Johannesburg, Randburg and Sandton, to Map Studio's *Street Guide to the Witwatersrand*, to Google maps, and considers the many retorts offered by actuality (or his observation of it) against these maps, street guides being a much used form of media in Johannesburg. Here we have a version of precisely the kind of reflexive observation in which certain forms of media are set against alternative versions of actuality, and then relayed, once again, via print and electronic media. The same raw, physical space of Johannesburg, as reflexively experienced over time, and written into Gevisser's narrative, complicates and unsettles the representations of the city in other media, in this case urban cartography. Fashioned as the explorations of a flaneur, Gevisser's narrative brings into sharp relief the play between cartographic representation and changing perceptions of the actual territory; he teases out the gaps between maps on the one hand, and lives that, in his (relayed) experience, transgress mere lines drawn on maps. It is an acutely considered, second look at spatial and social boundaries, how they are represented over time, and how people find ways around them.

Further, the narrative is frequently interspersed with old family photographs, that is, with pictorial evidence that speaks in a register different from the visual data of the maps, and from Gevisser's own prose, so that the book is experienced as multimodal, despite the fact that Gevisser is leading the reader by the hand, so to speak. To enrich the reflexive play, Gevisser combines this visual evidence with his own, considered interpretation of the various data he offers up for inspection. Still, this leaves interpretation open to a reader's further potential revisions (the reader's viewing of the photographs may, for example, yield divergent 'readings' of the visual archive thus presented). However, all of this – speaking resonantly to the postapartheid mood of impatience with fabrication, to the hunger for actuality and a keenness for sifting through relevant data – is bracketed within a larger story of true crime, a framing narrative that begins and (almost but not quite) ends the book. The framing tale is a compelling first-person witness account of an event in which Gevisser, along with two female friends, became the victims of a violent home invasion in Killarney, and were held hostage for almost three hours. This gripping tale, which, in its telling and public mediation via *Lost and Found* becomes an instance of true crime, not only frames the narrative, but functions as a kind of conditional clause in the story: if this can happen, then what do we make of everything else we know about our situation? As such, the robbery relativises Gevisser's own attempts at relativisation, in which social ills are shown to be remediable. Observations about Johannesburg, as with many cities, operate in a liminal space of constant self-revision. Martin J Murray notes that, in late-modern cities like Johannesburg, rampant capitalism promotes 'fertile ground for a kind of fugitive city building that stresses impermanence over stability, provisionality over endurance, and creative destruction over historical preservation' (*City of Extremes* xvi). In Gevisser's own words, 'I have found, to my perpetual surprise, that my home town eludes me, however assiduously I court it' (*Lost and Found* 19). In keeping with the city's perceived habit of chronic self-undoing and restless remaking, Gevisser's narrative uses pictures (in a manner reminiscent of WG Sebald's *Austerlitz*) as a way of catching both the fixity and the ephemerality of various moments in the city's life, and in the life of his extended family, over a period of about a hundred years.

The Johannesburg author links his own locating, making and refashioning of selfhood in this city of mirage-like forms to the mood of '*hüzün*' or 'fundamental melancholy' that Orhan Pamuk evinces about his native Istanbul (quoted in *Lost and Found* 38). However, even *hüzün*-type melancholy, in the case of Gevisser's Johannesburg, is fractured by the tendency of the city and its denizens to repress knowledge of Joburg's deferred margins, like the person or thing just beyond the frame of a photograph, which nevertheless manages to skew the proportions and relations of the picture itself:

> If there is a Johannesburg *hüzün* – if *I* have a Johannesburg *hüzün* – it must be found, somehow, in the relationship between the bucolic gardens of my Kodachrome childhood, wooded and green and irrigated, a world of swimming pools and sprinklers – and the harsh bleached landscapes just beyond its suburban walls. Pamuk's work has provoked me into thinking about how the visual archive I have been collecting for the past two

decades – photographs and maps – offers some route to an emotional truth: about what it means, to me, to be a South African, and about how my particular South African identity has been formed within the shadow of how I was defined – by family, by society, by the state. (39)

As if to underline this sense of doubling, of having to seek a more profound sense of home in the 'shadow' of what has been given and validated as home, Gevisser adds: 'I do not possess Pamuk's confidence: I cannot distil my national identity down into an essence such as *hüzün* and name it, the way he does…What I am trying to describe is not the boundaries that define South Africa (or, more specifically, Johannesburg), but the way that we South Africans define ourselves within, and across, and against, these boundaries' (39). If Johannesburg is, as Nuttall and Mbembe suggest, the 'elusive metropolis',[25] then its act of eluding, in the case of Gevisser, at least, results in the sense that being 'in' and 'of' the city requires a cancelling out of any form of containment – of being and feeling 'at home'. Johannesburg's inhabitants need to defy all that is pre-given, delving instead into forms of difference in a continual flux of self-reinvention and reconstitution. This near-impossible prerequisite for a sense of self, however contingent, may explain the phenomenon of fortified enclaves built upon a persistent substructure of class and ethnicity. Gevisser, in the postapartheid moment, is reconstituting the (vanished) moment of coming into consciousness as an anti-apartheid insider, occupying the paradoxical position of privileged white subject who wishes to refuse his privilege, but is everywhere constrained by a psycho-geography of boundaries, frontiers and underground spaces. From his narrative vantage point, the postapartheid present some 20 years into democracy, Gevisser retells the story of a life led within the confines of privileged white patriarchy: visiting Exclusive Books in Pretoria Street, Hillbrow – an intellectual haven in what was an otherwise stunted city; crossing the road and stealing glimpses at banned gay magazines in Estoril Books;[26] and hanging around on Sundays when multiracial pool-picnics were encouraged at his wealthy parents' home in Athol, near Sandton. These are moments that seem to herald interracial harmony and the toleration of difference; in the blur of Johannesburg's cruel ephemerality there was a deep stirring of counterfactual hope, an idealism that comes of living on an unsteady faultline.

However, Johannesburg proves to be too mercurial, too self-annihilating and unpredictably regenerative to cater to any such anti-apartheid idealism, even beyond the threshold of full democracy. Such a projection of hopefulness would appear to be far too unitary in nature for a city like Johannesburg, with its propensity to refract into unexpected and unpredictable 'lines of flight', to appropriate Deleuze and Guattari's phrase.[27] And so this coming-of-age of an anti-establishment figure, along with a superbly executed rendering of Johannesburg's Fischer/Gordimer generation, does not yield a workable telos, or, indeed, a sustainable outcome. For, despite Gevisser's acknowledgement of postapartheid's key gains – Constitutional Hill, a free press, gay rights, liberalised abortion laws, (imperfect but functional) welfare programmes – the entire story of this *Bildung*, already rendered unstable by the sense of a looming shadow in every photograph on display, is further destabilised when those very gains are shown to be subordinate to a greater criminal force, i.e. home invasion, robbery and random violence.

In Gevisser's rendering, the 'atrocity exhibition'[28] that he narrates, a detailed and sober rendering of true crime, is executed with some reluctance. For this crime story appears as a blot on his stylistically elegant and ultimately upbeat meditation on a life lived under signs of borders, boundaries and transgression. There is a sense in which Gevisser's book is *held up* (both in a temporal and a criminal sense) by the home invasion, seemingly against the author's inclination and better judgement. Of course, Gevisser *chooses* to reconstruct the book to incorporate the robbery, but it is a choice that presents itself as well-nigh unavoidable. A micro-story within the larger account of the robbery illustrates this sense of almost losing one's story to the forces of invasion. At the time of the attack, Gevisser had in fact completed a draft of *Lost and Found*, and he had brought this hard copy of the manuscript, with extensive handwritten edits, along with him on his visit to Bea and Katie on the night the break-in occurred. His book is virtually done. In the middle of the hold-up, Gevisser realises that the criminal act against his person might extend to the theft – and possible loss – of his near-finalised manuscript, along with the digitised version on various devices. He then narrates his panicked thoughts about this possibility.

> I knew the men would take all my technology, but would they take the manuscript? I debated asking them to leave it behind, but

thought better of it. I preoccupied myself by running through the options. If they killed us and left the manuscript, someone would find it and publish it. If they did not kill us and took the manuscript, I would have lost my book but I would be alive. If they killed me and took the manuscript, all would be lost. (256–257)

It later turns out that Gevisser, under the pressure of the robbery and the trauma he is experiencing, forgot that he had in fact backed up the manuscript, and that he had sent an electronic copy to his agent shortly before the attack. In conceptual terms, it is accurate to say that the marked-up manuscript is placed under a form of erasure. Although the manuscript was safe all along, its literary 'innocence' is corrupted, its former wholeness ruptured by the violent criminality of the event. Gevisser feels compelled to include the story of the robbery in an expanded version of what has now suddenly become an incomplete book. This, despite his reluctance to taint his Joburg story with a crime account: such a story breeds the kind of pessimism that Gevisser clearly feels is unworthy of the genuine hope that Johannesburg, and South Africa, in fact offer. So he tells his agent he needs another year to finish the story, which turns out to be a substantially altered account.

And so it is that a respected literary stylist finds himself writing a true-crime story. Gevisser makes bold efforts to mitigate this outcome by writing a conciliatory and affirmative closing chapter, ending with a touching portrait of an 'Open City' that is in stark contrast with the opening cameo of a 'Closed City'. But the 'true-crime' rupture of the narrative, itself constituting a dramatic 'break-in', registers an uptick in urgency, an acceleration of tempo, and a thrillingly readable alteration in what, up to that point, is a meandering, even languid account.

The acceleration in pace, along with a distinct sense of panic, is in no small measure attributable to the fact that the home invasion Gevisser narrates puts at risk not only the immediate physical integrity and wellbeing of Bea, Katie and himself, but also the very values – of boundary-breaching, of tolerance for others, of love and generosity – that *Lost and Found* implicitly and explicitly espouses. Throughout the book, frontiers and borders are figured as places to explore, and as liminal spaces in which transgression (for example, of sexual norms or political taboos) is experienced as a liberating act. Such crossings are also projected as acts of reconciliation and potentially loving human encounter. The home invasion, however, represents the transgression of limits in an unambiguously vile and dangerous manner. The good intentions implicit in Gevisser's stepping across established lines are negated, with raw criminality seeming to mock the liberal humanism elsewhere evident in *Lost and Found*. This creates an unwelcome schism, an apparent loss of plot.

How does Gevisser deal with this sense of ethical and actual rupture? On the one hand, the author factually – and tautly – recounts the details of the event, in all their banal brutality; significantly, however, he is at pains to 'humanise' the attackers, and have the attackers see him and his companions as humans, too. First, then, we read a chilling account of the robbers delivering a vicious slap to Gevisser's head, sending his glasses flying and leaving the near-sighted writer almost blind, after which they pistol-whip Katie. They proceed to upend the furniture, the TV included, thereby bringing to an end the episode of *The Slap* that the three friends had been watching; a fictional human 'drama' is supplanted by a real-life crime 'drama'. Not long after upending the TV, the robbers lead Bea off to the bedroom; when they fail to find the whereabouts of the safe, they sexually molest her instead. The situation threatens to become a homicidal rampage, but what Gevisser reads as a change in the robbers' tempo is brought about by Bea before she gets dragged off:

> I followed my breath, in, out, in, out, and heard Bea's voice, calm and clear: 'Excuse me,' she said, as if she was talking to someone at a book-club meeting, 'but we've just made tea, I think the cup's still hot, you'll see, and I was wondering if you'd give me a sip before you gag me, because my throat is feeling very dry.' (248)

A 'blind and disoriented' (247) Gevisser realises from 'motion' he senses in his peripheral vision, as well as sounds he can hear, that the robbers are complying with Bea's request for a sip of tea. 'I understood immediately what Bea had done,' the narrator writes, 'and what I needed to do, too.' He continues:

> It was as clear as anything I have ever thought, and I will never forget it. We needed to communicate with them. We needed to make them look after us. We needed to get them to acknowledge that we were human beings and not animals, not disposable, and

> then they might spare us. And then the revelation: this meant we
> needed to see them as human beings, and not animals, too, if we
> were going to survive. (248)

Gevisser is not entirely naïve about the fact that these men are violent
criminals with alcohol on their breath, and quite possibly resistant to
reasoning. The behaviour of one, 'the gangly pop-eyed man who had
smacked me', seemed 'high beyond reason', and 'so fraught was the
situation … that even the most careful, cooperative behaviour imagina-
ble might not have saved us' (248). But Gevisser persists in his Paton-
esque 'love rather than hate' approach; in so doing, he resists, both in
his behaviour on the night and also in his subsequent narrative, the
possibility of an 'atrocity exhibition' escalating into outright hatred,
leaving torn and broken bodies. This is a significant moment, and it
signals a divergence from mainstream true-crime narratives. Gevisser
is straining, both in the course of the actual event and in its mediation,
to reshape, and renarrate (or reorient), the incident, thereby eluding
an atrocity exhibition proper, or true crime pure and simple. In so
doing, however, we see Gevisser – as per Seltzer's analysis – adher-
ing to the criterion that true crime 'always tak[es] exception to itself,
always look[s] over its own shoulder, and by analogy, invit[es] viewers
to do the same' ('Murder/Media/Modernity' 13). One cannot help
wondering, however, whether the 'viewers' of this scene will come
to the same conclusions as the author in this instance. In view of the
constitutive role of narrative and media, Gevisser's conscious refusal
to surrender to the crime story, and his determination to 'humanise'
the attackers, marks a significant moment in postapartheid writing.
And yet the more meaningful act may be the actual reflexive parrying.
Moreover, despite the author's admirable attempts to steer away the
criminal transgression at the centre of his book, certain readers may
not be persuaded. Whether materialists or hardened sceptics, such
reader-observers may point to alternative understandings of the facts,
having considered the same raw data. In addition, many of the elements of the true-crime narrative are stolidly present in Gevisser's
stylish narrative: the 'shock of contact' that encodes a 'breakdown
in the distinction between the individual and the mass, and between
private and public registers' (Seltzer, *True Crime* 3); the 'excitations
in the opening of private and bodily and psychic interiors: the exhibition and witnessing … of wounded bodies and wounded minds in

public' (3). What is more, Gevisser's account chimes uncannily with Warner's sense of a 'mass public' being realised in 'the body it witnesses', within a larger 'disaster discourse' ('The Mass Public' 250). It is hard not to see *Lost and Found*, in its final instantiation, as a work in which it is possible for 'anonymous and dispersed publics [to] seek representations of mass subjectivity in spectacles of disaster, atrocity, and violence – in images, precisely, of suffering bodies' (Green 250). How else is one to read the events that Gevisser narrates other than to identify with the atrocity exhibition via deferred witnessing and referred pain? Warner, as noted above, writes that the 'transitive pleasure' of witnessing/injuring makes available 'our translation into the disembodied publicity of the mass subject' ('The Mass Public' 250), and *Lost and Found* invites precisely such a process, where a pathological public sphere is realised by reader-witnesses who *see* in the hurt bodies here represented a mass subjectivity to which they fearfully relate. This is, of course, one way of reading the book, and Gevisser himself provides an alternative way of taking the measure of the robbery (i.e. the 'humanising' argument). However, the fact that a counter-argument is deemed necessary testifies to the force with which the 'true crime' elements have infiltrated the story.

The narrated crime encounter in *Lost and Found* reveals, in addition, a significant amount of trauma: Bea is sexually violated and all three victims are bound, gagged and physically assaulted, all of which results in wounds to the psyche. Whether or not Gevisser and Bea's 'friendly' approach does indeed contribute to the fact that the robbers eventually leave the apartment without *further* hurting or injuring the three victims is of course open to debate. One could argue both ways. The more pertinent point, though, is the extent to which Gevisser is *invested* in the recuperation of his book from its seemingly temporary suspension, owing to an account in which an actual crime derails the plot.

At this point, it is useful to recall that in *Midlands*, Steinberg arrives at a similar conjuncture in his narration, with violence confronting elevated conceptions of the moral good (see Chapter 3). This, in short, is what the author calls 'endgame'. In one such signal instance, interlocutor Elias Sithole declares, in conversation with Steinberg, that when a white man 'marches onto your land and tells you he is going to interview your future son-in-law and decide whether he can live in your house, you take matters into your own hands, because nobody else is going to' (245–246). In response, Steinberg asks: 'You kill his son?' Sithole replies: 'Yes. It has come to that' (246).

Gevisser, by contrast, quite forcefully redirects his narrative, in the closing section of the book, via his narrative conceit of stitching a 'seam' of regenerative heterogeneity. Wandering through Hillbrow on one of his last peregrinations before returning to Paris, where he lives with his partner, Gevisser gazes up at Temple Israel, and finds himself reflecting upon what it represents. This old Hillbrow institution is today a scene of cultural syncretism, accommodating the union of a middle-aged black woman and a much older white man, the woman singing the Kol Nidrei 'like a regular, drawing out those mad Aramaic diphthongs with the intensely performed abjection the prayer requires' (331–332). Directing the reader, '[t]hink about what makes you feel at home', Gevisser continues:

> ...at home among strangers, leaning against the rails of the landing outside Hopey's flat [in Alexandra township, Johannesburg], or sitting among congregants in a reclaimed city *shul*, or walking on a city street or driving along it, looking left, looking right, as you move forward. For it is the Dispatcher's route that threads it all together, sending you out and bringing you home, sending you out and bringing you home, sending you out and bringing you home, stitching you together tighter and tighter until the stitches lose their individual definition and become a seam, a road, a river, the Sandspruit itself, holding page 75 and 77 together across its banks rather than keeping them apart...creating one life of the past and present, the rough and the smooth, black and white, Alexandra and Sandton, Bachelors and Maidens, your bound terror at the end of a gun in Killarney and your unbound release on the landing outside Hopey's flat...Welcome home. (332)

Gevisser's allusion to a seam stitching together heterogeneity recalls my own theory of the seam in a 2001 essay on South Africa in relation to a 'global imaginary' ('South Africa in the Global Imaginary'). In that essay, however, the emphasis falls on the simultaneous joining *and* pulling apart, a 'crisis of inscription' marked by the seam in South African writing. Gevisser reads the seam as a triumphant coming together, a homecoming that resolves the tension of 'bound terror at the end of a gun', and 'unbound release' in the event of a regenerative adult encounter with a childhood ally and friend – in this instance Hopey, the daughter of the servant who had worked for the Gevisser family. And yet, even in this finely wrought finale, an especially delicate act of narrative stitching, the return of the Killarney moment of 'bound terror' acts as the ultimate delimitation, marking 'home' and 'welcome' with an unbreakable cross-stitch, an ineradicable memory of pathology.

Nothing Left to Steal

Gevisser's *Lost and Found* may be read as a quest to determine the optimum manner of existence for the postapartheid citizen. This quest, namely, to find a revised locus of virtue – both personal and political – amid the evanescent blur of rapid social transformation, is more problematic than may appear at first glance. As in the case of Thobela Mpayipheli in Deon Meyer's *Heart of the Hunter* (see Chapter 2), issues relating to civic virtue remain contested. This explains to some extent Gevisser's reluctance to condemn his Killarney attackers outright. Instead, he hedges the matter by implicitly invoking the deprivation experienced by the perpetrators, their lack of access to socio-economic rights such as the right of access to social security.[29]

In stark contrast to Gevisser's open-ended approach to the matter of positively delimiting civic virtue one way or another is the booming voice of Mzilikazi wa Afrika in his 2014 nonfiction memoir *Nothing Left to Steal: Jailed for Telling the Truth*. Wa Afrika's book is a veritable loudhailing of his labours since the 1990s as an investigative reporter for various media outlets, the most prominent of which is the *Sunday Times*, a mass-circulation newspaper with an extensive digital footprint. Wa Afrika's narrative voice reveals little self-doubt or ambivalence about what it means to be a 'virtuous' postapartheid citizen. Indeed, his voice radiates a strong sense of political virtue, revealing scant patience for any notion that problematises the idea of a 'good' South African citizen. Wa Afrika would in all likelihood agree with Ivor Chipkin's argument in *Do South Africans Exist?* (2007) that a postapartheid South African national identity based on cultural, ethnic or territorial affiliations will not suffice.[30] The postapartheid democratic sphere, for Wa Afrika as much as for Chipkin, must be reimagined in such a way that citizenship is grounded in constitutional principles as well as practice, disregarding all forms of kinship, whether ethnic, racial or political (see Chipkin 24–25 ff; Ndlovu-Gatsheni).

However, what Wa Afrika encounters during the course of his investigative journalism is a very different culture: one of systemic malfeasance and misconduct involving businesspeople and elected officials, often based on political connections with the ruling elite, who by many accounts were mired in the corrupt practices of the previous regime. Wa Afrika's stance is relatively simple: for him, these practices are corrupt, unconstitutional and illegal. He finds evidence of lying, stealing and even killing across countless layers of business and government, and he exposes a criminal underworld that lays waste the 'democratic miracle' of postapartheid South Africa, mortally infecting its society in the process. With the help of several members of an investigative unit (Jessica Bezuidenhout, Stephan Hofstatter, Jocelyn Maker and Rob Rose) and the considerable resources of the *Sunday Times* newspaper, Wa Afrika uncovers and presents evidence of extensive criminality. The process of discovery is recounted in a mode of forensic detection, rendering a detailed record of crooked dealings in both business and government. Conducted, for the most part, on behalf of the *Sunday Times* and *Sunday World*, Wa Afrika's exposés target a broad readership. As systemic venality is revealed, Wa Afrika himself has guns shoved in his face, is repeatedly beaten up, wrongfully jailed, and targeted in assassination attempts; this is the thanks he receives for reporting on the misdeeds of powerful people and organisations. Ultimately, Wa Afrika's personal tale may be said to amount to true crime, in both its public and political instantiation. The abuses of due process that he recounts, and for which he provides detailed factual evidence, amount to a dossier in which truth – and the public good – are consistently shown to be under attack.

All the while, Wa Afrika positions himself as a heroic narrator, a locus of the good and the true. Without irony or self-deprecation, he invokes liberation icons such as Pixley ka Isaka Seme, Malcolm X, Stephen Bantu Biko and Nelson Mandela. For all this, Wa Afrika's work is novel – and significant – in several senses. For one thing, it undermines the perception that postapartheid discontent is largely located among displaced and/or despairing whites, on the one hand, and politically disaffected middle- to upper-class blacks on the other. Wa Afrika himself emerged from the rural poverty of Mpumalanga, with his mother's – admittedly tenuous – royal connections counting for little in material terms. His early life, from childhood to young adulthood, as narrated in the first third of *Nothing Left to Steal*, shows elements of self-development against the odds, combining the story of the activist with that of the emerging artist, in the tradition of literary icons such as Dennis Brutus, Alex La Guma, Es'kia Mphahlele and Mongane Wally Serote. Like Wa Afrika, all these writer-heroes outfaced structural and social limitations to become truth-bearers; their chronicles, especially but not only in autobiographical writing, bore witness to the *true* or *actual* state of affairs in South Africa, urgently calling upon readers, whether at home or abroad, to take cognisance of and to act against unconscionable practices that were killing human rights, not to mention human beings. This kind of writing – the soul and substance of struggle literature – brought about what Louise Bethlehem has called a 'resolute empirical dominant' in anti-apartheid writing ('A Primary Need' 378); that is to say, it deployed the communicative force of literature to bring actual conditions into view, since they constituted a lived reality that urgently needed to be addressed.[31] People were suffering and dying. Unlawful imprisonment and torture were rife,[32] an inbuilt part of the state's militarised, oppressive culture of governance across the length and breadth of the land. Such committed writing was vested with legitimacy by virtue of its global uptake among critics and social justice advocates. This was not, however, the case with much post-1994 literature, which changed conditions have compelled to seek more diverse, perhaps less urgent topics and issues for its daily work.[33]

Wa Afrika is one of a new generation of writers to emerge after 1994 who connects a sense of urgent witnessing – i.e. of public wrongs and unjust injury to individual citizens – with a history of anti-apartheid activism.[34] The deeds Wa Afrika bears witness to as a reporter include kidnapping, killing, large-scale financial fraud, extortion, human trafficking and abuse of political office; the sheer scale of such crimes merits a glance at the life he describes, validating as it does his act of witnessing.

Wa Afrika[35] was born in 1971 in Sibambayani, 'a village in the heart of Bushbuckridge', Mpumalanga, to parents without any formal education, who were divorced when he was four years old. His village had neither running water nor electricity (18). He was named Vusimuzi (Vusi), meaning 'the one who will raise the family from the ashes' (21). His mother tongue was Xitsonga, although he learnt to speak SiSwati at a young age, too (27). It is noteworthy that Wa Afrika traces, in his book, his family line on both the maternal and paternal sides, thereby authenticating an African ancestry. So, in addition to the details of maternal kinship to a royal African line (the Nguni

tribal prince Mpisane Nxumalo), the author narrates that his paternal lineage stems from the village of Zucula in the Gaza province of
Mozambique, with an ancestral relation to former Mozambican president Samora Machel (22).

Having meticulously set out his (orally transmitted) lineage, Wa
Afrika describes how he graduated from an innocent childhood to
political awakening during high school. As a boy in Bushbuckridge,
an area in which 'poverty was palpable and wretched' (26), he was an
ardent singer and musical 'noisemaker' (25–26). He also played soccer, and learnt karate. After enrolling at Qokiso High School in 1985,
within whose rudimentary structures he endured 'barbaric' initiation
practices (29), he met a friend called Nathaniel 'Nat' Makanete, a
13-year-old boy from Diepkloof, Soweto. Their friendship was initially based on a shared love for football, but the real bond came
when Nat explained to young Vusi that he had abandoned Soweto for
Bushbuckridge to flee 'politics' (31). In response to Vusi's question,
'Who is politics and why are you so afraid of him' (32), Nat patiently
'explained to me the history of our country' (32). This explication
proceeds via micro-stories about figures such as Hector Pieterson,
Winnie Mandela, Walter Sisulu, Steve Biko and Robert Sobukwe; the
story of organised resistance against racial oppression; and an explanation of the very term 'apartheid' itself, including the events signified
by the date 16 June 1976. And so, Wa Afrika 'loses his virginity in
politics', realising that although he had always been top of his class, up
until that moment he had actually known 'nothing of substance' (32).

Outlining the significance of Nelson Mandela's life story, Nat
puts it to the young Vusi that Mandela was jailed because he fought
for black people's freedom, and that he, Vusi, was 'a slave without
freedom: freedom of association, freedom of speech, freedom of the
right to vote' (32). Vusi learns about the African National Congress
(ANC), the Pan Africanist Congress (PAC), and the Azanian People's
Organisation (Azapo), all of which were 'banned by the apartheid
regime' (33). He is educated, too, about struggle figures such as
Teboho 'Tsietsi' MacDonald Mashinini, Abram Onkgopotse Tiro
and Solomon Kalushi Mahlangu, and about Steve Biko's death at the
hands of the South African Police (33). Wa Afrika declares:

> The information Nathaniel gave me was mind-blowing. I was
> scared and confused. It made me realize that for the past 13 years

of my existence, I had been blind. But like the blind man from Jericho, healed by Jesus Christ, my sight would be restored by this young man from Soweto. (33)

Nat continues to feed Vusi with political education, giving him copies of speeches of Abram Tiro and Nelson Mandela to study. Vusi repeatedly reads a banned copy of Mandela's address from the dock at the Rivonia Trial before burning it, as per Nat's instructions. Mandela's words etch themselves into the young boy's mind, with Wa Afrika later saying 'these words echoed in my head over and over again':

> 'I have fought against white domination and I have fought against black domination. I have cherished the ideal of a democratic and free society in which all persons live together in harmony and with equal opportunities. It is an ideal which I hope to live for and to achieve. But if needs be, it is an ideal for which I am prepared to die.' (34)

His younger self feels inspired, to the extent that Vusi writes his first poem, 'The Tears of a Blind Man', a lyrical rendering of a blind man's longing for humane treatment, but the only response is violent rebuttal at the hands of a brutal regime whose Calvinist God reigned supreme. Vusi begins writing songs and poems, working on a manuscript titled *Afrika My Bequest, Afrika My Patrimony* (35).

And so the activist-writer is born. The elements of his *Bildung*, as summarised above, are similar to those of many young activist-writers who came to political consciousness in the turbulent 1980s, and who gave expression to their politics through consciousness-raising, writing and speaking in popular community modes and forms. Writer-activists such as Andries Walter Oliphant and Chris van Wyk joined independent publishing companies such as Ravan Press, and much protest material was published in anti-apartheid literary publications such as *Donga* and *Staffrider*. The young Wa Afrika was a generation or so behind this struggle cohort (which included the likes of venerable poet Don Mattera), but the Bushbuckridge firebrand's story follows a similar trajectory, in particular the nexus of penmanship and political activism that came to be known as 'struggle writing'. Indeed, the kind of literary activism that Wa Afrika tapped into as a teenager in the 1980s was a powerful, socially meaningful domain, where 'conscientising' cultural forms issued forth in what radicals often thought of as 'praxis'. One only has to listen to recordings of Mattera reading his poems in community venues, or watch a video of performances of *Woza Albert!* in townships across the country, or listen to Mzwakhe Mbuli's oral tours de force to understand the power and suasion of activist writing and performance, and its infectious energy, not to mention its power of legitimation – lending a sense of righteous cause to revolutionary action.

The civic arena into which Vusi eventually poured his literary, cultural and political consciousness was journalism, thereby following a tradition stretching back to the previous century, starting with publications such as Allan Kirkland Soga and Walter Rubusana's *Izwi Labantu* (*Voice of the People*) in the 1890s. As a high school boy, Wa Afrika, together with his friend Nathaniel, made up a makeshift newspaper for circulation among fellow pupils. This 'paper' was a blank, lined, A4, 92-page 'exercise book' into which they pasted clippings from the (then) *Weekly Mail, New Nation, City Press* and *Sowetan* newspapers (37). They called it 'The Voice', and it caused a stir in their high school community, eventually landing them in the headmaster's office. This was after they had bought paint and written, in large letters, on the school wall: '*Siyayinyova!* Viva ANC!' Fortunately escaping any serious consequences (the ANC was still banned at the time, with any form of promotion held to be seditious), Vusi enrolled at Mzwangedwa High School – the first institution of learning he attended that had electricity, bathrooms and a laboratory (41). His English teacher, one Ronny Mkhari, encouraged his activism, and Vusi later came into contact with Stanley Mokoena, co-leader of the school's Student Representative Council (SRC). Mokoena had links with underground ANC structures. Soon enough, he took Vusi along with him to United Democratic Front (UDF) rallies, where the budding young poet recited in public. Mokoena later introduced him to Umkhonto we Sizwe operative 'BA', whom they met at a rendezvous outside Acornhoek. Soon afterwards, Vusi began helping BA in his underground operations, allowing BA to fill his schoolbag with weapons; these would later be picked up at Vusi's house by appointed agents, men who signalled their credentials by leaving behind a copy of the *New Nation* newspaper. One of the people facilitating the supply of these guns, which were sent in from Mozambique, was Mathews

Phosa, an ANC member living in Mozambique with the sanction of President Machel.

And so it was that Wa Afrika's life as an ANC comrade commenced. Upon his return from a UDF rally in Venda, where he had recited one of his struggle poems, he discovered that the police had arrested members of his underground cell in Bushbuckridge. In response, he rounded up other members of the cell, and they hid in nearby 'caves and bushes' (51). Then, on 9 October 1989, as he was returning home from the cave to collect food and clean clothes, he was arrested by a policeman hiding in the outside toilet of his house.

At this point, the next phase of his education began: the youthful Vusi was handcuffed and beaten up: 'When the other police officers arrived, I became a punching bag. I was assaulted with the butt of a gun, stomped with police boots and beaten' (51). The police ransacked the boy's house and confiscated his books and newspaper collections, including a copy of Malcolm X's *By Any Means Necessary*. Failing to find any weapons – which were in fact hidden inside a coal stove in the kitchen – the police took him off to the Mhala police station in Thulamahashe, where he was interrogated and tortured to the point of losing consciousness (51–53). And then, he writes, Mathews Phosa stepped in, hiring a lawyer to secure bail for Wa Afrika and others who were being held in custody; the provision of bail money enabled Wa Afrika to write his matric exams just a few weeks later. Before the youth left the overcrowded cell, however, he wrote on the wall: 'Mzilikazi: the warrior was here. Aluta Continua!' Not long afterwards, he felt inspired by a story told to him by a student at the University of the North, relating to the movie version of Alex Haley's book *Roots*. After securing a video copy, he watched it over and over again. Emboldened by the refusal of the slave Kunta Kinte to accept his slave name 'Toby', keeping instead his African name and thereby remaining true to his roots, Wa Afrika likewise decides to drop his English name 'Leonard', which he now regards as 'a slave name'. He writes: 'After weeks of soul-searching and toying around with different names and researching in the library, I announced to my friends and shocked classmates in the spring of 1989 that my new name would be "Mzilikazi wa Afrika", which simply means "Mzilikazi from Afrika". Mzilikazi means "a little path", and this would be the road of my journey in life' (57–58). Wa Afrika adds that he was inspired by the historical figure of King Mzilikazi, 'a fearless warrior and one of King Shaka's advisers'. Similarly, he now regarded himself as a 'rebel against the apartheid regime' (58). An important moment arrived when he received an invitation to attend the annual general meeting of the Congress of South African Writers (Cosaw) in Johannesburg. The letter was addressed to him as 'Mzilikazi wa Afrika'. His friend, Nat, had sent Cosaw the manuscript of *Afrika My Bequest, Afrika My Patrimony*. Wa Afrika duly travelled to Johannesburg and was booked into the Moulin Rouge Hotel in Hillbrow, a major event in his young life. To add to his excitement, a friend brought along copies of Mzwakhe Mbuli's first two recorded albums, *Change is Pain* and *Unbroken Spirit*; having listened to these, Wa Afrika felt 'blown away' and 'hooked on his poetry'. As a consequence, he felt compelled to change his way of writing. At the Cosaw AGM, he rubbed shoulders with 'some of the country's best writers and poets', despite being 'the youngest kid at the conference with no writing credit to my name' (59).

Such are the resonant details of Wa Afrika's *Bildung*. An adaptation of the rags-to-riches motif (with the 'riches' being the symbolic reward of political awakening), it also traces a lineage within the traditions of the ANC and the South African liberation struggle. And so, when Wa Afrika turns to professional journalism, first as a reporter for the *Witbank News*, later as a founder-member of *Mpumalanga News* and a reporter for the Africa Eye News Service (AENS) in Mpumalanga, and still later as a key member of the crack investigative journalism team at the Johannesburg *Sunday Times*, he does so with impeccable political and personal credentials. This is a career that culminates, moreover, in a slew of awards for his work as a reporter, including the Sunday Times Journalist of the Year Award (2003), the Standard Bank Sikuvile Journalist of the Year Award (2012 and 2014), the Taco Kuiper Award for investigative journalism (2011 and 2012) and the Vodacom Journalist of the Year Award (2011 and 2013), among other prizes, scholarships and prestigious nominations.

Wa Afrika's determination to hold to the principles of honourable behaviour informs his writing. For him, this is not an over-complicated matter: he sticks to his guns, remaining resolutely true to the revolutionary values he internalised by following the example of his oft-quoted heroes, such as Che Guevara and Mandela. This simple, resolute stance also leads to his sense of mission in exposing any and all examples of public behaviour that disgrace such values, regardless of their origin. And so, as noted earlier, one sees in his work a continuation, perhaps even a reinvention, of struggle writing; alternatively, one might describe this as a resurgence of politically invested writing that has as its aim the exposure of a pathological and corrupt public sphere.

What exactly is it, then, in the accumulated investigative journalism dispatches, the stories-behind-the-stories in *Nothing Left to Steal*, that is brought out into the open? The public larcenies themselves are already common knowledge: scandals involving the business world and bent politicians. A prime example is former ANC parliamentarian Tony Yengeni and his proven self-enrichment arising from the R43 billion arms deal between the South African government and various international dealers. In this event, an extensive swathe of high-level bribery is widely believed to have corrupted senior ranks of South African governance.[36] The accounts of how legions of postapartheid racketeers were exposed make up the bulk of Wa Afrika's book, including stories about slavery rings, corrupt practices in the civil service and an extensive culture of political killing (especially but not exclusively in Mpumalanga – such killings are ongoing in KwaZulu-Natal, too[37]). Taken together, this amounts to a tale of evil which, for all its apparent banality, is deeply corrosive.

So-called scandal fatigue, much like compassion fatigue,[38] might well render such revelations belated and somewhat boring, especially if merely catalogued as a series of misdemeanours. Perceived public exhaustion in relation to the reportage of political scandals (Munusamy, 'A New South Africa Syndrome'[39]) is itself a remarkable fact about postapartheid South Africa, especially when viewed from the perspective of 1994, with its rainbow-hued optimism. Exposés no longer carry the weight of the Watergate era of print journalism, or of Infogate (Muldergate) in South African newspapers in the 1970s. In the affectively volatile (rather than strictly factual) domain of new media, novel forms of narrative representation, or reanimation, are a prerequisite if the general reader is to experience reported crimes as forms of behaviour whose failure of civil virtue constitutes personal threat. This form of narrative presentation inevitably draws from elements of 'true crime', as I will suggest below.

The book's opening gambit, in which Wa Afrika recounts the story of two occasions on which he was arrested, once by the apartheid police (the SAP) and then, roughly 20 years later, by the postapartheid South African Police Service (SAPS), provides a consciously nonpartisan frame for the book as a whole. However, the more salient point, from a narratological point of view, is the taut, thriller-like style of presentation, emphasising – in an unconventional manner – the agency of the reporter-protagonist and the drama of his experiences:

> I was arrested on 9 October 1989, just weeks before I was to sit my matric examination, after an *impimpi* (police informer) told the police I had a couple of AK-47s stashed somewhere in my house. I was not a gunrunner but a political activist whose house was often used as a 'base' – a secret place where underground activities were taking place – to move weapons.
>
> After I was arrested, a police officer put a 9mm pistol into my mouth and threatened to blow my brains out.
>
> I was then assaulted. My uncle's house where I was staying alone at the time was raided and ransacked and everything turned upside down. But no guns were found, not even a single bullet.
>
> Little did they know the guns were hidden inside a coal stove in the corner of the house; the cooking pots on top were just a disguise. The stove had not been used for months. Had the guns been found, I would have faced potential treason charges and possible life imprisonment.
>
> I had a duty as one of the oppressed citizens of this country to make a contribution, no matter how small or big, to our struggle. Young as I was, my conscience would not allow me to fold my arms and wait for miracles to happen and for freedom to fall from the sky.
>
> Che Guevara said it loud and clear: 'The revolution is not an apple that falls when it is ripe. You have to make it fall.' (viii)

This account reveals a far more expansive, affective storytelling style than a conventional newspaper report permits. The focalisation, which places emphasis on Wa Afrika's personal sacrifice for the sake of the general public good, arouses sympathy for him – as befits a worthy or virtuous protagonist, a 'good guy', in crime-thriller terms. This affective slant is helped along as the hero faces bad-cop behaviour from policemen who are shown to be the dumb dupes of a morally dubious ruling clique. Without sacrificing the factually verifiable elements of the incident, the writer clearly borrows from the conventions of fiction – crime fiction in particular – as true-crime writing frequently does.

In the following scene, a similar narrative positioning is employed – not without irony: though the former regime has been relegated to the dustbin of history, along with its oppressive security apparatus, police officers of the new, democratic police service behave in a manner that is frighteningly familiar:

> My second arrest on 4 August 2010 made international headlines. I was arrested in front of television cameras and members of the South African National Editors' Forum (SANEF) on trumped-up charges. [This arrest occurred after Police Commissioner Bheki Cele was exposed by Wa Afrika and his colleague Stephan Hofstatter for involvement in fraudulent practices.]
>
> This illegal arrest was designed to intimidate me, harass me and humiliate me. Worst of all it was an attempt to get me fired from the job that was integral to everything that I am.
>
> I was arrested without a warrant and my house raided and ransacked without a search warrant. I was literally kidnapped, bundled into an unmarked police vehicle surrounded by heavily armed guards and then smuggled to Mpumalanga, more than 300km away from Johannesburg, in another unmarked police vehicle, without the knowledge of my lawyer, my family or my bosses.
>
> My release was only secured with a late-night High Court application, more than 30 hours later, when a judge ordered my immediate release. (ix)

Several points about this passage are noteworthy. The writing relies on stark facts, verifiable in themselves, and yet it offers far more than the mere facts of the matter. The arrests are illegal, as the High Court ruling suggests, but motives are attributed, putting the spotlight not only on the victim's vulnerability, but also on his valour in the face of brute force. The focalisation once again points to thriller models of narration. Wa Afrika's personal vulnerability is dramatised in the defencelessness of his actual body, and – typically of true-crime narratives – the reader is invited to identify with such vulnerability. In this way, the private-public divide is breached, and Warner's mass

subjectivity, referred to above, is enabled, figured as it is via identification with the wounded or wound-vulnerable body in a notably
pathological public sphere. Here, there is little public-sphere debate
(in the Habermasian sense), no considered reflection, at least in Wa
Afrika's dealings with authority in this story as a representative citizen. Elected representatives authorise illegal arrests and public intimidation with a disregard that the average reader might experience with
shock and disillusionment, especially given Wa Afrika's animation of
the story in a manner that exceeds mere reportage.

Remarkably, this telling reveals little of the doubt, the 'reflective
gap', a characteristic of the information-saturated dromosphere. It
carries the weight of certitude, as well as the moral authority of what
might be termed a reconfigured freedom fighter, now fighting a widespread perversion of truth and justice. And so emerges the heroism
of 'Mzilikazi', a fearless warrior, an emblem of moral rectitude that
seems long lost. Here and elsewhere in his memoir, the author projects the persona of a virtuous citizen who rejects any form of prevarication: Mzilikazi Wa Afrika is the face of a re-energised sense of
morality within the political sphere.

A recurrent event in Wa Afrika's narration is the use of law
enforcement to protect the wrongdoers against exposure, using the
force of the police to shut the messenger up – and in Wa Afrika's
case, to shut him away. Here, then, is a drama in which criminality is legitimated, thereby constituting a bigger saga, in storytelling
terms, in which truth is slain by a fully legitimate state, a democrat-
ically elected government that came to power with more than sixty
per cent of its citizens' votes. Wa Afrika's narrative implicitly asks
whether the ruling party can in fact withstand such a cold-blooded
wounding of legitimacy in what Mineral Resources Minister Susan
Shabangu in 2013 referred to as 'the national democratic revolution
that we scored as a result of the democratic breakthrough of 1994'.[40]
This is Wa Afrika's underlying theme. In his narrative, the location
of the struggle has shifted decisively from unjust minority rule to
unjust majority rule, as police operate in cahoots with a 'felonious
state'.[41]

Wa Afrika's story is not only telling, but true (compellingly so, it
seems). It is in such stories – solidly fixated on 'true crime' – where
the drama of postapartheid South African letters is often most vividly
located.

Postscript: Marikana

If there is one event in postapartheid history that concentrates all the elements of a pathological public sphere, and suggests that the country is as much in the grip of a wound culture as it is a (mal)functioning democracy, then it is the event known as the Marikana massacre. The salient details of this event – as extensively reported in the media at the time, and subsequently narrated in films and books[42] – are as follows: 34 people, most of them rock drillers at Lonmin platinum mines near Rustenburg in the North West province, were shot dead by members of the South African Police Service (SAPS) on 16 August 2012. The miners had been on strike for better wages, and in the week preceding the massacre, ten people had been killed in strike-related 'unrest' (a frequent euphemism for uprising), including two policemen and two Lonmin security guards. The Farlam Commission of Inquiry was set up by government to investigate the incident and report on its causes. The Commission found that the SAPS used a key witness, Mr X (real name withheld), to testify falsely in its favour; this was part of an apparent cover-up, since Mr X's evidence was shown, during cross-examination by Advocate Dali Mpofu and others, to contain what appear to be irreconcilable contradictions and lies.[43] Noted commentators, including Pulitzer Prize-winning photojournalist Greg Marinovich, writer/filmmaker Aryan Kaganof, sociologist Sakhela Buhlungu, and others (see below), detect in this event the conniving of capitalism and a neoliberal ruling elite to maintain the status quo, and in effect joining forces to counter the demands of mineworkers earning what appear to be pitifully low wages.[44] For many commentators, including family members of the slain miners, Marikana recalls the Sharpeville massacre of 1960, in which 69 people were gunned down by the South African Police (SAP), as well as the killings associated with the Soweto uprisings in June 1976, and the Bisho massacre in 1992.[45]

Comprehensively 'written up' in new-media forms also, Marikana signifies the salience of 'true' writing about 'crime' in the South African public sphere. (Marinovich refers to the killings as 'murders', as we shall see below.) Further, the events of Marikana suggest that South Africa's public sphere is characterised by pathology, and that the intersubjectivity[46] it elicits is strongly located in wound-culture media representations. In such depictions, ruptured and broken bodies stand in for a 'shocked' and generally dismayed mass public. In its media representations, Marikana blurs the line between the private and the public, bringing otherwise nonpublic and unknowable agony – a phenomenon that threatens the body politic as much as it hurts private bodies – into *affective* general view. Additionally, Marikana underscores the 'fiction' of transition, in the sense that the 'transition to democracy' itself, as in the 'silent revolution' or the 'Mandela miracle', is exposed as a myth. The 'transition' has not achieved any meaningful metamorphosis in living and working conditions for the poorest of the poor, despite gains in housing and social grants. Indeed, Marikana and its various retellings gesture towards the social importance of public forms of truth-telling over and above the broad, encompassing genre of fiction. The dramatic contests of truth and falsity vis-à-vis perceived life-and-death questions, relayed via a hypermediated wound culture, have in an important sense begun to resituate the culture of writing in the postapartheid context.

Following this line of thought, the dominance of nonfictional forms in postapartheid South Africa may be ascribed, in part at least, to the life-and-death nature of questions circulated and written about in digital relays, but also to the precarious status of 'truth' and, with it, the devaluation of the currency of truth-telling as a public good. It is no exaggeration to say that this perceived decline is the biggest 'story' out there. The hope and promise of the Mandela years and its aftermath could be said to be the grand narrative of the immediate postapartheid era, conditioned as it was by the enormous, if unsustainable, idealism that Mandela's presidency evoked. This *grand récit* underlies what must be counted as the two leading nonfiction epics of post-1994 writing: Nelson Mandela's *Long Walk to Freedom* (1995) and Mark Gevisser's *Thabo Mbeki: The Dream Deferred* (2007).[47] While Mandela's world bestseller sets a tone of optimism regarding the struggle for freedom, Gevisser's very title speaks to the unhappy turn of events in this saga of eventual victory against oppressive forces. As Gevisser writes in the introduction to his magisterial work,

> [f]or Mbeki and those around him, the possibility of a Zuma presidency was a scenario far worse than a dream deferred. It would be, in effect, a dream shattered, irrevocably, as South Africa turned into yet another post-colonial kleptocracy; another 'footprint of despair' in the path of destruction away from the

promises of uhuru. That some people in the ANC family felt this way about other people in the ANC family was a symptom, in and of itself, of the dream deferred. (xli)

By the time this book was being finalised (2016), the South African public knew all too well what Gevisser himself did not at the time he wrote his introduction (circa 2006/7). It is common knowledge, now, that the 'scenario far worse than a dream deferred', namely a double-term Zuma presidency, with runaway kleptocracy and a governing culture of clientelism and patrimonialism, confirmed, indeed exceeded, the fears expressed in the above passage. If Marikana shows anything, it is that racial capitalism remains as devastatingly exploitative under the command of a Cyril Ramaphosa[48] as it ever was under apartheid. Equally 'shocking' (in the 'true-crime' sense) were the attempts of the SAPS to manipulate evidence before the Commission. The Commission's final report, released to the public in June 2015, found that a 'prima facie' case could be made against both the national police commissioner, General Riah Phiyega, and North West provincial commissioner, Lieutenant General Zukiswa Mbombo, for approving a series of lies that were put to the Commission in their defence.[49] In February 2016, it was reported that Independent Police Investigative Directorate (Ipid) investigators had registered cases of defeating the ends of justice against Phiyega and Mbombo.[50]

Ramaphosa – one of the 'black capitalists in the mining industry' – certainly has 'many questions to answer', according to sociologist Sakhela Buhlungu (Letsoalo and Evans), particularly in the light of his well-documented email exchange with Police Minister Nathi Mthethwa and Minerals Minister Susan Shabangu. Referring to the strike, Ramaphosa infamously requested that 'concomitant action' be taken against 'criminals' (Marinovich and Nicolson). Buhlungu, a former trade unionist and activist, told a National Union of Mineworkers of South Africa (Numsa) special congress that 'the hand of Cyril was there in the mineworkers' deaths' (Letsoalo and Evans n.p.). Though he may claim that his words were 'taken out of context, the fact of the matter is that he was involved in the killing of the Marikana mineworkers', Buhlungu asserted (Letsoalo and Evans n.p.).[51]

And so, the narrative of the country's public sphere is one in which the alleged criminal liability of elected representatives – and the coercive forces at their disposal – becomes a matter of profound concern in the overarching narrative, namely the desecration of the Mandela myth. It is within this context that one might view the *Mail & Guardian* project of Niren Tolsi and Paul Botes, on the one hand, and an extraordinary series of photojournalistic dispatches by Greg Marinovich for the *Daily Maverick*, on the other. As online, multimodal and long-form nonfiction projects, they are characterised by a persistent refusal to abandon the story, to let go and move on to the next moment in the news cycle, the next version of 'now time' in a dromosphere that compresses time and space within a never-endingly anguished present. These journalists have approached the story of Marikana from various angles, both analytical and affective, covering the events of the massacre and its unfolding, in political and legal terms. A year after the massacre, Tolsi and Botes interviewed the families of the deceased, most of them in the rural Eastern Cape: they documented their living conditions, their sense of betrayal by the Zuma administration, and their general sense of loss and abandonment. Marinovich's penetrating stories amount to a compilation in which the truth is pursued over a period of many months. The urgency of the subject matter is visually rendered, too, in Marinovich's own series of accompanying photographs, graphic images that document the unvarnished evidence of the massacre. The underlying mode of these long-form dispatches is sharp forensic analysis in evidential mode, thereby recalling the work of Dlamini, Altbeker, Gevisser and Steinberg.

Marinovich is a something of a hybrid: as a photographer-filmmaker-author-journalist,[52] his credentials command respect, particularly as one of the four members of the 'Bang Bang Club', news photographers who braved the insurrectionary streets during the apartheid period, up until 1994. Nearly 20 years later, he found himself documenting the stories of the Marikana strikers, as well as the police torture that survivors allegedly endured in the wake of the massacre (Marinovich, 'Police Torturing'). In addition, Marinovich painstakingly analyses the data arising from the Farlam Commission. In one dispatch, which I consider below, Marinovich combines photographs and text to challenge the police version of the killings, as presented at the Farlam Commission, in a manner that speaks to the implausibility of the state's version of events.

In his key piece, 'The Murder Fields of Marikana. The Cold Murder Fields of Marikana', Marinovich points out that 'of the

34 miners killed at Marikana, no more than a dozen of the dead were captured in news footage shot at the scene' (n.p.). He goes on to add: 'The majority of those who died, according to surviving strikers and researchers, were killed beyond the view of cameras at a nondescript collection of boulders some 300 metres behind Wonderkop' (n.p.). It is noteworthy that the forensically exact narrative assumes some of the contours of true-crime narration:

> On one of these rocks, encompassed closely on all sides by solid granite boulders, is the letter 'N', the 14th letter of the alphabet. Here, N represents the 14th body of a striking miner to be found by a police forensics team in this isolated place. These letters are used by forensics to detail where the corpses lay.
>
> There is a thick spread of blood deep into the dry soil, showing that N was shot and killed on the spot. There is no trail of blood leading to where N died – the blood saturates one spot only, indicating no further movement. (It would have been outside of the scope of the human body to crawl here bleeding so profusely.)
>
> Approaching N from all possible angles, observing the local geography, it is clear that to shoot N, the shooter would have to be close. Very close, in fact, almost within touching distance. (After having spent days here at the bloody massacre site, it does not take too much imagination for me to believe that N might have begged for his life on that winter afternoon).

Despite its evidentiary precision, its attention to minute detail and its analysis of probability, backed up by Marinovich's own photographs of the scene (below), the literary-affective tenor of true crime irresistibly begins to bleed into the news report as the author speculates on the possibility of a man begging in vain for his life on a wintry day on what is clearly a desolate koppie in the veld.

This combination of, one the one hand, evidentiary discernment and, on the other, imaginative transport brings to mind what is widely regarded to be the ur-text of true crime: *In Cold Blood* by Truman Capote. Capote's book, which he himself described as a 'nonfiction novel', raises important questions about how nonfiction narratives draw energy not only from fictional techniques of storytelling, but also from fiction itself, that is, from imaginative invention, for their paradoxical effect of truth-telling in story form. Regarding the

The narrow spot between boulders where 'N' died

'literariness' of a nonfiction work such as *In Cold Blood*, Jerónimo Corregido contends:

> We perceive *In Cold Blood* as a literary text in spite of its non-fictionality, then, because of the artful form in which it is created, because of the unconventional uses of the language, because of its innovative inner structure; all in all, because of the *priom* or literary procedure that was used to create the story. What lies in the center of the narrative is its creativeness, its deviation from the conventional. As Jakobson said, a text becomes literature when the language presents 'an organized violence committed on ordinary speech'. The form in which a text is written determines its inclusion in the literary genre: it does not matter that the events narrated in *In Cold Blood* or in *Recuerdos de Provincia* actually happened or not; what matters is that those events are told in a way that redefines ordinary objects and ordinary behaviours, that deviates from everyday language in order to 'recover the sense of life, in order to feel objects, to make the stone stony' [Victor Shklovsky], in order to deautomatise the perception of reality. (n.p.)

In a social environment sapped by scandal fatigue, writing (and photography) play an important role in reinvigorating 'ordinary objects and ordinary behaviours'. This is especially true for the impassioned writer, and, however measured he may be, Marinovich is nothing if not impassioned in a long-form piece whose effect is sharpened by a series of startling photographs. In a notoriously poorly paid profession, Marinovich deals in the higher currency of truth, a particularly rare coinage in postapartheid South Africa. He employs unconventional and improvisational storytelling means, straining against the 'news' shell, the constraints of conventional journalism. Marinovich succeeds both in satisfying the evidentiary demands of writing in the forensic, social detection mode, and in making the 'story' as grippingly convincing as possible. His clear aim is to disclose the truth that lurks behind the postapartheid lie – in this case the whitewashed official version of the events of 12 August 2012 at Marikana. So he zooms in, literally and figuratively, on the Rustenburg rocks (the 'small koppie') where many miners were by many accounts hunted down and killed, recreating a sinister atmosphere of entrapment. Marinovich's marshalling of the available clues unavoidably conjures up the scenario of a secluded space in which the fleeing miners could be shot dead, at close range. In this telling, Marinovich's writing makes the 'stone stony' – to paraphrase Shklovsky on the importance of defamiliarisation or estrangement – and he does so by means of an intense and sustained focus on the boulders, and the doom that they portended for the miners who were killed in their shadow.

Further, Marinovich's reconstruction of what happened amid these outcrops of stone, mute witnesses to what he insists were premeditated slayings, could be said to have been driven by Corregido's[53] 'macropropositions' and 'micropropositions': a macroproposition 'represents the theme, or one of the themes, of a text…the global meaning of the discourse, at a semantic level of analysis' (n.p.); micropropositions, on the other hand, are 'the details and characteristics which entail the macrostructures', and they 'cannot be classified as non-fictional', some of them being 'deliberately fictional' (n.p.). In summary, the factual macroproposition of a typical Marinovich article introduces content imbued with a presumed truth, while the stylistic rendering of this larger truth, i.e. 'the global meaning of the discourse', borrows freely from fictional techniques. One such technique is the use of focalisation, the point of view or perspective through which the events of a narrative are presented, in this case the evidence as reported, and narrated, by eyewitnesses.

In the first instance, Marinovich starkly exposes to public view aspects which (he is at pains to remind us) were not shown in official, broadcast footage of the shootings. 'None of these events were witnessed by media or captured on camera. They were only reported on as component parts in the sum of the greater tragedy,' he writes. He then shifts – and sharpens – the perspective (further defamiliarising the 'known' events) by focalising this hitherto 'unknown' story via a witness:

> One of the striking miners caught up in the mayhem, let's call him 'Themba', though his name is known to the *Daily Maverick*, recalled what he saw once he escaped the killing fields around Wonderkop.
>
> 'Most people then called for us to get off the mountain, and as we were coming down, the shooting began. Most people who were shot near the kraal were trying to get into the settlement; the blood we saw is theirs. We ran in the other direction, as it was impossible now to make it through the bullets.
>
> 'We ran until we got to the meeting spot and watched the incidents at the koppie. Two helicopters landed; soldiers and police surrounded the area. We never saw anyone coming out of the koppie.' ('The Murder Fields of Marikana' n.p.)

This story is in stark contradiction to the official version that has 'muti-crazed' mobs threatening police who were compelled to defend themselves. Themba's simple and uncomplicated telling is rendered thus: 'Most people who were shot near the kraal were trying to get into the settlement; the blood we saw is theirs. We ran in the other direction, as it was impossible now to make it through the bullets.' The self-evident logic, the rationality of his narrated account, is enhanced by the preciseness of the punctuation, the semicolons and periods. Themba goes on to describe the pincer-like advance of the police: 'Two helicopters landed; soldiers and police surrounded the area. We never saw anyone coming out of the koppie.' Such stylised micropropositions are deployed in support of a macroproposition that is fully committed to uncovering the truth – an entirely non-negotiable truth:

> It is becoming clear to this reporter that heavily armed police hunted down and killed the miners in cold blood. A minority

were killed in the filmed event where police claim they acted in self-defence. The rest was murder on a massive scale. (n.p.)

The depersonalisation at this point of the narrative voice is noteworthy, as Marinovich refers to 'this reporter', thereby claiming objectivity in his rendering of events. He then returns to a witness focalisation, which he tellingly introduces by invoking academic integrity in the task of seeking out the truth:

> Peter Alexander, chair in Social Change and professor of Sociology at the University of Johannesburg, and two researchers interviewed witnesses in the days after the massacre. Researcher Botsong Mmope spoke to a miner, Tsepo, on Monday 20 August. Tsepo (not his real name) witnessed some of the events that occurred off camera.
>
> 'Tsepo said many people had been killed at the small koppie and it had never been covered (by the media). He agreed to take us to the small koppie, because that is where many, many people died,' Mmope said.
>
> After the shooting began, Tsepo said, he was among many who ran towards the small koppie. As the police chased them, someone among them said, 'Let us lie down, comrades, they will not shoot us then.'
>
> 'At that time, there were bullets coming from a helicopter above them. Tsepo then lay down. A number of fellow strikers also lay down. He says he watched Nyalas driving over the prostrate, living miners,' Mmope said. 'Other miners ran to the koppie, and that was where they were shot by police and the army** with machine guns.' (** *Several witnesses and speakers at the miners' gathering referring to the army, or amajoni, actually refer to a police task team unit in camouflage uniforms and carrying R5 semiautomatic files on the day. – GM)* (n.p.)

Marinovich reminds his readers that the police took several days before they released statistics. 'The number 34 surprised most of us,' he notes. 'With only about a dozen bodies recorded by the media, where exactly had the remaining miners been killed, and how did they die?' He continues: 'Most journalists and others did not interrogate this properly. The violence of the deaths we could see, again and again, was enough to contend with. The police certainly did not mention what happened outside of the view of the cameras.'

However, in service of the macroproposition of an overarching, encompassing truth, Marinovich marshalls a degree of observation seldom seen in reporting on this event: 'The toll of 112 mineworkers (34 dead and 78 wounded) at Marikana is one of those few bitter moments in our bloody history that has been captured by the unblinking eye of the lens. Several lenses, in fact, and from various viewpoints.' This, he proposes, 'has allowed the actions and reactions of both the strikers and the police to be scrutinised in ways that undocumented tragedies can never be. Therefore, while the motives and rationale of both parties will never be completely clear, their deeds are quite apparent.' Having provided validated and reliably witnessed micro-detail about what actually took place under cover of the boulders, Marinovich returns to his macroproposition:

> Thus developed a dominant narrative within the public discourse. The facts have been fed by the police, various state entities and by the media that the strikers provoked their own deaths by charging and shooting at the forces of law and order. Indeed, the various images and footage can be read to support this claim.
>
> The contrary view is that the striking miners were trying to escape police rubber bullets and tear gas when they ran at the heavily armed police task team (our version of SWAT). The result was the horrific images of a dozen or so men gunned down in a fusillade of automatic fire. (n.p.)

Later in the story, Marinovich, having set out with economy as well as stylistic variation the macro- and micropropositions, seems to opt for a 'true-crime' flourish. The chilling shock of imagining the details of the scene, as rendered below, and presented in the accompanying photographs, serves the higher, overarching aims of truth-telling:

> The yellow letters speak as if they are the voices of the dead. The position of the letters, denoting the remains of once sweating, panting, cursing, pleading men, tells a story of policemen

hunting men like beasts. They tell of tens of murders at close range, in places hidden from the plain sight.

N, for example, died in a narrow redoubt surrounded on four sides by solid rock. His killer could not have been further than two meters from him – the geography forbids any other possibility. (n.p.)

J and H were shot down alongside each other

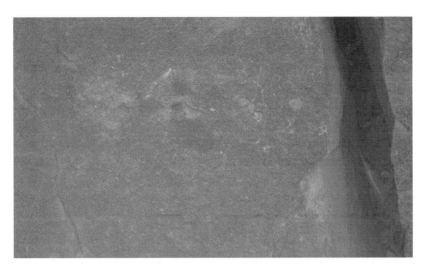

A bloody handprint bears witness to someone's effort to remain standing

Not content to leave the matter here, with an exposed murder scene, the subject of much official prevarication and protestations of innocence, Marinovich asks: 'Why did this happen?' He then analyses the events of the preceding days, when strikers and police clashed, and several lives were lost. More witness accounts cast further doubt on police versions of events, and so, too, does a satellite photograph of the killing fields with its various 'koppies', an examination of Lonmin's 'corporate communication' on the incident, and a detailed analysis of the weaponry used by police:

> The weapons used by the majority of the more than 400 police on the scene were R5 (a licensed replica of the Israeli Galil SAR) or LM5 assault rifles, designed for infantry and tactical police use. These weapons cannot fire rubber bullets. The police were clearly deployed in a military manner – to take lives, not to deflect possible riotous behaviour. (n.p.)

Marinovich concludes his extraordinary exposé with some hard-hitting statements. By entreating the reader, '[l]et us be under no illusion. The striking miners are no angels', he seeks to avoid accusations of unwarranted bias in favour of the miners. He continues:

> They can be as violent as anyone else in our society. And in an inflamed setting such as at Marikana, probably more so. They

are angry, disempowered, feel cheated and want more than a subsistence wage. Whatever the merits of their argument, and the crimes of some individuals among them, more than 3,000 people gathering at Wonderkop did not merit being vulnerable to summary and entirely arbitrary execution at the hands of a paramilitary police unit.

In light of this, we could look at the events of 16 August as the murder of 34 and the attempted murder of a further 78 who survived despite the police's apparent intention to kill them.

Back at the rocks the locals dubbed Small Koppie, a wild pear flowers among the debris of the carnage and human excrement; a place of horror that has until now remained terra incognita to the public. It could also be the place where the Constitution of South Africa has been dealt a mortal blow. (n.p.)

Whether what Marinovich here concludes is true, and to what degree, is perhaps less immediately relevant to our purposes than the manner in which he has chosen to narrate the details of a watershed event in postapartheid South Africa. This form of writing/representation amalgamates personal observation; third-party witnessing; relentless inquiry; unstinting evidentiary nous; and a commitment to forms of representation that combine maximum communicative force and improvisational, hybrid forms of writing, as well as photographic evidence. It is a communicative package that borrows strongly from (and in fact instantiates many features of) creative nonfiction, all the while acknowledging also the porousness of fiction and nonfiction. The 'crime scene' or violated public sphere, where postapartheid pathology emerges into public view, seems insistently to require such modal innovations, which in turn require adjustments of interpretive lenses. Marinovich's narratives about Marikana have since been published in book form (*Murder at Small Koppie*), but their first life as affectively loaded digital relays within a hypermediated wound culture is a symptomatic indicator of the location of the most acute pain in postapartheid writing.

7

Fiction's response

If it is fair to claim that nonfiction writing has garnered attention to the point where it seems to have eclipsed fictive forms,[1] one cannot but wonder what the retort of fiction might be to such a situation. As noted in Chapter 1, Antjie Krog has stated, 'I want to suggest that at this stage imagination for me is overrated' (Twidle, 'Literary Non-Fiction' 5), while Marlene van Niekerk has been quoted as saying that Altbeker's *Fruit of a Poisoned Tree* 'almost convinces one that fiction has become redundant in this country'.[2] What underlies assertions such as theirs is the sense that the sheer scale of postapartheid's failure to deliver on its promises – and the need to document this perceived condition – has edged out imaginative or fictive writing as the country's leading form[3] of literary intermediation.[4] For a long period in South Africa's literary history, fictive forms prevailed as the locus of ultimate literary value, as suggested by the Nobel awards achieved by Nadine Gordimer and JM Coetzee. Many authors have, in their own way, imagined a brave new future, but in the face of a 'neocolonial outcome of an anticolonial struggle' (O'Brien 3; Pechey 153), and a postapartheid public sphere widely perceived to be pathologised and felonious, where does 'invention' go? The imperative for writers, as we have observed, is more often found to be the exploration of actual, material conditions, and in so doing to establish the veracity of perceptions that emerge under conditions in which South Africans, according to Rian Malan, continue to occupy separate 'kingdoms of consciousness' (Twidle, 'Literary Non-fiction' 16). Recall, also, Steinberg's metaphor of 'coordinating between deaf people'.[5] In the face of an event such as Marikana, for example, what is more urgent – 'reimagining' the event, or finding out the deliberately obscured facts behind this catastrophe? What, indeed, is left for the imagination? And yet, despite the sense that one simply cannot 'make this shit up', as Twidle subtitles his essay on nonfiction,[6] it is precisely because this 'shit' is so egregious that a crucial question begs to be asked: how might fiction respond to such conditions, and what form might this response take?

South African literature has, as suggested above, a proud history of truth-telling, carried on the wings of a courageous and often inventive fictionality. Representative works from the postapartheid period include: JM Coetzee's *Disgrace,* Imraan Coovadia's *Tales of the Metric System,* Achmat Dangor's *Bitter Fruit,* K Sello Duiker's *The Quiet Violence of Dreams,* Nadine Gordimer's *The House Gun,* Mandla Langa's *The Lost Colours of the Chameleon,* Zakes Mda's *Ways of Dying,* Etienne van Heerden's *30 Nights in Amsterdam,* Marlene van Niekerk's *Agaat,* Eben Venter's *Trencherman,* Ivan Vladislavić's *The Restless Supermarket,* and Zoë Wicomb's *David's Story.* Such works challenge, though in different ways, a simplistic setting apart of fiction and nonfiction; it has, indeed, long been clear that neither fictionality nor nonfictionality is a watertight category, with a unique claim to truth or the 'real' real.[7] Fiction, as we know, uses 'made-up' stories only as a kind of surface guile that enables the telling of 'truths', and, as has been argued since Aristotle, such insights may go deeper than the mere factuality of nonfiction. Still, given the fact that today's readers are drawn towards surface forms which yield gratification by way of both facts and affect, fiction faces a significant challenge. The emphasis on discovery rather than invention, and on satisfying a quantifiable reality hunger among the reading public, acts as a weathervane for writers. Specifically, then, we can consider how postapartheid fiction might respond, were such a proposition to be put forward for rhetorical purposes, on two counts: (i) reality-embedded modes of representation in nonfiction form (with a high quotient of surface materiality and affect) are better suited to convey the immediate content, and charge, of wayward events as they unfold; and (ii) modes of representation that are faithful to the facts, eschewing 'imaginative' or 'fictive' manipulation, are more appropriate for intermediating the pathological public sphere of postapartheid, with its attendant social ills. This chapter deals with these two challenges to fiction in two parts, enabling a 'response' in each case. In the first instance, regarding modes of representation, there is an engagement with Ivan Vladislavić's 2010 novel *Double Negative*, a type of fictionalised memoir. I then turn to the work of K Sello Duiker, Phaswane Mpe, Lauren Beukes, Henrietta Rose-Innes and Imraan Coovadia for examples of how recent fiction has in fact 'reported' on various instances of postapartheid pathology, as focalised by fictional subjects.

Vladislavić's 'response' presents a signal act of underplotting when confronted by an overwhelming external reality. For the purposes of this chapter, *Double Negative* opens up a conceptual space, one that allows for the possibility of considering similar acts of underplotting, accounts wherein the author's voice acts as a medium through which postapartheid cities may reveal their unplottable, wayward trajectories. In such cases, fictional(ised) forms can be seen to break through, as it were, into the keenly felt materialities, as well as the abrasive surfaces, of the postapartheid public sphere. One such fictional rupture, K Sello Duiker's *The Quiet Violence of Dreams*, is taken into view as a work that exemplifies the documentary turn typifying much post-1994 writing: it demonstrates a kind of plotlessness – or plot loss – that is key to relaying the *felt* realities of a world in which death and madness emerge as overwhelming forces. Fiction has the advantage of rendering a world thus experienced uniquely legible, by means of a language whose main purpose is empathetic identification,[8] or proxy experience. In Duiker's novel, the very ground, and the everyday 'data', of a reimagined 'real'[9] is pathology and madness, as witnessed in Tshepo's Valkenberg period and occasioned partly by rape and killing (acts indirectly committed by Tshepo's father against his mother). The novel draws much of its discursive force from similar currents – violent assault and murder – in contemporaneous testimony before the Truth and Reconciliation Commission. A desire (or need) to document is likewise evident in Phaswane Mpe's *Welcome to Our Hillbrow* – yet another signal postapartheid fictional work in which a pathological city is seen to overwhelm its citizens. Both works, in different ways, build on the foundation of Mda's novel of the early-transition period, *Ways of Dying*, where the struggle between the creative imagination and death is staged as the definitive challenge in the postapartheid milieu. In novels by Lauren Beukes and Henrietta Rose-Innes, experiencing subjects find themselves caught up in plot contortions that signify profound dislocation, a lack of anchorage in an irrational social order. Finally, Imraan Coovadia's novel *Tales of the Metric System* is approached in terms of its search for – indeed expression of – a certain whimsy, an unexpectedly humorous fissure, in the seemingly intractable kleptocracy that contaminates the post-apartheid public sphere.

Fictional 'negatives' of the documented real

In *Double Negative*, Vladislavić enfolds within the story he tells a series of documented visual encounters – or, more accurately, he allows key visual imprints of the outside world to enter the darkroom of fiction, in much the same way as lines and shapes emerge on a photographic print once it is placed in developer solution. The optic encounters so embedded in *Double Negative* are mediated by what one might, following Coetzee, call the novel's inner workings:[10] fictionalised meditations on how art, in particular visual forms, sometimes intermeshed with verbal data, size up South Africa's gritty social realities. *Double Negative* was first released as a joint product, in a large, slipcase package, with David Goldblatt's *TJ-Johannesburg: Photographs 1948–2010*, a series of monochrome studies set in the city of gold, also known as Egoli. *Double Negative* was thus forged as a verbal account in dialogue with photography, both in its very materiality – a fictional(ised) work inside a larger package containing a book of pictures – and as a written work that seeks to mediate moments and images that have also been captured through the medium of photography. It therefore resorts to the crossover medium known as ekphrasis,[11] i.e. 'the verbal representation of visual representation' (Heffernan 3). *Double Negative* is, then, intrinsically about the dialogue between different forms, principally the verbal and the visual, in conveying images of Johannesburg as the city reflects (or refracts) – and its inhabitants negotiate – changing conditions, from the time of apartheid to the postapartheid period.

Furthermore, Vladislavić's fictionalised memoir charts the evolving style or manner of this dialogue over several key decades in South African history. In so doing, the author asserts the capability of fictional forms to describe and investigate the surfaces of visual forms (including, in *Double Negative*'s third section, 'Small Talk', the new media), whereas visual media, by their very nature, cannot so contain fictional forms. Herein lies the core of *Double Negative*'s engagement with – indeed response to – the challenge of documentary forms in nonfictional mode. *Double Negative* asserts, in its formal organisation, that it is capable of doubling the act of picture-making: paralleling the chemical process in which photographic film is developed, the visual datum of the protagonist's (photo-mediated) world emerges gradually, doing so by means of ekphrasis. Naturally, this is a conceit, in that the illusion of visuality (and therefore the documented 'real') is achieved in a written, fictionalised form. Still, this doubling, in which visual data, a form of 'nonfictional' representation, is both contained and relativised within fiction, represents a noteworthy moment in postapartheid writing. The ample allowance in *Double Negative* for external imprinting (as in a photograph), including 'real' characters that are doubled into fictional 'negatives', implicitly asserts fiction as a 'panharmonicon'[12] form; accordingly, it may be described as multi-modal, with the capacity to contain and 'play' other forms.

Key to this intersection of the verbal and the visual, as suggested above, is the fact that Vladislavić underplots his writing. This is the case not only in *Double Negative*, but elsewhere, too, notably in *The Restless Supermarket* (2001) and *Portrait with Keys* (2006), Vladislavić's non-fiction tour de force. It is as if the outside world, with all its quirks and quiddities, dictates the writing process. (Of course, Vladislavić's some-what outré eye is the other vital element, the window through which this 'dictation' flows.) In a manner similar to Coetzee's understanding that 'stories finally have to tell themselves' and that 'the hand that holds the pen is only the conduit of a signifying process' (*Doubling the Point* 341), Vladislavić opens himself to being written by the story (or stories) of actual conditions. And the story that so writes itself, in this conceit, is the postapartheid metropolis, in particular (but not only) Johannesburg.[13] In thus orchestrating his writings, Vladislavić engages directly with the challenge that a 'surface' form such as documentary photography poses to the power of fiction as a meaningful or purpo-sive agent in postapartheid intermediation.

In order to appreciate the structural response of fictional(ised) forms to the claims of critics who perceive of 'surface' forms as eclips-ing the potency of fiction, it is necessary to examine such claims. This is because 'surface' is often aligned with the idea of reality hunger, and of media representations of the actual, the here and now. In their con-troversial essay 'Surface Reading: An Introduction', Best and Marcus make the case for a reading practice that eschews 'symptomatic reading', along with 'psychoanalysis and Marxism as metalanguages', in favour of what they invoke as a mode of reading belonging to the 'now' (1). Writing in 2009, the authors suggest that '[i]n the last decade or so, we have been drawn to modes of reading that attend to the surfaces of texts rather than plumb their depths' (1–2). Symptomatic reading, they argue, 'took meaning to be hidden, repressed, deep, and in need of detection and disclosure by an interpreter' (1). In contrast to this, in contemporary times 'so much seems to be on the surface', they claim, citing images of torture at Abu Ghraib being made immediately available on the internet, and real-time coverage of Hurricane Katrina showing the state's 'abandonment of its African American people'; such images and coverage render the demystification of deep texts irrelevant, in Best and Marcus's argument (2). In the course of their essay, Best and Marcus make the case for 'attention to surface as a practice of critical description', the critic thereby avoiding the trap of seeking hidden truths beneath the text's surface to the extent that there is a failure properly to describe what the text is in fact 'about' (11); they argue for seeing surface 'as the location of patterns that exist within and across texts' rather than skimming over such designs as one seeks out supposedly concealed subtexts (11); quite unapologetically, they advocate for a reading of surface as 'literal meaning' (12), relishing what the text 'shows' rather than what it seemingly hides. Further, among other more recent approaches to reading, they allude to the work of the New Formalists, who see the task of the critic as restoring the artwork to its 'original, compositional complexity', cultivating a kind of 'learned submission' (14) to the work itself. Focusing in their opening section on 'Reading "The Way We Read Now"', Best and Marcus link the argument about newer modes of reading to new-media forms of representation, such as the internet and other forms of what they call 'real-time coverage' (1–2; see also Chapter 6 of this volume).

The debate that has ensued around surface reading is a lively one. However, the more interesting turn in this critical dialogue about rejuvenated forms of reading, from the point of view of postapartheid writing, was made by Sarah Nuttall in 2011. Invoking as her title the phrase used by Best and Marcus, i.e. 'The Way We Read Now', she applies it to South African writing in general. Nuttall opens her argument with a provocative gambit: 'Not many people around here seem to think that literary studies has problems – but I do' ('Way We

Read Now' n.p.). Echoing the claims of Best and Marcus, she asks, rhetorically:

> Haven't we come now towards the end of a way of reading that has evolved into a big sophisticated machine since the 70s but may no longer be right for its time? Don't we feel a little tired now of critique as we have come to know it, of the work of detection involved in identifying the Marxian or psychoanalytic symptom? (n.p.)

Like Best and Marcus, Nuttall appeals to the salience of new-media forms when she argues that '[i]n this new century of ours, the surface (the screen, the interface, but also the skin-like surface of a (literary) text) is emerging as a much more potent space than it used to be'. She cites Rita Felski, who describes 'suspicious reading' as an 'asocial emotion' and a 'low-grade affective stance'; for Felski, as for Nuttall, suspicious reading involves 'under-reading [the text's] affective powers', and like Shields, whom she also cites, Nuttall encourages attention to the 'reality phenomenon'. In addition, she supports Bruno Latour, who advocates moving away from an excessive emphasis on ideological demystification ('Way We Read Now' n.p.). Nuttall proclaims that, for her, '[contemporary] South African novels were just not getting anywhere near the edge of the South African present in its most interesting forms', leading her, in her own research, to a consideration of paintings instead. Nuttall enlarges this argument in her contribution to *Print, Text, and Book Cultures in South Africa*, citing the work of affect critics such as Elaine Freegood, Anne Cheng, Eve Sedgwick and Leah Price ('Rise of the Surface').

Arguments such as those proposed above represent a set of concerns which converge in a striking manner with emphases identified in previous chapters of this book. This is particularly evident in the prominence of 'reality' phenomena in nonfiction writing in post-apartheid South Africa, and the embedding of such writing within new-media forms characterised by 'surface'. In formulating her argument, Nuttall sets up Vladislavić as a fictional trader in the 'hidden and unrecoverable' (see quotation below). A useful way of taking stock of Nuttall's arguments is, I suggest, to allow Vladislavić a fictional response, thereby setting up a putative dialogue construed after the fact (of course, Vladislavić at no point actually refers to Nuttall's claims, nor does he make any broad reference to postapartheid fiction). The benefit of the debate so construed is entirely impersonal and conceptual: it broadens and deepens a set of issues that are of central concern to writers, critics and readers of South African writing.

For Nuttall, Vladislavić's writing typifies that of an older school where 'surface' is largely inactive, or used as a foil for hidden depths that require symptomatic or 'suspicious' reading. She writes:

> Even as Vladislavić examines the surfaces of the city, its truth lies in all that is hidden and unrecoverable, and in a lens that for all its sophistication, amounts to a nostalgic vision of the Johannesburg of his childhood. For Vladislavić, the truth of the city is largely to be found in its underneath – a literal underneath, its history, his own memory, its figures of marginality, its psychic effects and an archaeology of words in its written texts. His is a vocabulary of critical excavation. ('Rise of the Surface' 420)

Leaving aside certain points about which scholars might wish to argue,[14] the main argument here casts Vladislavić as a writer whose nostalgia cripples his capacity to see the city's truth, to read its 'surface' signs.

A careful reading of *Double Negative*, however, unsettles Nuttall's proposition. Not only does this work reveal an acute awareness of surfaces, in all their materiality, but it also encodes, within the author's own self-awareness, a lively debate about precisely the claims of 'surface reading'. This is something that is staged rather than asserted, and it is, moreover, achieved within three successive temporal frames, one in the pre-transition years, one in the mid-transition period (the 1990s), and one in the postapartheid present (i.e. the temporal setting of the work itself, which was first published in 2010).

Vladislavić's three-part fiction is premised on the speculative 'what if' that informs mimetic works which depend on imaginative immersion in a presumed, correspondingly accurate, or metonymically representative, rendition of 'reality'. This 'what if' question can be put more or less as follows: what if one could escape the blur of time and then capture, in a moment, or a series of moments, the true nature of the 'real'? What does one gain, or lose, in such a pursuit? Vladislavić seeks to answer this question in three separate fictional narratives: one about documentary photography in the anti-apartheid era, exemplified by David Goldblatt; one about failed communication or 'dead letters' – in the story itself, unclaimed mail – in the immediate aftermath of apartheid; and one about digital, continuous capture in the current era, something that one might see as a widespread response to 'reality hunger'. It will be immediately obvious, even from such capsule descriptions of these sub-narratives, that Vladislavić's fictional(ised) assay relates precisely to questions about the surface of the 'real' and *how surfaces relate to* their representational capture; also, that *Double Negative* does so in a series of mutating forms. In some ways, then, both Nuttall and Vladislavić are dealing with surface forms and their valence, apart from one essential difference: Nuttall seeks to question the 'reach' of work such as that of Vladislavić, whereas Vladislavić's enquiry can in fact be seen to be reaching for larger, more encompassing perspectives on the matter of representation.

The first and second sections of *Double Negative* engage in an implicit dialogue about cross-modal representations, as I have argued elsewhere ('So, What Should Academic Critics Be Doing?'). My current focus, however, is the third and final section, entitled 'Small Talk'. Protagonist Neville has returned to South Africa after spending a large part of the 1990s (the transition period) in London, learning to become a photographer who specialises in 'frozen moments'. One of a generation of returned-from-exile artists, Neville finds inspiration in the work of Saul Auerbach, a David Goldblatt[15] figure (and, by implication, that of Auerbach's contemporary Nadine Gordimer). Neville might be said to represent a generation of artists who found themselves in the interregnum, the period between apartheid and what was to follow, people with a leg in both worlds. Such artists, *Double Negative* suggests, occupy a troubled psychological space which, characterised by rupture and reconnection, produces an unsettling sense of alienation. As Neville says, shortly after his return, '[g]rafting memory to experience had turned out to be painful' (145). He adds: 'There was so much to be recovered, yet so little felt familiar, and the scraps that did had become resistant. A gap had opened up between me and the known world' (145). If the generation that came before Neville, the Goldblatts and the Gordimers, bore witness to apartheid in 'hard', or fixed, mimetic modes[16] (i.e. still photographs and realistic fiction), then the generation that succeeds Neville (and, by implication, Vladislavić) is of an equally distinct character, working in more fluid forms. This generation's representative in *Double Negative*, Jane Amanpour (echoing Christiane Amanpour, the

television and online journalist), is a blogger/reporter/artist/digital bricoleur who wishes to interview Neville for a feature in a community
newspaper. She is a multimedia artist whose work straddles multiple
domains, from the 'hard', actual world to the more playful, simulacral
digital sphere. She writes highbrow and lowbrow book reviews in her
blog, along with scraps of advice on how to cope with daily life, and is an
artist of the 'reality phenomenon'. Almost indiscriminately, Jane waves
a digicam as she moves through the world, and then loops the images
into her blogs, thereby blending visual media and print media. She is,
therefore, an integrator, a collage artist whose work shuttles between the
real and its rechannelled forms. Her work could hardly be more different
from Neville's static, 'frozen' images, and Neville's pictures, in turn, are
equally distinct from those of Auerbach. Collectively, these three figures
form the basis of Vladislavić's analysis of the ongoing evolution of artistic
mediation, from apartheid through postapartheid to post-postapartheid.

Neville takes Jane on a guided tour through his world of 'threshold'
photography, in which he captures people who, quite literally, occupy
liminal spaces, the 'line' between private and public worlds – next to
their postboxes and the high-security outside walls that are so typical
of Johannesburg. Jane, in turn, distinguishes herself as a 'reality' artist in her eager invitation to him to penetrate the threshold with her,
the exterior surface of a property that is occupied by one of Neville's
subjects, and to which he needs access. Though Neville declines her
offer, Jane nevertheless forges ahead, disregarding his warning to 'be
careful': 'Miming some sort of SWAT team procedure, she slipped
through the gap in the gate with the digicam cocked' (159). The subject of Neville's study in this instance is one Antoine K, a refugee from
the Democratic Republic of Congo (DRC), who lives in Malvern,
an old part of Johannesburg, in a house fronted by a makeshift wall
'patched together with sheets from bus shelters and billboards' (159).
Advertising fragments are visible – '[b]est prices, the wall said, fresh
petrol' (159) – and the postbox itself is a recycled paint can, a 'Wall
& All tin with a slot cut in the bottom. Pebble Beach, according to the
label, ran in horizontal streaks along the tin, defying gravity' (159–
160). This is classic Vladislavić, writing up an urban, visual mesh of
styles, temporalities and yearnings that coalesce or collide on the exterior surfaces of aspirational Johannesburg. In so doing, Vladislavić
gives voice to the cacophony of the postapartheid urban spectacle,
transforming what might otherwise remain an everyday banality into

the shimmering surface of his prose. This is a far cry from the writer for whom 'the truth of the city is largely to be found in its underneath', and whose vocabulary is one of 'critical excavation', as Nuttall suggests ('Rise of the Surface' 420). Instead, Vladislavić seems beguiled by the materiality of surfaces, their jauntiness, and their refraction of the mix-and-match bricolage of urban spaces. Such surfaces bespeak a city of sly wit and astounding asymmetries – of wealth and yearning, gaucherie and nouveau chic, mishmash and 'design' of a kind that begs to be seen and appreciated, even if only by a flaneur.[17] His readers are, of course, unable to actually *see* the physical objects in his prose, so Vladislavić employs ekphrasis, which may in many senses be regarded as his métier, his way of exposing to view the chaotic spaces, the tacky surfaces, the grit and the grubby glamour of the postapartheid metropolis. And such 'surfaces' are nothing if not simultaneously visual, aural and olfactory, relayed with flourishes of touch, smell, taste and other senses, too.[18] One of Vladislavić's distinctive marks of 'fictionality', especially in his later work, is his ability to *style* the ekphrasis, the record of the surface, by lending poise and artistry to the visual/verbal representation of seemingly random objects in his world. Such surfaces are suggestive in an immediate, literal way, capturing what is actually out there, but they are also suggestive in more extended senses, pointing to new alignments in the cultural and sociopolitical spheres of the postapartheid metropolis. Vladislavić's work is therefore a rich source for new materialist critics whose readings would be rewarded as they mined these texts for more resonant meanings – they may even encounter depth-charges along the way.

As noted above, Vladislavić's protagonist chooses to ignore Jane's invitation, and does not venture beyond the threshold of Antoine K's gate. When she returns from her reconnaissance into this 'backyard' world, she exclaims: 'It's a village back there! You'd never say so, but there must be twenty shacks behind this wall, a whole shanty town in the middle of a suburb. I reckon there could be a hundred people living here. Do you want to take a look?' (160). Neville's reply is a curt 'no thanks'. Jane continues:

> 'You'd get some great shots. It's like the kasbah or something, all these twisty alleyways between the shacks, really beautiful. There's one shack made of ten different materials – iron, hardboard, scraps of lumber, you name it – but the whole thing's been painted eau de

Nil. It's an artwork. Have you been to Zanzibar? It's like that, except the scale's all weird because everything's been reduced to fit on one plot. Maybe it's three-quarter scale like Melrose Arch. It has that sort of charm, although it's very different, of course, I don't mean to suggest. When you're done, you should look around.' (160)

Once again, Neville refuses: 'I'd rather not' (161). When pushed by Jane's blunt 'Why?', he answers: 'I don't want the inside story' (161). Ironically, this particular Vladislavić double refuses what Nuttall calls 'critical excavation', here described as the 'inside story'. Later, Neville cannot avoid seeing what Jane has discovered beyond the threshold: as an artist of the backstory and the documented fragment, Jane zooms in with her digicam, and then shoves the footage under Neville's nose:

I went with her into the maze of Antoine's village, twisting and turning between the shacks, on and on as if the place were endless. Once she came to a dead end, quickly doubled back, and found another path. The shacks were so close together, you could reach out and touch the walls on either side. A tangible community. You would not need to go next door for a cup of sugar, you could simply lean out of your window. She swung around a corner, jaunty and unafraid. A woman stooping over a plastic basin of laundry started when she saw her, and then stood up with her foamy hands on her hips, laughing. She focused on the laughing woman and then on a king-size bottle of Sta-soft. 'Hello ma. Who are you? Tell me your name and what you're doing.' But the camera made the woman shy and she turned away, hiding her face. The camera bobbed and reeled again along the ironclad streets, as if it had been set adrift on a raft. Bits of sky flickered into the lens, dented walls fell like shutters, layers of trampled earth flew up. She turned to look back. A gang of kids were following her, excited and alarmed. She focused on a girl with braids standing out stiffly like a crown of exclamation marks all around her head. (178)

This verbal relay of visual material constitutes an ekphrastic account, incorporating a kind of ready-made, new-media display. This is perfectly appropriate to a digital-travel bricoleur such as Jane Amanpour, and it is noteworthy that the latter bears a striking resemblance to the backstory curator who, for Nuttall, is best equipped to catch the 'now' – an ability to capture the moment, which, she argues, seems lacking in the case of Vladislavić. However, if Neville at times resembles the figure of an older practitioner perceived to be out of touch with 'reality', then the author does not permit him this luxury for very long, as the above passage suggests.

In thus writing up a vivid visual record, Vladislavić succeeds in capturing – by 'playing' literary forms – the surface, that which is visible to the eye. The literary domain here serves as a record of the 'now', but it also comments (implicitly) on the 'now's' registers of mediation – something only a 'thick' medium[19] can accomplish. Vladislavić's capacity to 'play' with literary forms, and to bring to light reciprocal relations between surface and depth, calls into question any pessimism concerning the current capabilities of 'the literary' in the postapartheid context. The author shows characters reading across as well as down as they puzzle over their world; he exposes the artifice of art making, and he infects it with the 'real'.

Double Negative, then, brings 'contrapuntal' or polyphonic modalities into being. In the words of Neel Mukherjee:

> One of the substantial pleasures of the book is the way Vladislavić has made non-fiction in its many forms – critical theory, the essay, (the illusion of) memoir – rub against the domain of storytelling...It is also a masterclass in making one art form – photography – speak within and through the containing vessel of another, the novel, and creating contrapuntal music out of it. (n.p.)

Double Negative in fact goes a step further, in that the contrapuntalism identified by Mukherjee goes beyond photography, embracing new forms such as the multimedia blogging that is Jane Amanpour's forte. As a result, it seems difficult not to read this work as a staging of the rival claims not only of photography and prose, but of textual depth and surface forms of the real. In the process, the disjunctures of both form and temporality – which, as argued in the chapters above, are key to postapartheid writing – are addressed, or faced up to, if not resolved.

Cities of the dead

If Vladislavić's implicit response to the claims of nonfiction and surface forms of the real is to bring the very textures of such forms into play within the novel, then K Sello Duiker and Phaswane Mpe's fictions exemplify a similar visual sensitivity to the outside world. Like *Double Negative*, Duiker's *The Quiet Violence of Dreams* and Mpe's *Welcome to Our Hillbrow* are underplotted novels that exhibit the alert, sceptical documentary style typical of postapartheid writing. These are not so much 'stories' as records of shattering experience under remorseless social conditions. Not to put too fine a point on it, the personal predicaments of both writers' protagonists are terminal. Their respective scenarios are uncomfortably close to the authors' personal lives – both Duiker and Mpe died early deaths as a result of precisely the kinds of conditions described in their novels, which might accurately be described as semi-autobiographical fiction, or fictionalised memoir, a marked tendency in postapartheid writing, as indeed is demonstrated by Vladislavić's writing, too. In the overbearingly oppressive worlds described by Duiker and Mpe, more than the minimum necessary fictional invention would be superfluous. There is too much going on already, too much death, and too much disease.

Duiker's protagonist, Tshepo, is a young man whose corrupt father, a mafia figure with connections to the postapartheid underworld, organises a 'hit' on his own wife, Tshepo's mother, not only to avoid culpability – she has incriminating information on him – but also to benefit from an insurance policy on her life. Such is the craven bottom line, the ethical graveyard, of the world Tshepo inherits. Clearly, this scenario acts as a metonym, with extortion and evasion of responsibility the order of the day in a larger social reality. Like most things in Tshepo's world, the planned 'attack' on his family spins out of control, with the attackers raping him for good measure, too, after gang-raping and then murdering his mother. This, narrated almost casually, as if it is nothing to be too surprised about, is Duiker's version of formative childhood experience in postapartheid conditions. After such an introduction to the imprint of the outside world, it is, ironically, no surprise to find this child of Mandela's long struggle for freedom incarcerated in Cape Town's Valkenberg psychiatric hospital. Tshepo has been involuntarily admitted after being found wandering the streets of Cape Town in a state of apparent numbness as a consequence of 'cannabis-induced psychosis'. The 'madhouse' of Valkenberg is a veritable sanctuary from the world of zombies outside its walls.[20]

Tshepo is but one of many death-driven flaneurs of the postapartheid city. From within the gates of the asylum, Tshepo reveals

that 'madness' is the métier of public life. The asylum becomes the
inverted locus of reckoning, providing a perspective from which the
'outside' is recognised as the actual site of sickness, sending a feeling
subject such as Tshepo into psychic shock. He has the clear realisa-
tion that '[i]n here everyone knows that there are more crazy people out there, and that most of them are politicians, lawyers, judges,
accountants and bankers. It seems only a matter of chance that we are
in here and they are out there' (*Quiet Violence* 161).

What is more, the supposedly liberated South Africa that Tshepo
inherits is run by a patriarchal order with criminal propensities which
are figured directly in the person of Tshepo's father, who is well 'connected', and whose overriding focus is the accumulation of money
and goods, in the process sacrificing his wife and child to what Tshepo
terms the 'Mafia' (97). This is the same world that Niq Mhlongo picks
up on in his novel of undisguised scorn for postapartheid venality,
Way Back Home, where slick wheelers and dealers mockingly squeeze
BEE-style legitimacy for every last ounce of single-malt gain. By contrast, however, Tshepo's economic survival is limited, upon release, to
the world of gay prostitution: his previously unsuccessful attempts at
selling commodities while waiting on tables are upended as he himself
becomes a commodity, sold to the highest bidder. In many senses,
Quiet Violence is an epic documentary of the everyday, 'ordinary' real
(in Ndebele's terms), circa 2000, in which the postapartheid social
order is definitively queered. Put differently, it is only from the margins, from a 'queer' space, that a feeling subject such as Tshepo is able
to disassociate from the macho brutality of the patriarchy he inevitably enters upon reaching adulthood. Duiker describes a social order
in which criminality and violence are fundamental, as is evident when
two of Tshepo's friends, Chris and Zebron, rape him, and a third,
Jacques, who is associated with satanism and 'evil', turns against him
after initially accommodating him in his home.

A trenchant critique of Duiker's novel by Alla Ivanchikova, who
reads it in conjunction with a post-Soviet novel,[21] identifies a turn
towards consumerist subjectivity in both the South African as well as
the Soviet 'post' zones, where a sense of political disillusionment is so
pervasive that it is almost nonchalantly accepted. This is clearly evident in Tshepo's cynical comment that 'Dolce e Gabbana kicks more
ass than any bill of rights', and that 'on the dance floor it doesn't matter which party you voted for in the last election … [t]hey want to see

how creatively you can fuse mall shopping with flea market crawling
and still remain stylish' (*Quiet Violence* 37). For Ivanchikova, transitional identities in postapartheid South Africa, as much as in post-
socialist Russia, 'try to reconstitute themselves through the discourse
of commodity consumption and self-sale. What we see there [i.e. in
both societies] is a hyperinflation of one's commodity status coupled
with profound anxiety about this process' (2). Understanding oneself
as a commodity 'presents an important promise while also posing a
threat' (2). Ivanchikova continues:

> [I]n both novels the protagonists eventually exit the realm of cir-
> culation as commodities and are presented as 'trash' or waste.
> Instead of realizing their full potential as enfranchised consum-
> ers in a transnational market economy, they become what I call
> 'trash citizens' – discovering that waste is, inevitably, the dialecti-
> cal counterpart of every commodity. Both novels could be read as
> allegorical in regards to post-socialist Russian and post-apartheid
> South African national identity. The hyperinflation of commodity
> status in both novels and the resulting rhetoric of disillusionment
> is a response to the ideological vacuum and uncertainty that
> defines the post-socialist or post-apartheid condition – a situation
> that consumerist ideology promises to resolve, but fails. (2–3)

This reading strips bare the pathos of what the male prostitutes at
Steamy Windows call the 'brotherhood', a pseudo-philosophy by
which the men selling sexual gratification seek to understand their
work in terms of a 'commitment to being sexual visionaries with the
fervour of artists' (*Quiet Violence* 376). Despite the genuine tenderness
of touch and feeling that Tshepo offers in many of his sex sessions
with clients – a kind of generosity that is generally lacking in non-
consumerist interactions in 'normal' society – he is later reminded
by a fellow 'black stallion', Cole, that 'this whole brotherhood thing is
very convenient' for the white bosses of the gay sex-for-sale business,
a point that Tshepo must reluctantly accept. Ivanchikova notes that
the identification of the consumer with the commodity being sold
means that to be a subject one is forced to become a saleable object.
Or, as Zygmunt Bauman famously put it: '[I]n the society of consumers no one can become a subject without first turning into commodity, and no one can keep his or her subjectness secure without

perpetually resuscitating, resurrecting and replenishing the capacities expected and required of a sellable commodity' (*Consuming Life* 12). For Ivanchikova, both novels 'expose the contradictions of commodity fetishism when it extends itself into the world's margins, bowels, and slums — contradictions that cannot be easily, if ever, surpassed' (8). Furthermore, while 'commodities present themselves as a common language, offering a semblance of universality, a utopian vision of the equality and "brotherhood" or "sisterhood" of commodities', in an ironic twist, the 'language of refuse in the novels replaces the language of commodities as more universal' (8). This is precisely what takes place in the concluding pages of Duiker's novel. Following the death of his father, Tshepo returns to the streets, wading through actual, rotting garbage that signifies his (fast-fading) existence as a branded 'black stallion' sex commodity. During a psychotic episode where he goes walkabout in Khayelitsha, 'a pig digs its snout into a pile of rub-bish' (578), while the foul, 'splattered' innards of a dead dog stink to high heaven and no one bothers to take them away (578). Dislocated and distraught, Tshepo walks like a lost man in and around Cape Town, having reverted to his original state of disarray. He drifts to his birthplace of Johannesburg, where he joins the sprawling community of migrants in Hillbrow. The novel implicitly suggests that the only home that is possible for Tshepo is to be found among those with no home, those who, like him, are compelled to find makeshift commu-nities in places permeated by the reek of putrefaction, for the 'scent of death is everywhere' (551).

Hillbrow is where Duiker's novel ends, and it is where Mpe's story begins, as if the two narratives were conjoint. Indeed, both were pub-lished in 2001, and both emanate from, and confront, what comes across as a kingdom of the dying. 'NARRATION FROM THE DEAD, OF THE DEAD, ADDRESSED TO A READER IN THE POSITION OF THE DEAD', reads a heading introducing *Welcome to Our Hillbrow* as part of a compara-tive literary studies course presented by the University of Warwick. Lecturer Ross Forman's heading not only encapsulates the essence of Mpe's novel, but also speaks of a certain critical metanarrative inform-ing the reception of Duiker and Mpe as postapartheid authors.[22] As writers of the dead zone, both authors are emblematic of a unique moment of literary invigoration that was prematurely snuffed out. Duiker died by his own hand at the age of 30, and Mpe succumbed to what is believed to have been an AIDS-related illness at age 34.[23]

Mpe and Duiker died within two months of each other, in 2004/5, and there was much grief at their loss.

The mournful metanarrative that enshrouds these two writers underscores a widely held conception that Duiker and Mpe together signify a marked turn, or a hardening, in postapartheid writing, one in which the contest between the counterpoised options evident in *Ways of Dying* – pathology and death on the one hand, and creative reinvigoration on the other – is firmly decided.[24] It is not the content alone of Mpe and Duiker's fictions that speaks of such a lethal turn, but the fact of these writers' untimely passing, too: while the annihilation of ongoing literary power and promise is mourned, this incorporates a far greater actual loss. The tragic sense of ruinous waste has become a standard trope in comment on these two authors, including what might in other circumstances be regarded – even dismissed as – merely anecdotal. However, there exists also a publication in which Mpe and Duiker are memorialised as emblems of cultural and human spoliation writ large. Edited by Mbulelo Vizikhungo Mzamane, and consisting of poems, tributes, short pieces and critical essays, under the title *Words Gone Two Soon: A Tribute to Phaswane Mpe & K. Sello Duiker*, the book freezes in time a moment of mourning that also has significant symbolic power. Published in the mid-2000s, the collection is a lament not only for two young writers cut down prematurely, but for the mortal wounding of postapartheid democracy.

Published by Umgangatho Media & Communications, the project was originated by wRite Associates, who administer the South African Literary Awards, or SALA, in conjunction with the South African Department of Arts and Culture. In his preface, Morakabe Raks Seakhoa states that the project was 'conceived in grief and pain' (Mzamane vi). The book features an introduction by Mzamane; poems by, among others, South African poet laureate Keorapetse Kgositsile and Gabeba Baderoon; and tributes by a range of people who knew both writers.[25] There are also interviews featuring writers, editors and associates of both writers, and stories by Maakomele Manaka, Nadine Gordimer, Njabulo S Ndebele, Can Themba and Marcia Nkululeko Tladi, inter alia. The criticism section features essays by McQueen Motuba, Osita Ezeliora, Pamela Nichols, Rob Gaylard, Lizzy Attree, Meg Samuelson, Madala Thepa, Es'kia Mphahlele, Mbulelo Vizikhungo Mzamane and Andries W Oliphant. Apart from the content of these various pieces, the sheer orchestration of public figures (literary and otherwise) in this valedictory cause speaks to a collective sense of loss.

The critical writings are especially revealing. Opening the 'Criticism' section, McQueen Motuba writes that the characters in Mpe's and Duiker's novels resemble what he calls a 'new national hybrid', which he further describes as the 'kwaito/hip-hop genera-tion, the model C youth' (161). They are characters 'grappling with identities that were not quite white, but not black enough to be black' (161). Not only were Mpe and Duiker voices of a new and hybrid generation, as Motuba suggests, blurring older certitudes and lines of struggle, they also inherited a (literally) sick world in which suicide and sex and mortal illness seemed inescapable. Mpe and Duiker lived out their final years in the midst of a national HIV epidemic, with then president Thabo Mbeki, along with minister of health Manto Tshabalala-Msimang, propounding denialist positions that effec-tively deprived HIV-positive people of life-saving medication.[26] It should therefore come as no surprise that *Welcome to Our Hillbrow* is riddled with images of disease and dying. According to a *New York Times* report in 2006, based on an interview with then deputy minis-ter of health Nozizwe Madlala-Routledge, one in eight of the world's HIV infections at the time was to be found in South Africa, and the country witnessed, every day, '1,000 South Africans...infected with HIV, and 800 more...killed by AIDS' (Wines n.p.). Many commen-tators in this period used the term 'genocide' in relation to the Mbeki administration's extreme reluctance to roll out antiretrovirals for the treatment of HIV and Aids.[27]

It therefore makes sense that, as Lizzy Attree writes in *Words Gone Two Soon*, the nation, and the city, become in Mpe's and Duiker's work a 'community of disease', or 'an acknowledged sick zone' (189).[28] Attree, referring to the centrality of the city in Mpe's book, invokes the established idea that cities are emblematic of 'diseases of the social body' (353). Attree adds, however, that, more literally, 'the body becomes a discursive formation', and that '[o]nce the HIV virus has intersected with the body, the body becomes a site of struggle or mourning, it resonates with political, economic and sexual connota-tions' (189). Implicitly concurring with this more general emphasis on the dominance of death tropes, Samuelson – who sees Mpe and Duiker as 'two of the most evocative inscribers of post-apartheid city-space' – points to *Welcome to Our Hillbrow*'s 'persistent crossing of the border between life and death' ('Crossing Borders' 197). '[T]he city celebrated in Mpe's fiction,' she adds, 'is undeniably also a space of death' (197).

It is therefore fair to argue that South African writing in the wake of Mpe and Duiker, whether overplotted genre fiction or underplotted fictionalised forms, has found itself negotiating a criminal public sphere and a deathly if not deadly social environment. As Mpe and Duiker's emblematic works suggest, this is the world – and the literary landscape – South African writers after 2000 have inherited. Fittingly, the crime novels of Makholwa, Brown, Tlholwe, Meyer, Orford, Nicol and others take it as a generic given to open with a corpse, either violated or mutilated. Marlene van Niekerk's postapartheid epic *Agaat* is an account of a life conducted in a manner that offers the mortally ill matriarch, Milla, little but a mordant awareness of error and waste in her deathbed ruminations. Van Niekerk's 2010 play, *Die Kortstondige Raklewe van Anastasia W*, presents the postapartheid world from the perspective of a funeral parlour that routinely feeds off death. It is a lament for a morbidly diseased country characterised by cynical cruelty and opportunistic killing, where decomposition and decay are, consequently, overpowering tropes.[29] Similarly, Ingrid Winterbach's *The Road of Excess* is narrated by an artist who walks a tightrope, faced with the imminent threat of disease and annihilation, and the actual narration, as much as the country it depicts, is quite literally obsessed with 'going under' (as implied in the Afrikaans title, *Die Benederyk*). The narrative culminates in up-and-coming young artist, Jimmy Harris, turning his own demise into a video art-installation, as if little else is possible or relevant in the domain not only of life, but also art.[30]

Unlikely though it is that such writing has the capacity to shape the struggle for civil standards in South Africa's public life, it is certainly effective – at least from a literary point of view. Marlene van Niekerk, upon being nominated for a Man Booker International Prize in 2015, addressed this very question in a manner that seems to border on despair ('Maak Só'). She expresses scepticism about the ability of writers, regardless of form, to act in the public interest. 'It is, and remains,' she writes, 'a difficult task to be a so-called writer in this violent and unsafe country, and I would in any case prefer to call myself an investigator and an experimenter.' Tellingly, she observes: 'One must be aware that if you experiment and want to publish your experiments, there is always the possibility that you will be attacked from both the right and the left.' Van Niekerk is unequivocal in acknowledging the social limits experienced by the (white, female) writer: 'Further, I am painfully aware that, as a result of the physical danger in which everyone and everything in this country find themselves, writers and artists in general cannot investigate all the things that they might want to.' Drawing an analogy between the writer and an archerfish, in which the above-water 'target' is 'the dominant power and the relationship between the dominant power and global financial capitalism', Van Niekerk continues:

> Increasingly I think that the lazy fascism of the governing regime is succeeding, without bureaucratic and systemic refinement, but simply via a policy of laissez-faire, in achieving the same result as bureaucratized Apartheid-fascism did with its outspoken, racially fascist laws: an oppressed, apathetic, scared, bullied public who are rendered helpless by social immobility, economic inequality, and poor, irrelevant education, and who are allowed by undisciplined and aggressive policing and ineffectual law enforcement to murder, rape, rob and intimidate each other, both physically and emotionally. All of this while a kleptocratic regime enriches itself recklessly and without any sense of shame whatsoever. (My translation, n.p.)

Van Niekerk ends with the words 'perhaps it is all a little too much' ('*miskien is dit alles te swaar*'), suggesting a deep sense of anomie with the whole project of writing in South Africa. It is as if she is signalling that, without giving up on her lifelong struggle to expose the sins and shortcomings of successive regimes, she nevertheless feels that the odds have become almost unbearably loaded against 'so-called writers', particularly when confronted by an '*afgeknoude*' ('bullied' and therefore worn-down) general public; this means that not only is there indifference from above, but that much the same applies among the citizenry. No one seems to care any longer, or not enough people care to make a difference, beyond being robotic consumers in a system of global capitalism, and all of this while the governing kleptocrats get away with murder, or laugh all the way to the bank, depending on one's metaphor, on a daily basis. For all the likelihood that it may fall on deaf ears, Van Niekerk's carefully timed public statement nevertheless alters the terms of any literary argument in South Africa: from a debate about modes of writing in postapartheid to the usefulness of writing at all, as if prevailing social-order issues result in writing itself becoming (almost) redundant.

Breaking the stalemate: Genre blends and fabulation

Lauren Beukes and Henrietta Rose-Innes have, in the conditions alluded to above, opted for fabulations suggestive of a *beyond*, an alternative to the apparent stalemate the fictional imagination is faced with in having to process the daily data of degeneration, decay and death. Indeed, both Beukes's *Zoo City* and Rose-Innes's *Nineveh* put into play their protagonists' predicaments of contingency, risk and insecurity – their unhomeliness – in fictional amplifications that are noteworthy also for a degree of exuberance. (This is true also of Coovadia, whom I discuss later in this chapter.) In so doing, to some extent at least, they respond to the implicit dilemma posed in Mda's *Ways of Dying* – pathology and death on the one hand, creative reinvigoration on the other – by *combining* instead of placing these options in opposition to each other. The binary is turned to generative amplification, and the ebullience of fictional expression in the work of both Beukes and Rose-Innes gives expression to states of *intensified instability* that are portrayed as 'realistic' givens. This is done in such a way that the female heroes in both cases evince a deep unease that runs parallel with an insuppressible, creative chutzpah. The novels bring into relief a newfound sense of social and generational deracination among born-frees who came of age in post-2000 South Africa: both Katya Grubbs (*Nineveh*) and Zinzi December (*Zoo City*) are cut off from, or in a state of deadlock with, their parents, and live in crumbling urban edifices beyond the putatively safe enclosures conventionally offered by family. Both are literally unhomed at the conclusion of their respective stories, although this state is a mere continuation, if an intensification, of their initial positions. The conditions of their lives underscore generational drift and uprooting amid scenes of social decay that are amped up to a degree that borders on the carnivalesque. Both Katya and Zinzi, at the beginning of their stories, have a place to live: for Zinzi it is a ransacked, dilapidated building in Hillbrow called 'Elysium Heights', and for Katya a crumbling old Cape Town house with a gaping crack down its side, surrounded by homeless drifters and situated across the road from a park that is being dug up for 'redevelopment'. Both novels may be read as expressive of a desire to break out of and destabilise the local condition described by Van Niekerk as 'the relationship between the dominant power and global financial capitalism'. In the process, both protagonists are uprooted, both physically as well as generationally, and without much prospect of any change or improvement.

One of many digital commentaries describes Lauren Beukes's *Zoo City* as 'a noir detective pagan cyberpunk novel'.[31] *Zoo City* is, indeed, the novel that hatches Beukes's escape from the limitation of a mainly local readership, precisely because of the lure of speculative fiction (SF) elements blended with laconic, worldy noir, and hip-cool familiarity laced with cyberpunk style (future-oriented, high-tech, low-life). These accents give the book an immediate global reach. The tone is laid-back-manic, with comic touches, and the narration is racily descriptive in its rendering of a ruined Johannesburg within a global scene in which over-the-edge urban life is fairly common. Here, then, is a *District 9*-variant of Johannesburg, a Hillbrow ('Zoo City') of 'animalled'[32] people living grungy make-do lives on the ragged edges of law and lawlessness. *Zoo City*, like *Nineveh*, is a book that shakes up the realistic elements it convincingly presents; it is a fabulated remix that transports the reader into an altered register of speculation, a 'what if' that posits defamiliarised, fresh nuances of being in post-apartheid city spaces. Building on the work of Mpe, Duiker, Moele, Mhlongo and others, Beukes and Rose-Innes succeed in providing upbeat accents of response, and responsiveness, despite a pervasive condition of unhoming. Narrated in the voice of the zany Zinzi, the tone of *Zoo City* is almost flippantly acquiescent. This is a protagonist that is is way beyond bemoaning her lot. Beukes's characters make of what might otherwise be seen as terminal conditions an urban adult playground, a terrain they master with savoir faire while dealing with the detritus, the dirty warrens and the sheer ruin of late modernity. This depiction is spiced with Johannesburg particularities such as *amaShangaan* bags in a city that is 'all about the cheap knock-off', as Zinzi says (7). Explicit SF/fantasy inventions blended with this kind of baseline realism achieve a special appeal as dystopian life is piquantly characterised by suggestions of *muti* (and similar local details) in what was once the 'Golden City'. Ironically, Egoli in the province of Gauteng, the place of gold, is a city both unexceptional (just another

post-industrial crime-ridden city) and otherworldly, or exotic, by virtue of a certain postcolonial grit. Writing in the *Guardian*, Gwyneth
Jones comments that 'this is the other face of cyberpunk, a face
we've seen too little of in the past decade … an information-drenched
world that has become haunted' ('*Zoo City* Review'). According to
an (anonymous) digital commentator, 'the realism of Johannesburg
seemed nearly as exotic as the fantastic elements', in a novel that has
the 'edgy cool of cyberpunk'. Significantly, *Zoo City* joins the growing
ranks of 'postcolonial science fiction' as a consequence of its 'local'
detail despite its worldly locale, 'privileging … a perspective from the
inner-city margins of post-apartheid society' (Dickson 67).

Zoo City thus succeeds in relativising, within a global cyberpunk
stylistic matrix, a postapartheid public zone that shows advanced
sociopolitical and economic derailment; the novel succeeds in doing
this despite a marked sense of over-emplotment, in the course of
which the action almost spins out of control, especially towards the
book's conclusion. Details of the greasy Johannesburg so realistically
depicted in *Zoo City* are blended with fantastic elements, specifically
animal familiars.[33] Here is an example of the book's first-person narration, in the voice of protagonist Zinzi:

> I pause to buy a nutritious breakfast, aka a *skyf* from a Zimbabwean
> vendor rigging up the scaffolding of a pavement stall. While he
> lays out his crate of suckers and snacks and single smokes, his
> wife unpacks a trove of cheap clothing and disposable electron-
> ics from two large *amaShangaan*, the red-and-blue-checked bags
> that are ubiquitous round here. It's like they hand them out with
> the application for refugee status. Here's your temporary ID,
> here's your asylum papers, and here, don't forget your compli-
> mentary crappy woven plastic suitcase. (6–7)

A *skyf* – a loose cigarette – serving as a 'nutritious breakfast' is of
course indicative of the couldn't-care-less lifestyle of one who is
already marked, or 'animalled' (*Zoo City* 8 ff.). Zinzi carries a sloth
on her back, her animal familiar marking her out as a criminal outcast.
She and others like her are lower than 'untouchable' (86) in Joburg's
post-postapartheid social hierarchy, now less race-obsessed and more
concerned with class. Zinzi, who spent time in jail for alleged involvement in the murder of her sibling Thando, is perceived as a 'psychotic

junkie zoo bitch who killed her brother' (284). Nevertheless, Zinzi has a devil-may-care attitude, despite her outsider status, and a life that is worlds removed from the middle-class existence that many still enjoy.

Zinzi is involved in email scams, so her position is hardly innocent, although she eventually abandons the activity in a plot that is a heady brew of detection and escape. Zinzi wearily works away at her job of promoting the email scams as a means of paying off her debts to an old dealer, whose drugs she had once recklessly indulged in. However, in exploiting her talent for finding things (a gift that comes along with her sloth familiar and her 'animalled' state), Zinzi takes on a missing-persons case – thereby incurring further obligations. She is soon in over her head with manipulative operators who are proficient in witchcraft, Afripop and extortion. Finding her way out of this mess results in Zinzi being caught up in sophisticated criminal syndicates from which she only just manages to extricate herself. Zinzi's position at the end of the novel is tenuous at best, with the police coming after her as she drives off into an indeterminate unhomed future, with little more than a bag of counterfeit notes to rely on.

Beukes, then, resorts to a dense weave of plotting within a stylish mash-up of subgenres, thereby carving out a space for writing that speaks to transnational audiences in a reconfigured range of fictional accents. *Zoo City* does this in a way that is reminiscent of the film *District 9*, but Beukes echoes the pastiche-play of music group *Die Antwoord*, who blend (g)local detail and social commentary in an energetic, effervescent (even egregious) cultural mishmash, or mash-up. Critics find themselves grasping for terms that are adequate to Beukes's unique collocation of style and voice in *Zoo City*: 'There are elements of noir, urban fantasy, psychological thriller, not to mention a bit of not-so-thinly veiled social commentary,' comments Justin Landon, who eventually settles for 'urban noir magical realism' (n.p.).[34]

Whatever terms are employed in relation to *Zoo City*, from the point of view of postapartheid writing they inevitably amount to a reconfiguration of form and content that provides *a way out*: an escape from generally underplotted (and perhaps dreary, mostly depressing) literary realism that defers in sombre tones to a problematically occulted 'out there'. *Zoo City* is also a way out of the relatively small, somewhat provincial space of 'SA Lit', given the shrinking intellectual attention from South African literary academics inside the country's handful of universities, and the fact that the country's literature is increasingly folded into 'world literature' paradigms or other conceptualisations of postnational literary networks.[35] Beukes has forged global connections, turning to US-based horror stories as a way of speaking to larger, more diverse audiences and, in the process, freeing herself to write in a different key. The overall effect may be one of loss, however, in terms of engagement or immediate relevance.[36] Beukes has broken loose from what some perceive as an uncomfortable and perhaps claustrophobic confinement within the walls – both historical and sociopolitical – of 'writing South Africa'.[37] This move is of course concomitant with increased connectedness in a globalised world where the significance of space or place or indeed displacement has taken on revised nuances. Beukes speaks from the point of view of a generation that is both impatient with – and exhausted by – the severities of politico-ethical engagement, or postmodern circularities. While the appropriation of genre conventions is a pathway to global markets (crime, horror, cyberpunk, chick-lit, sci-fi), it also marks the transnational mash-ups so characteristic of similarly densely plotted strains of postapartheid writing.[38]

Zoo City and Henrietta-Rose Innes's *Nineveh* share a sense of anxiety, as Shane Graham contends: 'Perhaps the most apt single word to characterize the mood and attitude of South African culture in the twenty-first century is "anxious"' ('Entropy of Built Things' 64). In suggesting that this anxiety centres on underground irruptions, Graham identifies 'two particular clusters of post-millennial anxiety found in urban South Africa' (64): the first is 'a dread of invasion, contamination, infestation', while the other amounts to 'encroachments of the new, alien, and other' (64). The motifs of subterranean caves and excavations, which Graham reads as fear of invasion and contamination, are also what link *Nineveh* and *Zoo City*. Whereas Zinzi in *Zoo City* reconnoitres underground drains and other subterranean channels for loot, Katya Grubbs in *Nineveh* mines underground channels and dark crevices for unwanted 'pests'.

In Rose-Innes's *Nineveh,* the protagonist is a pest-control expert called Katya who is hired to clean up an infestation of insects at a brand-new Cape Town housing development. Called 'Nineveh', it is located on wetlands that lie on the eastern side of the peninsula. Crucially, Katya chooses not to kill these 'pests', but rather to remove them humanely. The infestation consists of curious beetle-like creatures which multiply uncannily when it rains. This invasion causes the pristine real-estate project to run aground, pitting 'development capital' against the forces of an insect world that burrows up from below and infects the supposedly clean entrepreneurial money invested in an otherwise buoyant Cape Town property market. Katya eventually discovers that it is in fact her violent, renegade father – to whom she has not spoken for seven years – who is responsible for the Nineveh mess that she is contracted to clean up. A pest-extermination operator of an earlier generation, Len Grubbs scorns his daughter's frequently ineffectual methods of 'humane' bug-clearance, and her rather dubious attempts at ethical practice and harmonious co-existence with the natural world. Katya herself is presented as far from perfect, and does in fact take short cuts when she's tired, turfing out bugs next to the road, and using one of her father's dirty tricks: re-implanting bugs she has just removed from a property, so ensuring follow-up business. Len's own approach to pest clearance is firmly based on 'man versus nature', or tooth-and-claw tactics; he is 'a lifelong vermin man, an exterminator' (20). This is an aspect, also, of his racial supremacism – the ideology that underpins much of the imperial-colonial project in Africa, and one which Katya's generation is trying to slough off. Unbeknownst to Katya, her father was initially given the pest-removal job at Nineveh, but he cheated to the point that he got himself fired. As the Nineveh capitalist-kingpin Martin Brand tells her, '[Y]our dad ripped me off quite spectacularly, you know that? Len Grubbs. Took my money, fucked around, fucked off' (17). Len has a similar perspective on the man he calls 'that cunt Brand', who was 'quibbling about payment from the get-go. Stiffed me in the end. So I thought, stuff him. When the job ended I made sure I left a calling card or two. Took certain precautions' (103). Katya finds herself drawn unwittingly into her father's revenge against the developer and his brand of capitalism as Len re-infests Nineveh with pestiferous insects, opening an underground channel for them to infiltrate the site. He also uses this channel to pilfer building materials, copper wire and the like, selling them to street traders for further on-selling in an expanding informal economy that (also) operates outside of the law and on the margins of venture capital. As Graham puts it:

> Rose-Innes' Cape Town dramatizes what Martin Murray [in *City of Extremes*] says about the postmodern city where the 'powerful role

of the private real estate industry in promoting the marketability of landed property as a malleable commodity creates fertile ground for a kind of fugitive city building that stresses impermanence over stability, provisionality over endurance, and creative destruction over historical preservation'... Or more precisely, *Nineveh* shows us the psychological effects of this constant state of impermanence and flux on city dwellers. ('Entropy of Built Things' 68)

Such 'psychological effects' include a sense of deracination – a kind of internal exile which is at once political, cultural and economic – that is keenly felt by South Africans born around the turn of the twenty-first century, the so-called millennials. Graham goes on to argue: 'Insofar, then, as Rose-Innes' novel reflects contemporary anxieties over the encroachments of global capitalism and its technologies of surveillance and control, it also reveals to us the blind spots and interstices that inevitably disrupt those technologies in an unsustainable and entropic world system' (71). Despite the stylistic buoyancy that characterises *Nineveh* (and, indeed, *Zoo City*), the processes mentioned by Graham come at quite a cost for a character like Katya, who (like Zinzi at the end of *Zoo City*) finds herself adrift in an unstable city:

The further [Katya] drives, the better she feels. She likes to put distance between herself and her father. It's necessary, she thinks, to both of them. She is like a ball of string unravelling, always connected, but lighter the further she goes. She turns left and right down familiar streets; up over Main Road, past the hospital and onto the highway. She drives, she drives. There is no rush now, no particular place to go. No permanent address. Katya's sleeping in the van these days. Nights are warm. This might seem dangerous in a place like Cape Town, but actually it's surprisingly easy. In the back of the van, nobody can see her; she parks in quiet suburban side streets. The van has bars, after all, and can be locked from the inside. And who's going to hijack a van with cockroaches painted on it?... She cleans herself in shopping-centre bathrooms. It isn't the easiest way to live, but it's also not impossible. (*Nineveh* 205)

Not only does this achieved state of rootlessness echo the conditions in the closing pages of *Zoo City*, it is also remarkably similar to the outcome of Eben Venter's *Wolf, Wolf*, in which protagonist Matt Duiker also ends up sleeping in a car (on the Rondebosch Common) after being disinherited by his recently departed (and agonistically loved-hated) father. All three novels – which are definitively post-postapartheid – present conditions in which the compelling issue is the disorientingly fluid, insecure state of contingency that immerses citizens of post-2000 South Africa, one that offers scant anchorage within a rampantly self-serving society. Here, the masses that exist below the poverty line are routinely condemned to criminal status, regardless of race. Beukes's protagonist is a black woman, Venter's is a gay Afrikaner scion who has been disinherited from the wealth (but not exonerated from the sins) of the fathers, and Rose-Innes's is a rootless white woman who similarly rebels against – and is tainted by – the law of the father (whose wrongs she attempts to redress). Still, all three novelists succeed in crafting resourceful characters, survivors of a new sort, and lively fictional fabulations within realistic frames: Beukes in morphing a recognisably ordinary post-postapartheid scene into a zany dystopia; Rose-Innes by creating a fable-like, friskily exaggerated yet lovingly drawn-out story of the dismantling of a bricks-and-mortar project by the concerted action of insects, a parable of the weak undermining the strong; and Venter by creating a queer counter-consciousness infused with sexual-cultural 'difference' that scandalises Afrikaner norms of the past, but offers no new homecoming except to live on the edge. This, of course, is the key issue in all three works: what might once have been 'home' has been superseded by conditions spawned by neoliberalism and aggressive capitalism – including patronage capitalism – in which entirely new forms of (driftless) agility are required for the individual to survive.

Measuring the odds

It is with a touch of whimsy that Imraan Coovadia assesses the post-apartheid situation in his 2014 novel *Tales of the Metric System*. This is a telling novel, and one that smartly combines the inventiveness of fiction with the solidity of documented South African history over the past 50 years or so – from the introduction of the metric system in the early 1970s to the 2010 World Soccer Cup. Coovadia introduces a deceptively disordered array of characters in successive historical frames, which are presented with a keen sense of factual accuracy.

The historical vignettes, or episodes, are vertically mined for details of time and place, but their horizontal spread is especially significant: 1970 – Neil Hunter (a version of assassinated anti-apartheid activist Rick Turner) and his wife endure the smug conservatism of a white, English-speaking boarding-school master in Durban; 1973 – a young black man has his pass stolen in a Durban hostel, an event that introduces the novel's observation of theft as a standard behaviour in South Africa among all classes and periods; 1979 – South Africanised descendants of indentured labourers from India claw their way up the social ladder in Phoenix township, Durban; 1985 – anti-apartheid exiles gather at the Soviet embassy in London; 1990 – an innocent youth is 'necklaced' in an act of 'people's justice' by a mob in Tembisa; 1995 – the now-affluent, politically connected Phoenix crowd attend the World Rugby Cup, displaying garish nouveau-riche tendencies; 1999 – Peter Polk, a version of playwright Athol Fugard, reproduces TRC testimony in a film; 2003 – a character called 'Sparks', based on the late presidential spokesman Parks Mankahlana, dies of AIDS in the thick of President Mbeki's genocidal denialism fiasco; 2010 – a third generation of oddly hopeful though still criminally enmeshed characters watch the opening game of the 2010 World Soccer Cup; and then, recalling the murder of Hunter, the plot doubles back to 1976, the date with which the novel closes.

The motif of common theft that binds disparate characters and timeframes in *Tales of the Metric System* suggests that kleptocracy has been the dominant phenomenon from apartheid right through to postapartheid and the post-post period, too. In the world of Coovadia's novel, it is the ultimate measure of things, making a mockery, throughout, of publicly professed sociopolitical idealism. However, Coovadia manages to import a certain whimsy into the personal lives of the younger generation of characters: Sherman, who operates a racket in which people's cellphones are stolen on the streets of Cape Town and then sold back to them, is drawn into a relationship with Shanti, who happens to be one of his casual, everyday victims. (She is also the niece of Uncle Ashok, who is modelled on convicted postapartheid fraudster Schabir Shaik.[39]) The somewhat unlikely relationship seems to flower despite, and in the midst of, the country's merry materialism, its casual culture of theft and shady dealings. It is as if Coovadia is suggesting that the younger generation has shrugged off the burden of the past, whose measures and reckonings have so ignominiously suffered defeat. This accounts to some extent for the juxtaposition at the novel's conclusion of the youngest and the oldest of the generations featured in the story, with the latter failing to realise its exalted vision of a just and better life, and the younger characters managing to rescue some sense of makeshift love – or of joy, at the very least – despite the country's many earlier failures in 'measuring up'. Coovadia's play on the ideas of measures and measuring up deserves some attention.

In the penultimate section of *Metric System*, we learn that smart, almost-15-year-old Shanti is an aspirant author who has declared her intentions to write her 'memoirs'. However, her phone is pickpocketed on Greenmarket Square in downtown Cape Town on the morning of South Africa's big day in 2010, when Bafana Bafana (the national soccer team) will play the opening game of the Soccer World Cup against Mexico at Soccer City, Soweto. Following the loss of her phone, Shanti's companion Joris tries phoning her number and discovers that the (surprisingly friendly) thief is happy to sell the phone back to her. They are invited to come to a building called Molteno Mansions, where they can pay a 'finder's fee' of R200 to secure the deal. Once there, they encounter Sherman, the good-looking city slicker with a gold earring who had earlier relieved Shanti of her phone. Shanti finds him attractive despite knowing that he had stolen from her. The social environment of the unkempt flat in Molteno Mansions is oddly jaunty and casual, as if thieving is nothing out of the ordinary. So much so, in fact, that they all decide to have a party and bring out some Castle beers.[40] Later, together with Joris, Shanti returns home to her parents' opulent house in Bishopscourt, where a party to celebrate the World Cup is being held. She looks around her fancy home, which is playing host to, among others, her decidedly dubious Uncle Ashok:

> Shanti was dissatisfied. She looked around at the women in nice outfits and necklaces and rhinestone belts. There was black meat piled on platters on the long table in the dining room, candles on rubber boats in the swimming pool. Suddenly it revolted her taste. She wanted to buy nothing in her life, to become vegetarian and subsist on salads, to go out of the security gate, find the unfriendly poor, and let them pick the skin off her bones. She wanted to cross over to the other side, the side of Joris and

> Sherman, the side of Yolanda who cleaned their house and of
> Amrita who could do no harm. From this other side she would
> see the obvious wrongness of life inside the gate, jeer back at it,
> and be awakened into some new consciousness. Money, like life,
> like oxygen, corrupted you. It didn't know what counted. (359)

Shanti here voices a key sense that, amid all the competing measures
of what constitutes the social good, from the 1970s through to 2010,
it is money – with all its morbid effects – that is the master metric,
and which has governed motivation, despite its being the measure
that 'didn't know what counted' (359). Having voiced what amounts
perhaps to the thematic punchline in Coovadia's novel, Shanti goes
on to do something that seems completely counter-intuitive: she
phones the thief who had stolen from her and invites him over to her
parents' nouveau-riche mansion in Bishopscourt. Remarkably, and
yet perhaps also predictably, once arrived and installed as a guest,
Sherman pickpockets her Uncle Logan's phone while enjoying the
family's Cuban-cigar hospitality. Sherman is of course a small-time
crook when measured against the likes of Uncle Ashok. When Shanti
hears from her Uncle Logan that his phone has gone missing, she
knows what to do. She pulls Sherman aside and takes him up to her
room, where the following exchange occurs:

> 'I meant, did you take my Uncle Logan's telephone?'
>   'Yes, I did, chicken. But only to prove that I had the talent. It's
> waiting for him downstairs on the kitchen table.'
>   'Am I going to find out that you took anything else?'
>   'Nothing except your heart. Or do I have that already?' (364)

Here, theft undergoes a transformation from a sinister activity – as
portrayed in the stories of Mr Shabangu, a kleptomaniac who himself
witnesses a community necklacing for the crime of stealing – to a form
of 'talent', including stealing a heart, securing affections and, with
that, the palace the princess lives in. Sherman's generation appears to
have adopted casual theft as a means to 'get even'. At one stage during
their earlier party at Molteno Mansions, he had said to Shanti: 'In the
end everybody makes money except ordinary people like me and you.
We must also have the chance to make money. We also have the right
to have our fun' (347). And how else to make money but to do what

the country's leaders and leading citizens are perceived to be doing – take it, steal it, finagle it, any way you can.

It is as if Coovadia is here registering that, despite the prevailing practice of plunder, which has gained broad acceptance among an otherwise disparate citizenry, the newer generation will come up with more creative forms of engagement, even if it must be via such an unfortunate thing as theft. In such a grossly unequal society where leaders, not to mention leading citizens, engage in and defend various forms of thievery, who is to say that people on the street should not find a certain joy in aping such behaviour, modifying it and scaling it down, or up, depending on opportunity and talent – including that of seduction?

★ ★ ★

Negotiating boundaries of variously forbidding kinds has long been the motor force behind writing in South Africa. As I have argued elsewhere ('South Africa in the Global Imaginary'), the poetics of the 'seam' remains suggestive, not only for the way it conceives of writing that stitches together asymmetrical ethnicities, traditions and voices, but also for a sense of the cross-modality that continues to characterise the region's writing. This chapter has sought to demonstrate that 'fiction' and 'reality' (or truth) converge and collide in multiple ways, confounding any separation between the domain of literary fiction and that of 'harder' forms of nonfiction. It seems undeniable that postapartheid conditions seem increasingly to favour a receptive space that is more concerned with *the facts*, with unadorned 'reality' than 'fiction', preferring nonfictional, new-media-related forms that emphasise and amplify affect and bring the materialities of surface into greater prominence. And yet, as Vladislavić's *Double Negative* so clearly demonstrates, along with the works, discussed above, of Beukes, Rose-Innes, Venter and Coovadia, literary fiction will continue to assert its panharmonicon capacity to 'play' other forms.

It is worth recalling, too, that some of the country's greatest works have been amalgams – that is, cross-modal blends – of 'fiction' and 'reality'. Two epic postapartheid examples are Nelson Mandela's *Long Walk to Freedom* and Charles van Onselen's *The Seed is Mine*. Both works are stories about the life and times of a single character – the one styled as autobiography and the other as biography – and while both speak through the registers of the real, or the factually documented, their structuring borrows heavily from the conventions of fiction. Indeed, narrative reconstruction of the real cannot but make use of 'fictionality', which Richard Walsh argues is a 'a communicative strategy, and as such…is apparent on some scale within many nonfictional narratives, in forms ranging from something like an ironic aside, through various forms of conjecture or imaginative supplementation, to full-blown counterfactual narrative examples' (7). Conversely, Walsh adds, 'much fiction serves communicative functions, of both non-narrative (essayistic) and narrative (documentary) kinds, which do not exclusively belong to the rhetoric of fictionality' (7). While such cross-supplementation is common to all literatures, it is distinguishable in South African writing by the special urgency in writers' attempts to tell the right story, or to get the story right. Therein, indeed, lies the deep, exhilarating paradox of the literature as a whole, the continuum from apartheid to post-postapartheid. We will need to plot our way carefully, to make sure we get this story right.

Notes

1   Introduction

1   For a comprehensive essay that covers most of the areas of engagement in literature after 1994 in survey form, with excellent individual capsule analyses, see Rita Barnard, 'Rewriting the Nation'. On the 'open-endedness' of this literature, see Elleke Boehmer ('Endings and New Beginning' 51); on its 'inchoate and amorphous' nature, see Daniel Roux ('A Post-Apartheid Canon?' 43); see also Frenkel and MacKenzie, 'Conceptualising "Post-Transitional"', and Ken Barris, 'That Loose Canon'.

2   Tutu, former Anglican archbishop of Cape Town, is widely credited with inventing this term.

3   See De Kok and Press, *Spring is Rebellious*.

4   The title of a novel by Heinrich Troost.

5   The phrase 'dream deferred' is borrowed from Gevisser's *Thabo Mbeki: The Dream Deferred,* which in turn derives it from Mbeki's familiar invocation of Langston Hughes's expression 'a dream deferred' (Russell 23). Towards the end of Mbeki's presidency, Russell writes, one of Mbeki's aides reworked the expression into a text message, bemoaning what he (the aide) described as a 'corrupt and sycophantic culture in the ANC', with 'too many predators, brigands, incompetents and phoneys' jumping onto the ANC bandwagon. Russell claims that Ramaphosa rolled his eyes at this and said: 'It's not a dream deferred but betrayed.' This recalls former Congress of South African Trade Unions (Cosatu) secretary-general Zwelinzima Vavi stating in 2010: 'We're headed for a predator state where a powerful, corrupt and demagogic elite of political hyenas are increasingly using the state to get rich.' See Steenkamp. Much more has since been written – there is a veritable literature on the betrayal of the dream, the most recent of which is Justice Malala's *We Have Now Begun Our Descent.*

6   On the rapid escalation of such protests since 2004, see Peter Alexander, 'Rebellion of the Poor'. For an example of newspaper reporting on service protests, see Nashira Davids in *The Sowetan,* 'The Year that Anger Boils Over'. Njabulo Ndebele, writing in the wake of the Marikana massacre, describes grassroots movements that are '[d]isillusioned by a liberation movement from which they expected radical sympathy', and

asks: 'What led a movement of 100 years of struggle to misinterpret the actions of the poorest of its followers and turn them into enemies? Widespread "service delivery protests" may soon take on an organisational character that will start off as discrete formations and then coalesce into a full-blown movement. Such a movement, perhaps the source of new energy for civil society, will owe little to the ANC and the tripartite alliance' ('Liberation Betrayed by Bloodshed'). Ashwin Desai and Richard Pithouse, writing in a special issue of the *South Atlantic Quarterly* on the South African transition, comment: 'Although the black elite became rapidly richer and the white poor became rapidly poorer the stark fact is that in general terms whites got richer and blacks got poorer. The government's own statistics agency concludes that in real terms: average black "African" household income declined 19 percent from 1995 to 2000, while white household income was up 15 percent. Across the racial divides, the poorest half of all South Africans earn just 9.7 percent of national income, down 11.4 percent from 1995. People have been putting their bodies in harm's way and fighting revolutionary struggles to stay in the places where apartheid put them, to retain access to basic services like water and electricity, and to resist exclusion from education. Not even the most cynical anticipated that the millennial hopes that fueled the struggles against apartheid would be crushed like this' (843).

7   Mangcu, *To the Brink* (xiv and elsewhere). The term 'nativism' was popularised by Kwame Anthony Appiah in his book *In My Father's House*, in which he devotes a chapter to 'The Topologies of Nativism' (47–72). See also Chapter 2 of this volume, note 12.

8   On the effect of neoliberal capitalism on economic transformation, see Michael H. Allen, *Globalization, Negotiation*; Patrick Bond, 'Mandela Years'; Anthony O'Brien, *Against Normalization*; and various contributors to the special issue of *South Atlantic Quarterly*, 'After the Thrill is Gone: A Decade of Post-Apartheid South Africa' (ed. Grant Farred and Rita Barnard), discussed below, in the main text. On Thabo Mbeki's 'Native Club' politics, see Chapter 2 of this volume; on public corruption, see Feinstein, *After the Party*; on the 'phenomenology of crime', see Steinberg, 'Crime' (28). For an outsider's point of view on a 'Rainbow Nation that has long since lost its sparkle', see Alec Russell, *Bring Me My Machine Gun* (xx) (Russell is the former Johannesburg bureau chief of the *Financial Times*). See also *Recovering Democracy*, where veteran antiapartheid activist Raymond Suttner writes that he 'wrestle[s] with, and tries to capture, the sense that something is missing in the existence of many South Africans, something they thought was theirs, which is now under threat, slipping away or even no longer there. That "something" is democracy' (xv). Suttner adds that in writing the book he 'was very conscious of a feeling of distress, disempowerment, demoralisation, defeatism and disappointment, arising from a sense that the state of affairs prevailing in South Africa is not what many would like to see and that there is little that can be done to change this' (xvi).

9 O'Brien argues further that by 'neocolonial' (with its resultant 'normalization'), he is referring to 'the interest of foreign and local capital in pre-
serving the structural inequalities of South African racial capitalism that
oppress the everyday lives of black working people' (3–4). He continues:
'Arguably, even after giving full credit to the reforms under way in infant
mortality and other primary health care, electrification, the water supply,
housing, and land claims, these inequalities are being remedied in the
new regime in an ameliorative rather than a structural fashion and show
fewer signs of any sweeping structural remedy now that the acceptance
of neoclassical economic orthodoxy by the African National Congress
(ANC) in its macro-economic programme known as GEAR (Growth,
Employment and Redistribution) – under pressure from local and international capital – will continue to prevent it. The general outcome thus
remains the reproduction of a de facto racist status quo in urban and
rural South Africa, even as the white monopoly on state power and on
some sections of capital slowly gives way to a semblance of black stew-
ardship' (4).

10 Special issues on crime writing in South Africa include *Current Writing*
25.2 (2013), with articles by Sabine Binder, Priscilla Boshoff, Claudia
Drawe, Elizabeth Fletcher, Elizabeth le Roux, Jessica Murray, Sam
Naidu, Margie Orford, and Anneke Rautenbach. A special issue of *scru-
tiny2* (19.1 [2014]) contains articles by Jonathan Amid and Leon de
Kock, Colette Guldimann, Elizabeth le Roux and Samantha Buitendag,
Caitlin Martin and Sally-Ann Murray, Sam Naidu, and Antoinette
Pretorius. Jean and John Comaroff's book, under the title *The Truth about
Crime: Knowledge, Sovereignty, Social Order*, is due from the University of
Chicago Press.

11 I am grateful to Jean and John Comaroff, who used this term in a seminar
called 'Crime and Writing' at the Department of English at Stellenbosch
University in May 2011.

12 See Carrol Clarkson, *Drawing the Line*, on questions of transitional
justice.

13 The Comaroffs are worth quoting at some length on this point: 'Among
all the things that have been said about the spread of democracy since
the end of the Cold War…one thing stands out. It is the claim that
democratization has been accompanied, almost everywhere, by a sharp
rise in crime and violence…that the latter-day coming of more or less
elected, more or less representative political regimes – founded, more
or less, on the rule of law – has, ironically, brought with it a rising tide
of lawlessness. Or, put another way, that political liberation in postcolonial, posttotalitarian worlds, and the economic liberalization on which
it has floated, have both implied, as their dark underside, an ipso facto
deregulation of monopolies over the means of legitimate force, of moral
orders, of the protection of persons and property. And an unraveling of
the fabric of law and order. This may not be all that easy to demonstrate
empirically; it depends in large part on how democracy and criminality,
past and present, are measured. But, as popular perception and party

platforms across the planet focus ever more on escalating crime, and on the "problem" of dis/order, the co-incidence certainly seems to be beyond coincidence' (*Law and Disorder* 1–2).

14 See Comaroff and Comaroff, *Law and Disorder.*

15 See Bayart, Ellis and Hibou, *Criminalization.* On the difficulties of democratic 'consolidation' after the fall of authoritarian regimes in general, see Linz, *Breakdown*; Linz and Stepan, *Breakdown: Europe*; Linz and Stepan, *Breakdown: Latin America*; and Valenzuela, 'Democratic Consolidation'.

16 In Mamdani, *Citizen and Subject* 27–34.

17 Thomas Piketty launches the first chapter of his study on runaway world capitalism in the twenty-first century with a discussion of the Marikana killings in South Africa in 2012 following protests for higher wages at one of Lonmin's platinum mines. On Marikana, see Chapter 6 of this volume.

18 The Protection of State Information Bill, commonly known as the Secrecy Bill, is a contested piece of legislation that proposes to regulate the classification, 'protection' and dissemination of state information. Critics of all hues see the Bill as undermining access to information and the rights of journalists. The Bill was passed by parliament on 25 April 2013, after much public protest, but President Jacob Zuma declined to sign it into law, sending it back to the national assembly for reconsideration. However, as Philip de Wet writes in the *Mail & Guardian*, the withholding of information by the state continues to be a significant trend (See De Wet, 'Transparency Deferred').

19 In a comment on slipnet.co.za in 2011, Margie Orford wrote: 'I did not choose the genre because it was a genre. It just seemed to me that the only literary protagonists that could traverse South Africa's stratified society with any kind of plausibility were cops and journalists (pathologists too, but they are bound to their gurneys most of the time, so to speak). Also, the question facing South Africa – why is it so violent? – is so simple. It is the simple question that a good investigative journalist asks, that a good cop asks, that a good citizen should ask. The answers are complex though – much more complex than I ever imagined. And it is particularly that study of violence – intimate and public, economic and political – that is so fascinating. Crimes – of all sorts – are in many ways symptoms of an individual, a social, a political and an economic pathology. And a crime draws together people who would often never meet (apart, I imagine, from incest or domestic violence victims) in a non-criminal life' (see De Kock, 'Roger Smith'). Michael Titlestad, Deborah Posel and Achille Mbembe comment that '[c]rime may not be the whole story of South African life, but it is the story most often told' ('Crime and Punishment' 2).

20 For other examples of this preoccupation in political science, sociology and other disciplines, see Patrick Bond, 'From Racial to Class Apartheid'; Emmanuel Chukwudi Eze, 'Transition'; Adam Habib, *South Africa's Suspended Revolution*; Neil Lazarus, 'The South African Ideology';

Tom Lodge, *Politics in South Africa*; Zine Magubane, 'The Revolution Betrayed?'; and John Saul, 'Starting from Scratch?'.

21 These are the words of Francine Prose, who, writing in the *New York Times*, adds: 'Steve and Jabu [the novel's main characters, a biracial couple] know former comrades who, under the new regime, have become exactly the kind of people – greedy, venal, corrupt – they have always most despised' (n.p.).

22 For example, Kirsten Holst Petersen, introducing the edited collection *On Shifting Sands*, says in her opening line that '[i]t is not a revolutionary observation that South Africa is at a crossroads' ('An Altered Aesthetics' i).

23 See Clarkson, *Drawing the Line*, on Jacques Rancière's use of the term 'aesthetic act' to 'refer to any event, or speech, or encounter that makes it possible to reset social perceptions of what counts and what matters, especially in relation to questions of social justice and to questions of political and legal identity' (2), drawn from Rancière's work *The Politics of Aesthetics*.

24 On the concept of adequation in relation to South African crime fiction, see Amid and De Kock, 'The Crime Novel' 62–64.

25 See David Shields, *Reality Hunger*.

26 On the fate of 'SA Lit', see Chapman and Lenta.

27 See, for example, Audrey R Chapman and Hugo van der Merwe, *Truth and Reconciliation*; Adrian Guelke, *South Africa in Transition*; William Mervin Gumede, *Thabo Mbeki and the Battle for the Soul of the ANC*; Ulrike Kistner, *Post-Apartheid's Human Rights*; Katherine Elizabeth Mack, *From Apartheid to Democracy*; Rich Mkhondo, *Reporting South Africa*; Martin J Murray, *Revolution Deferred*; Katherine S Newman and Ariane De Lannoy, *After Freedom*; Deborah Posel and Graeme Simpson, *Commissioning the Past*; Philippe-Joseph Salazar, *An African Athens*; Robert Schrire, *Critical Choices*.

28 See John Kane-Berman's *South Africa's Silent Revolution*.

29 The subtitle of a documentary film by Michael Henry Wilson.

30 Nuttall and Michael comment on the deferral of the present in postapartheid, or what they express as 'the absence of the present' in much postapartheid expression (*Senses of Culture* 317).

31 The work of Katherine Boo, Truman Capote, Ta-Nehisi Coates, Joan Didion, Dave Eggers, Norman Mailer, Janet Malcolm, Studs Terkel and Binyavanga Wainana come readily to mind. See David Schmid, 'The Nonfiction Novel'.

32 See, for example, Darryl Accone (*All under Heaven*); Stephen Clingman (*Birthmark*); JM Coetzee (*Youth; Summertime*); Jacob Dlamini (*Native Nostalgia; Askari*); Mark Gevisser (*The Dream Deferred; Lost and Found in Johannesburg*); Sita Gandhi (*Sita – Memoirs of Sita Gandhi*); Peter Harris (*In a Different Time*); Fred Khumalo (*Touch My Blood*); Antjie Krog (*Country of My Skull; Begging to be Black*); Sindiwe Magona (*To My Children's Children; Mother to Mother*); Rian Malan (*My Traitor's Heart; Resident Alien*); Fatima Meer (*Prison Diary*); Phyllis Naidoo

(*Footprints in Grey Street*); Njabulo Ndebele (*Fine Lines from the Box*); McIntosh Polela (*My Father, My Monster*); Karel Schoeman (*Die Laaste Afrikaanse Boek*); Jonny Steinberg (*Midlands; The Number; Three-Letter Plague*); among others.

33 For David Attwell and Barbara Harlow, writing in a special issue of *Modern Fiction Studies* entitled 'South African Fiction after Apartheid' (published in 2000), the 'liberalism of the new order is more accommodating than a revolutionary culture could ever be, to the re-invention of tradition, to irony, to play' ('Introduction' 4). See also Barnard, 'Rewriting the Nation'; De Kock, 'Does South African Literature Still Exist?'; Frenkel and MacKenzie, 'Conceptualizing "Post-Transitional"'; Samuelson, 'Scripting Connections'; and Titlestad, 'Afterword' 189; among others.

34 See Grant Farred, 'The Not-Yet Counterpartisan'. Attwell and Harlow argue that the 'so-called "miracle" of the South African transition' finds its corollary in the 'continuing legacy and discomfort of compromise: the effort to rebuild a society whose underlying social relations and even attitudes remain substantially unchanged' (2). For them, 'apartheid's legacy remains evident in extensive poverty, educational deprivation, and a warped criminal justice system which, because it was developed as an instrument of political oppression, seems incapable of dealing with ordinary crime' (2). Like Sanders, Attwell and Harlow see ambiguity rather than achieved transformation as characteristic of the both the TRC and the transition, contending that 'ambiguity seems to be the distinguishing feature of a transitional South Africa' (3). South African literature since 1990, they argue, 'has taken upon itself the task of articulating this larger predicament' (3), and 'its fields are the experiential, ethical, and political ambiguities of transition' (3).

35 The transitional 'cusp time', as Elleke Boehmer formulates it (45), is fixed in both popular and intellectual discourse. Even in 2015, in a time that one imagines should be post-transition, or post-postapartheid (as Michael Chapman puts it), political commentary, both inside and outside the country, lay and professional, frequently invokes the promise – and disillusion – of the 'rainbow nation' as a standard trope. Al Jazeera, for example, reporting on xenophobic attacks in South Africa in April 2015, states: 'Since the end of apartheid, groups of South Africans have exacted xenophobic violence against other African nationals. Outsiders are typically shocked, since this behavior appears at odds with the country's marketing of itself as a "rainbow nation" and with the ruling African National Congress' long history of Pan-Africanism' (see Al Jazeera). A Reuters report on the same, among many similar instances, is headlined 'South Africa's "Rainbow Nation" Turns Dark as Immigrant Attacks Rise' (see Serino and Mapenzauswa). Philip de Wet, reporting in the Johannesburg-based *Mail & Guardian*, quotes a young migrant from Burundi as follows: 'People should not be happy about the fact that they are attacking us because South Africa talks about "the rainbow nation" and diverse cultures but right now they are not practising what they

teach us' (see De Wet, 'Zuma Straddles'). Finally, Desmond Tutu himself, commenting on the xenophobic attacks in various parts of South Africa in 2015, stated: 'Our rainbow nation that so filled the world with hope is being reduced to a grubby shadow of itself more likely to make the news for gross displays of callousness than for the glory that defined our transition to democracy under Nelson Mandela. The fabric of the nation is splitting at the seams' (see Cohen).

36 Including Rita Barnard, Patrick Bond, Ashwin Desai and Richard Pithouse, Emmanuel Chukwudi Eze, Shaun Irlam, Neil Lazarus, Michael MacDonald, Zine Magubane, and Adam Sitze.

37 See also Derek Hook (197 and elsewhere), who writes in psychosocial vein about 'multiple, split or juxtaposed temporalities' in postapartheid South Africa.

38 Titlestad ('Tales of White Unrest') expresses this idea in a discussion of David Medalie's volume of short stories *The Mistress's Dog*, where, in 'Crowd Control', Titlestad discovers the workings of what he terms a 'mezzanine ontology'.

39 I am cross-referencing here Malvern van Wyk Smith's concise history of South African literature before the transition to democracy, *Grounds of Contest*.

40 This is a comment made by Steinberg at Yale University in 2013 during a seminar following the award to him of a Windham-Campbell Prize (personal notes).

41 As Steinberg writes, '[t]here are some who say that Grey is Magubane, that the man they found conning and tricking in The Point, the one who started the 26s, is the one Nongoloza had sex with. Nobody says this version in front of a 26. A 26 who respects himself will kill you if you say it to his face. But people say it behind the 26s' backs' (*The Number* 233). See also Chapter 2, 'Nongoloza and Kilikijan' (62, especially), on iron-tight rules about who could sleep with whom, based on interpretations of the Nongoloza story; and Chapter 7, 'Crossing the Never-Never Line' (152), on how the dispute about whether homosexuality is sanctioned has never been resolved.

42 One must always be aware, of course, that the categories named as 'fiction' and 'nonfiction' are porous and codependent, the one term relying on the other for its meaning, and both containing elements of the other. The debate about the relative truth-telling valence of fictive and non-fictive forms goes back a long way, to Aristotle, who argued that poetry was more serious and philosophical than history. It will be obvious that supposedly true narratives can falsely use nonfiction forms – as in the case of James Frey's *A Million Little Pieces* – to communicate untruths or inaccuracies. On a deeper level, and this may well be true of Frey's book, a different kind of 'truth' may be operative in fictional narratives (see Walsh 36–37). See also Tom McCarthy's essay 'Writing Machines', in which he writes: 'There's been a lot of talk in recent years about reality in fiction, or reality versus fiction.... It's disheartening that such simplistic oppositions are still being put forward half a century after Foucault

examined the constructedness of all social contexts and knowledge categories; or, indeed, a century and a half after Nietzsche unmasked truth itself as no more than "a mobile army of metaphors, metonymies, anthropomorphisms…a sum of human relations…poetically and rhetorically intensified…illusions of which one has forgotten that they *are* illusions" (and that's not to mention Marx, Lyotard, Deleuze-Guattari, Derrida etc.)' (21). In full awareness of such interdependency, this book nonetheless recognises that writers of nonfiction, whether or not such work is styled as 'literary nonfiction', depend in their *moments of articulation* on a relation to their material that is primarily evidential in an actual and documented sense rather than in an imagined sense, including cases where the imagined (or reimagined) work is of a documentarily fictive nature. Such a relation to one's material has significant ethical consequences with regard to the status of truth claims, which are, of course, always relative.

43 See 'His Role in the Truth and Reconciliation Commission'.

44 See 'Truth in Translation'.

45 One should also note that a semi-religious discourse of redemption, as voiced by Archbishop Desmond Tutu as chair of the TRC, among other such instances, played into the redemptive thrust in general, as many writers have observed. See, for example, Audrey Chapman and Bernard Spong, *Religion & Reconciliation in South africa*; Megan Shore and Scott Kline, 'The Ambiguous Role of Religion'.

46 The TRC's notion of truth was, of course, never uncomplicated, as Shane Graham points out in *South African Literature after the Truth Commission*, with various understandings of truth being acknowledged in the TRC's final report: forensic or factual truth; personal and narrative truth; social truth; and healing and restorative truth. There is, as Graham suggests, an inevitable tension between factual truth and psychological or personal truth (*South African Literature* 29), and competing truth functions created difficult paradoxes and ambiguities, rendering the notion of a 'recovery' or 'excavation' of truth severely problematic.

47 Pre-1990s literature in South Africa was also densely populated with nonfiction, and a similar sense reflected the need to set down the actual, often spectacular, bizarre or unbelievable facts about what was going on at grassroots level, so to speak. Ndebele, in 'The Rediscovery of the Ordinary: Some New Writings in South Africa', quotes TT Moyana as saying that '[a]n additional difficulty for the creative artist in South Africa, especially the black writer, is that life itself is too fantastic to be outstripped by the creative imagination' (42). Many other writers have made similar statements about the 'unreality' of the 'real' in apartheid South Africa, and the corpus of memoir and autobiography is substantial in the years before the transition was ever even conceived, from Sol T Plaatjie to Es'kia Mphahlele to Emma Mashinini to Ellen Kuzwayo (see, for example, Judith Lütge Coullie, *The Closest of Strangers*; Lauretta Ngcobo, *Prodigal Daughters*). However, the post-transitional scene sees a new, urgent emphasis on a different kind of detection of the real: no

longer what was 'wrong' in and with apartheid, but how the postapartheid project itself is playing out, and whether the reality squares with the claims. A great deal is at stake in this question – in fact, the success of the entire project of the 'quiet revolution'. For a comprehensive survey of autobiographical works in the post-transitional period (that is, from about 2000 to 2010), see Annie Gagiano, 'South African Life Stories'.

48 See Leon de Kock, 'Ethics Knot Leaves Poetry at Sea'.

49 Garman adopts her 'field' theory from the work of Pierre Bourdieu.

50 One should not forget the rich tradition of memoir and autobiography in the 1950s and 1960s, including the works of Peter Abrahams, Herman Charles Bosman, Alfred Hutchinson, Noni Jabavu, Todd Matshikiza, Bloke Modisane, Es'kia Mphahlele and Richard Rive. The critical difference between apartheid and postapartheid autobiographical narratives is the intervening political settlement, which fundamentally altered the political perspective at the heart of remembering.

51 Such works include memoirs (see examples in note 32 above), including Albie Sachs's *The Soft Vengeance of a Freedom Fighter* and Gillian Slovo's *Every Secret Thing*; true crime stories (Antony Altbeker's *Fruit of a Poisoned Tree*, Mandy Wiener's *Killing Kebble*); fictionalised memoir (Diane Awerbuck's *Gardening at Night*, Dominique Botha's *False River*, Nadia Davids's *An Imperfect Blessing*, Finuala Dowling's *Homemaking for the Down-at-Heart*); political exposés/thrillers (Andrew Feinstein's *After the Party*, Peter Harris's *In a Different Time*); extended political story-essays based on individual experience (Jacob Dlamini's *Native Nostalgia*, Anton Harber's *Diepsloot*); biographies (Stephen Clingman's *Bram Fischer: Afrikaner Revolutionary*, JC Kannemeyer's *JM Coetzee: A Life in Writing*, Shaun Viljoen's *Richard Rive: A Partial Biography*); crime fiction infused with the data of actual incidents (Erica Emdon's *Jelly Dog Days*, Jacques Pauw's *Little Ice Cream Boy*); historical sagas narrativised for popular reading (the later works of Charles van Onselen and the historical nonfiction of Karel Schoeman, to name only two examples). See also Gagiano, 'South African Life Stories'.

52 *The Spear* was a painting exhibited at the Goodman Gallery in Johannesburg in 2012, which depicted the country's president, Jacob Zuma, in a 'heroic, revolutionary pose, with his penis hanging out', as *Time* magazine put it in a report on 23 May 2012 (see Perry). The painting sparked a major public row and the filing of court papers for defamation, as well as the vandalisation of the painting (see Wikipedia entry on *The Spear*). The process of reclaiming precolonial identities in her Miscast exhibition during the 1990s was complicated, artist-curator Pippa Skotnes argues in a *Poetics Today* article, by 'their depiction in museum exhibits and displays as "living fossils" alienated from history and culture' ("'Civilised off the Face of the Earth'" 299).

53 Major forerunners to these 'spoken word' poets include Mzwakhe Mbuli and Lesego Rampolokeng.

54 On 'creolization', see Nuttall and Michael 6–10.

2   From the subject of evil to the evil subject: Cultural difference in postapartheid South African crime fiction

1   For special-issue treatment, see *Current Writing* 25.2 (2013), which is devoted to crime fiction in South Africa, with articles by Sabine Binder, Priscilla Boshoff, Claudia Drawe, Elizabeth Fletcher, Elizabeth le Roux, Jessica Murray, Sam Naidu, Margie Orford, and Anneke Rautenbach. Another South African journal, *scrutiny2*, published a special issue on the same topic in 2014, with pieces by Jonathan Amid and Leon de Kock, Colette Guldimann, Elizabeth le Roux and Samantha Buitendach, Caitlin Martin and Sally-Ann Murray, Sam Naidu, and Antoinette Pretorius. Other articles include Anderson, 'Watching the Detectives'; Titlestad and Polatinsky, 'Turning to Crime'; and Warnes, 'Writing Crime'. For a book-length study on the larger southern African zone, see Primorac, *Whodunnit in Southern Africa*. For an idea of the kind of content on website debates, see De Kock, 'Roger Smith'.

2   See, for example, De Kock, 'Roger Smith', in which a range of academics weigh in on the matter in the comments section following the review of Roger Smith's crime thriller *Dust Devils* on the SLiPnet website. of the SLiPnet website following the review of Roger Smith's crime thriller *Dust Devils*. I first raised the issue of crime novels and sociopolitical content in 2010 in the South African *Sunday Independent* newspaper in a review of Mike Nicol's novel *Killer Country* (see 'Hits Keep Coming'), followed it up in 2011 in the Johannesburg-based *Mail & Guardian* weekly in a review of Nicol's *Black Heart* (see 'High Noon in the Badlands'), and again in 2013 in the *Cape Times*, in a review of Nicol's *Of Cops and Robbers* (see 'Hardboiled Noir'). The *Sunday Independent* used my comments on crime fiction as possibly the 'new political novel' as the basis for a series of opinions by, among others, Imraan Coovadia, Mbongeni Buthelezi and Kelwyn Sole (see Corrigall).

3   See De Kock, 'Off-colour'.

4   For Nicol's reported statements about his own crime writing, see De Kock, 'Roger Smith'.

5   For example, police procedural, noir, fallible detective, nonfiction 'inside stories' about the resurgent social monster called 'crime', social biographies of known public thugs, and still more.

6   Bhabha, *The Location of Culture*; Said, *Orientalism*; Spivak, *In Other Worlds*; Young, *Colonial Desire* and *White Mythologies*.

7   Attwell, *Rewriting Modernity*; Brown, *Voicing the Text*; Comaroff, Jean and John, *Of Revelation and Revolution*; De Kock, *Civilising Barbarians*; Hofmeyr, *'We Spend Our Years'*; Wylie, *Savage Delight*.

8   See Dietrich.

9   See Dubow.

10   See Tim Soutphommasane, *The Virtuous Citizen*, for an extended discussion of the classic concept of 'virtuous' citizenry, derived as it is from Graeco-Roman traditions, and taken up, inter alia, by Rousseau in his

idea of a social contract, and by Thomas Jefferson and John Adams. See also Hamilton.

11 See Ndlovu-Gatsheni, *Tracking*; Finlay.

12 Mangcu's public pronouncements on matters of race appear to have changed somewhat in the period between the publication of *To the Brink* (2008), when he wrote that '[e]ven though I have not always been a great supporter of non-racialism as a strategy for struggle, I never had any doubt that the ultimate aim of our struggle was the creation of a non-racial democracy' (122), and the time of my completing this book (2016), when public heat on the topic of race was turned up considerably. See, for example, Mangcu's opening essay in his edited volume *The Colour of Our Future* (2015), entitled 'What Moving beyond Race Can Actually Mean', in which he proposes that Albert Luthuli's use of the term 'nonracial democracy' (in Luthuli's vision of a 'multiracial society in a nonracial democracy') should be replaced by the term 'anti-racist democracy' (*Colour* 9–10). In the context of 2015 and the #RhodesMustFall movement's strongly race-accented 'decolonisation' thrust, 'anti-racist' carries a charge of black racial solidarity, not to mention impatience with 'whiteness' more generally as a projected aggregate of recalcitrant self-privileging in post-postapartheid (after 2010), a time of acute want among the poor and accelerated sociopolitical crisis. 'Anti-racist' in such a context is a long way from 'nonracial' and from *To the Brink*'s critique of 'racial nativism' (see *To the Brink* xiv, 5, 6 and 12 for further uses of this term) as evidenced, for Mangcu, in Thabo Mbeki's rule in the mid-2000s. Mangcu's call, in 2008, for the observance of 'irreducible plurality', as against an overprivileging of a single racial category, appears to have been overtaken by a far greater accentuation of black solidarity in a context of racial antagonism.

13 See Allen; Bond, *Elite Transition*.

14 For example, Mngxitama wrote as follows in the *Mail & Guardian* in 2013: 'In 1994, the ANC accepted political power in exchange for maintaining the apartheid economic status quo. This presented the challenge of how black people were going to enter the economy, and so white capital extended to the ANC government its tried-and-tested corruption – its unethical business model that took the shape of black economic empowerment. In short, just like their white counterparts, black people had to steal and exploit to enter the economy. Political connectivity is the key to riches. We have watched as people associated with the ruling party accumulate wealth at shocking speed – and all this without any dismantling of apartheid economic structures. They simply joined in' ('Our Corrupt Economy is Built on Theft' n.p.).

15 A shack-dwellers' movement to leverage better housing in South African cities. See 'Abahlali baseMjondolo'.

16 By 'classical liberalism' I mean the conventional understanding of this term as given, for example, by Richard Hudelson, when he writes that 'a commitment to the liberty of individual citizens' is central to 'classical liberalism of the nineteenth century' (37); its 'core commitments', writes

Hudelson, are '[f]reedom of religion, freedom of speech, freedom of the press, and freedom of assembly' (37). Classical liberalism also holds that 'the underlying conception of the proper role of just government [is] the protection of the liberties of individual citizens' (37). On the history of the term liberalism and its contested nature over time, see also Duncan Bell.

17 On neoliberalism, see Wendy Brown, *Undoing the Demos* and 'Neoliberalism'.
18 See Orford's comment in De Kock, 'Roger Smith'.
19 On forms of 'allegory' in this sense, see also Rita Barnard's discussion of the film version of Fugard's *Tsotsi* in 'Tsotsis'.
20 See, for example, 'EFF: The Nazi Debate'.
21 Of course, one need only mention the name Vusi Pikoli and similar examples to find real-world cases of such collateral damage.
22 See Altbeker, *Fruit of a Poisoned Tree*; Bloom, *Ways of Staying*; Chipkin, *Do South Africans Exist?*
23 Such writers include Andrew Brown, JM Coetzee, Imraan Coovadia, Finuala Dowling, Lisa Fugard, Damon Galgut, Nadine Gordimer, Michiel Heyns, Fred Khumalo, Mandla Langa, Sonja Loots, Angela Makholwa, Zakes Mda, Deon Meyer, Thando Mgqolozana, Niq Mhlongo, Kgebetli Moele, Sifiso Mzobe, Margie Orford, Sarah Penny, Henrietta Rose-Innes, Diale Tlholwe, Heinrich Troost, Etienne van Heerden, Marlene van Niekerk, Eben Venter, Ingrid Winterbach, Rachel Zadok, and still others.
24 See De Kock, 'South Africa in the Global Imaginary' 289, for a contextualisation of Rüsen's interjection.

3   Freedom on a frontier? The double bind of (white) postapartheid South African literature

1 My own description, in 'South Africa in the Global Imaginary' (273).
2 I have made similar arguments myself in 'Judging "New" South African Fiction in the Transnational Moment'; 'Does South African Literature Still Exist?'; and 'A History of Restlessness: And Now for the Rest'.
3 This argument, cast in a slightly different way, is also, made by David Medalie ('Uses of Nostalgia' 35–36). See, in addition, Michael Titlestad, writing about Medalie's collection of stories *The Mistress's Dog*, on the idea of what he styles, borrowing from a story by Medalie, 'mezzanine ontology' in postapartheid writing (briefly discussed in Chapter 1 of this volume). Titlestad ('Tales of White Unrest' 119–120) argues that 'post-transitional' is a 'compromised' term: 'Prior to the liberation of South Africa, writers were haunted by a sense of approaching catastrophe and inspired by the hope for liberation. We lived, the dominant literary ideology asserted, in what Antonio Gramsci called an "interregnum": the old was dying but the new could not be born. What remained for authors in the context of this crisis was to put their shoulders to the wheel of history. In a sense, this logic – of being subsumed by historical process

and necessity – continued through the first decade of democracy. For most authors, though, this teleological rumbling forward is no longer an option: many instead reflect lives caught in-between an old order that has – quite rightly, and to the relief of all right-thinking individuals – disappeared, and the uncertainties of the future.'

4   See also West-Pavlov 166–170 on 'plural temporalities' in postcolonial conditions, citing Dipesh Chakrabarty, Achille Mbembe and Edouard Glissant.

5   Of interest in this regard is the spate of novels in the postapartheid period that return to telling the country's history, or major events in this history, in ways that cater to a sense of the future-anterior or the will-have-been. I am thinking here, for example, of Willem Anker's *Buys*; Russel Brownlee's *Garden of the Plagues*; Nadia Davids's *An Imperfect Blessing;* Zakes Mda's *Heart of Redness*; Claire Robertson's *The Spiral House*; Dan Sleigh's *Eilande*; James Whyle's *The Book of War;* and Ingrid Winterbach's *To Hell with Cronjé*; among others.

6   Mark Seltzer, *True Crime* 11; see Chapter 6 of this volume.

7   See also Silber and Geffen, Leggett, and Burger. Mandla Lionel Isaacs, writing in the *Daily Maverick* (April 2015), cites figures from the UN Office of Drugs and Crime as rating South Africa the 11th most violent country in the world.

8   See Lucy Valerie Graham, *State of Peril.*

9   Kynoch cites Charles van Onselen's *New Nineveh*, Clive Glaser's *Bo-Tsotsi* and Don Pinnock's work on street gangs in Cape Town, *The Brotherhoods*, among others.

10 Citing South African Police Service statistics, Steinberg ('Crime' 27) illustrates white 'misreading' of crime by the following example: In the remote town of Lusikisiki in the Transkei, where the only white face one is likely to see is that of a doctor from *Médecins Sans Frontières*, 109 murders were reported in 2003, and 76 in 2004. By contrast, in the rich white suburb of Parkview in Johannesburg, two murders were reported in 2002, and one in 2003. None of these three victims was white.

11 According to Altbeker ('Puzzling Statistics' 2), only two countries, Colombia and Swaziland, had higher murder rates than South Africa circa 2005, when his article was published. Misha Glenny writes in *McMafia* that '[c]rime sucked the lifeblood from the new South Africa like a deadly leech, leaving it debilitated and wracked by fear and insecurity', adding that '[s]tories of murder, carjacking, extortion, rape, mugging, gang warfare, and more drugs littered the pages of the local and international press' (187).

12 See the sections headed 'Neo-Noir 2' in Chapter 5 of this volume, and 'Cities of the dead' in Chapter 7, where writers Angela Makholwa, Phaswane Mpe and K Sello Duiker respectively are discussed in relation to crime and corruption. See also my discussion of *Tales of the Metric System* by Imraan Coovadia in Chapter 7. Other works of relevance in this regard include *Bitter Fruit* by Achmat Dangor; *The Lost Colours of the Chameleon* by Mandla Langa; *Black Diamond* by Zakes Mda; *Dog Eat*

Dog, Way Back Home and *Affluenza* by Niq Mhlongo; and *Counting the Coffins* by Diale Tlholwe.

13 See also the edited collection *Should I Stay or Should I Go? To Live in or Leave South Africa* (Richman).

14 As evident, for example, in nonfiction works such as Steinberg's *Midlands*, *The Number* and *Three Letter Plague*, Ivan Vladislavić's *Portrait with Keys*, as well as fiction such as Deon Meyer's *Heart of the Hunter*, Coovadia's *High Low In-Between*, Phaswane Mpe's *Welcome to Our Hillbrow* and Mda's *Ways of Dying*.

15 *Ways of Staying* was written amid the xenophobic attacks that occurred in 2008, and it reports on the aftermath of these killings.

16 See De Kock, *Civilising Barbarians* 141–187.

17 See Agamben, *Homo Sacer*.

18 A related concept is the 'civil imaginary', on which see During, and De Kock, 'Sitting'.

19 Cornwell, in his introduction to the *Columbia Guide to South African Literature in English since 1945*, cites anthropologist Robert Thornton as suggesting that 'South Africa seems likely to remain in permanent transition, just as it once seemed to exist perpetually just ahead of apocalypse' (7).

20 See Deborah Posel, 'The People's Paper'.

21 Such as, for example, Jacques Pauw's *Little Ice Cream Boy* and Chris Marnewick's *Shepherds and Butchers*.

22 This is precisely what Bloom, Steinberg and Altbeker, among others, do. An interesting recent addition is Anemari Jansen's *Eugene de Kock: Assassin for the State*, following in the tracks of Pumla Gobodo-Madikizela's *A Human Being Died that Night: A South African Story of Forgiveness* in which Gobodo-Madikizela interweaves interviews she conducted with Eugene de Kock with stories from the Truth and Reconciliation Commission; to this she adds her own considered reflection as a psychologist about the nature of evil and forgiveness.

23 See Hayden White, *Tropics of Discourse*.

24 Ginzburg cites art historian Aby Warburg's famous line 'God is in the detail[s]' (22), generally thought to be the origin of the phrase 'the devil is in the detail' (96).

25 See, for example, Ndebele's *Fine Lines from the Box*.

26 The Inkatha Freedom Party was led by Chief Mangosuthu Buthelezi, a compromised political figure who participated in the National Party's 'Bantustan' political system of 'separate development', one of apartheid's major structural pillars. The Boipatong massacre on 17 June 1992, in which 45 people were slaughtered, was a major example of suspected 'third force' complicity. In this massacre, members of Inkatha living in KwaMadala Hostel attacked residents of the nearby Boipatong township on the southern outskirts of Johannesburg.

27 Implicitly borrowing the term 'long conversation' from Jean and John Comaroff's major work *Of Revelation and Revolution*, in two volumes.

28 Krog made these comments at an international poetry festival at the Spier wine estate outside Stellenbosch (dubbed 'Dancing in Other Words'; see De Kock, 'Ethics Knot', as reported verbatim from a transcription of the voice-recorded panel).

29 See De Kock, 'Ethics Knot'.

30 See Shields, *Reality Hunger.*

31 All the evidence, both anecdotal and published, suggests that nonfiction generally outsells fiction (see also note 3, Chapter 7), and that 'true crime' does better than crime fiction. This is reflected in the rising tide of 'true crime' in both English and Afrikaans literary culture. Steinberg, one of the most competent practitioners of creative nonfiction among postapartheid writers, won the Yale University Windham-Campbell Prize in 2013.

32 See Livingstone's *Missionary Travels and Researches in South Africa.* For a discussion of Livingstone's 'field science' in the context of missionary colonialism in South Africa, see De Kock, *Civilising Barbarians* 162–170.

33 Steinberg was a member of the National Union of South African Students (Nusas) and attended UDF meetings as a Nusas representative. Shireen Hassim writes as follows about the growth of internal resistance in the 1980s: 'During the course of the decade, the primary location of resistance shifted from exile to internal and localised forms of resistance to apartheid … In broad terms, democratic visions were understood as emerging from the grassroots, political organisations were 'people driven' as opposed to elite-driven, took localised forms and aimed at laying the basis for reconstruction of political order after apartheid' ('The Limits' 48). See also Adler and Steinberg, *From Comrades to Citizens.*

34 The post-transition period saw a high incidence of political murders in KwaZulu-Natal. See David Bruce, 'Political Killings'.

35 I have defined 'bad' difference elsewhere in this book as follows: racial and cultural difference, as affirmed by the South African Constitution, particularly in its clauses guaranteeing equality, suggests a symmetry whereby the component parts of a diverse society enjoy equal rights. This may be termed 'good difference'. On the other hand, however, conditions in South African society have, since 1994, produced what may be termed 'bad' or corrupt difference, which uses the legitimising politics of cultural difference (identity politics) to achieve asymmetrical gain, often at the expense of others. 'Bad' difference is, then, the abuse of political privilege in order to leverage preferment, often under the guise of egalitarian practice. One example of this is the South African arms deal, while another is President Jacob Zuma's relationship with the Gupta family, which enables privileges such as the use of a military airfield for private purposes. 'Bad' cultural difference in such cases enables corrupt collaborative practices in state as well as private-sector dealings characteristic of comprador societies.

36 This fits with the demise of the 'young lions', or the ANC Youth League and its loss of power and influence. See Simon Allison, 'Young Lions'.

37 The trope of apocalypse can be detected in any number of 'classic' South African works of literature, including JM Coetzee's *Life & Times of Michael K*; Nadine Gordimer's *July's People*; Alan Paton's *Cry, the Beloved Country*; Karel Schoeman's *Promised Land* (translation of *Na die Geliefde Land*) and Eben Venter's *Trencherman*; among others. See also Cornwell (in *The Columba Guide*), quoting anthropologist Robert Thornton on the link between transition and apocalypse.

4 The transitional calm before the postapartheid storm

1 Many, if not most, scholars in English departments in South Africa have dropped 'SA Lit' in favour of various cultural studies, transnationalisms, book histories, posthumanist preoccupations, ecocritical foci, among other agendas – see my article on this ('The "Confessio" of an Academic Ahab'). South African literature studies are arguably more robust in the current period in the UK, where several English departments maintain teaching agendas in the field.

2 Though often wrongly dated by critics as a 1995 publication, *Ways of Dying* was first published in 1991 by Oxford University Press Southern Africa before being taken up internationally in 1995 by Picador. This nuance of dating is more than just incidental, as the year 1991 places the book at the very early stages of transition, and locates its actual writing in what one might call the conceptual stage of transition making, when many were emboldened by ludic positions being taken in the literary-critical community.

3 See Oxford University Press Southern Africa, 'Zakes Mda: The Story behind *Ways of Dying*' – described on the video site partly as follows: 'Zakes Mda talks to Oxford University Press Southern Africa about his book *Ways of Dying*'.

4 See also Brink's phantasmagoric 1998 novel *Devil's Valley*, along with the critical endorsement of 'magical realism' in the work of Mda especially, but also in fiction by Brink, Mike Nicol and Ivan Vladislavić – see, in critical commentary, Derek Barker ('Escaping the Tyranny'); Gail Fincham (*Dance of Life*); Gerald Gaylard (*Marginal Spaces*); Paulina Grzeda ('Magical Realism'); Sten Moslund (*Making Use of History*); and Christopher Warnes ('Chronicles of Belief').

5 In the work of, for example, Coetzee, Gordimer, Mphahlele, Ndebele, Vladislavić, the 'Soweto Poets', Lesego Rampolokeng, and experimental black theatre in the 1980s – including *Sizwe Banzi is Dead*, *The Island*, *Woza Albert!*, *Asinamali* and *Sarafina* – among others. See also Attwell, *Rewriting Modernity*.

6 See, among others, Clough and Halley, *The Affective Turn: Theorizing the Social*; Rita Felski, 'Suspicious Minds'; Marguerite La Caze and Henry Martyn Lloyd, 'Editors' Introduction: Philosophy and the "Affective Turn"'; Brian Massumi, *Parables for the Virtual: Movement, Affect,*

Sensation; Eve Kosofksy Sedgwick, *Touching Feeling: Affect, Pedagogy, Performativity.*

7 See, in particular, the comprehensive critique by Ruth Leys, 'The Turn to Affect'.

8 This is Hannah Arendt's objection in *The Human Condition*, where she writes: 'Division of labor is based on the fact that two men can put their labor power together and "behave toward each other as though they were one." This one-ness is the exact opposite of co-operation, it indicates the unity of the species with regard to which every single member is the same and exchangeable' (123).

9 Such as, for example, Damon Galgut's *The Good Doctor*, Eben Venter's *Trencherman*, Duiker's *The Quiet Violence of Dreams* and Mhlongo's *Affluenza*, among others.

10 See De Kock and Pieterse, 'A Vast Domain of Death'.

11 According to Grzeda, the magical realist phase was given form in works by Brink (*Devil's Valley, The First Life of Adamastor, Imaginings of Sand*); Matlou (*Life at Home and Other Stories*); Mda (*She Plays with the Darkness*); Wilma Stockenström (*The Expedition to the Baobab Tree*); and Vladislavić (*Missing Persons* and *The Folly*); although I would add Anne Landsman's *The Devil's Chimney*, Van Heerden's *Ancestral Voices* and Chris van Wyk's *The Year of the Tapeworm*.

12 The withdrawal of 'big government' across the world is a political act, one that has widespread ramifications on individual lives – for example, austerity measures in the UK, affecting social benefits; shrinking education and arts funding in Australia; and the case of postapartheid South Africa, where a similar 'hands-off' and 'leave it to the market' approach has resulted in the devastating effects of underdevelopment (apartheid) remaining mostly in place for the majority of the poor. See Patrick Bond, 'From Racial to Class Apartheid'; Adam Habib, *South Africa's Suspended Revolution*; Neil Lazarus, 'The South African Ideology'; Tom Lodge, *Politics in South Africa*'; Zine Magubane, 'The Revolution Betrayed?'; and John Saul, 'Starting from Scratch?'. On neoliberal forms of governmentalisation, see Loïc Wacquant's *Punishing the Poor* and his 'Crafting the Neoliberal State'.

13 Jacob Zuma is reported as having said this in 2008. See, for example, Mthethwa.

5 Biopsies on the body of the 'new' South Africa

1 On neo-noir (in chronological terms, generally post-1990s, and in thematic terms, a more expansive and less restrictive version of classic noir), see Hirsch (4–22) and the various essays in Mark T Conrad's edited volume *The Philosophy of Neo-Noir*. See also De Kock, 'Off-colour'.

2 See De Kock and Graham, 'A Candy Castle Built on a Septic Tank'. In *Mixed Blood*, Smith's character Jack Burn states: 'I made a mistake bringing us here. This place [Cape Town] is like, hell, I dunno, a candy castle built on a septic tank' (99).

3   On the concept of adequation in relation to South African crime fiction, see Amid and De Kock (62–64).

4   Although I use the term 'emplotment' in *Civilising Barbarians* in the manner of Hayden White in his major work *Metahistory*, my use of the term in this book is closer to the sense of plot and emplotment theorised by Brooks in *Reading for the Plot*, namely as a vehicle of interpretative causality (see Brooks 27, 35, 48).

5   On the very day on which I first drafted this sentence, Raymond Suttner wrote as follows in the *Daily Maverick*:

> Let us look at who lies dead on the ground or dying from gunshot wounds or writhing from the impact of rubber bullets. Who are those who fill prisons, either as awaiting-trial or convicted prisoners? Who are the homeless or those living in ramshackle huts that easily catch fire or are flooded? Who walk through sewerage in the streets where they live? Who hide at the sight of police, even if they have committed no wrong? Who may be assaulted or killed, generally with impunity, by police? Are these citizens treated any differently from those who were victimised under Apartheid?
>
> Who are the protesters who are dispersed and forced to inhale tear gas, even if they are young children? Who are the children who die as a result of falling into pit toilets? Who are forced to drink polluted water? All of these form part of the same section of the population, the majority of the inhabitants of South Africa, black people, who were nationally oppressed under Apartheid. ('The Persistence of the Past in the Present' n.p.)

6   See also Rehana Rossouw's *What Will People Say?* as a fictional exposition of precisely such conditions, but written in a style of gritty realism.

7   Most notably, Piketty's *Capital*, which starts off with the case of the police massacre of miners in Marikana as a prime example of the consequences of disproportionate wealth gaps.

8   See Andrew Faull, 'Corruption in the South African Police Service'; 'Something Very Rotten'.

9   As depicted in the acclaimed postapartheid movie *Jerusalema*.

10 See De Kock, 'Off-colour'.

11 Kruger writes of Johannesburg in 1996 that as murder and violent crimes soared to rates four times that of the United States, 'edginess deepened into apocalyptic visions of a "long day's journey into Jo'burg night"' (*Imagining* 151). See also Breytenbach in 'Mandela's Smile' and Mbembe in 'Our Lust for Lost Segregation'.

12 The blurbs appear on the opening pages of the Pan Macmillan paperback and e-book versions of *Killing Kebble*, and in the interview at the end.

13 On the prevalence of the term 'miracle' in this regard, see Beall, Gelb and Hassim.

14 Mamdani is quoted by Roland Czada (2) as saying, in 1998: 'When I came to UCT [University of Cape Town] nearly two years ago, I was aware that the notion of South African exceptionalism had stained the South African intelligentsia with a prejudice that was more than just

skin-deep. What I was not prepared for was the ferocity with which it would be defended.' See also Mamdani 27–34.

15 Wiener writes that in December 2006 *Beeld* newspaper carried a story saying that Liberty Life had paid out about R10 million, while Discovery had paid out R20 million (*Killing Kebble* 467).

16 It is not clear why only black editors (seven in all, with one assistant editor) were present at the 'hugely controversial' briefing, which Wiener describes thus: 'In 2003, ex-prosecutions boss Bulelani Ngcuka "outed" Brett Kebble at a hugely controversial off-the-record briefing with black editors, held to update them on the progress of the investigation into allegations against Zuma' (*Killing Kebble* 124).

17 South African History Online gives the following summary of Zuma's involvement with Shaik and the court case relating thereto: 'During his tenure as Deputy President of South Africa, Zuma was also involved in controversies, which resulted in legal problems for Zuma. In 2002, Zuma was implicated in a major corruption scandal, in connection with the trial of his close associate Schabir Shaik. The state alleged that Zuma used his position in government to enrich himself by benefitting from Shaik and companies involved in the procuring of arms for the state. It was further alleged that he violated "The Code of Conduct in Regard to Financial Interests" to which all cabinet members are bound. In Shaik's court case, Judge Hilary Squires said that Shaik, Zuma and Alain Thetard – the local director of an arms company involved, Thomson (later Thint) – met in Durban and agreed that Zuma would receive R500 000 a year in return for protecting the arms company from any investigation regarding its role in the arms deal acquisition, which became a serious issue for the country. Bulelani Ngcuka, then National Director of Public Prosecutions, and Maduna, now Minister of Justice, announced at a media conference that the National Prosecuting Authority's (NPA) decision was not to prosecute Zuma for corruption; however, Shaik was to be charged for fraud and corruption. Ngcuka had said that although Zuma was clearly involved, the NPA did not have a winnable case against Zuma. Shaik at his trial said that the financial relationship between Zuma and himself were loans made in friendship and not as a result of corruption. He had realised that Zuma was experiencing severe financial difficulties. Nevertheless, on 2 June 2005, Shaik was convicted at the Durban High Court on two counts of corruption and one of fraud relating to bribes he allegedly paid to influence Zuma in order to win government contracts for Shaik's company, Nkobi Holdings. On 6 November 2006, the Supreme Court of Appeal (SCA) in Bloemfontein, Free State Province, upheld Shaik's fraud and corruption charges and he was set to begin his 15-year sentence at Durban's Westville Prison. The five SCA judges agreed with Judge Squires' findings that Shaik had made 238 payments to Zuma totalling R1.2 million and that it was not because of their friendship.' (See 'Jacob Gedleyihlekisa Zuma' n.p.)

6 Referred pain, wound culture and pathology in postapartheid writing

1 See Nicholas Carr, *The Shallows*, on reading practices in the age of digital content; on the rise of 'surface', see Stephen Best and Sharon Marcus.
2 As noted elsewhere in this book (see note 42, Chapter 1), the categories of fiction and nonfiction are porous and codependent, the one term relying on the other for its meaning. Still, the orientation towards what is nominally 'nonfiction', in contradistinction to what is seen as 'fiction', remains important for what one might call the nature of a writer's 'moment of articulation', as I argue in the note referred to above, since there are important ethical considerations at play in one's approach ('fictional/imaginative' or 'factual/evidential') to one's material, especially under contested conditions.
3 See Lauren Berlant, 'Properly Political', Michael Hardt, 'For Love or Money', and Eve Kosofsky Sedgwick, to name a few, who have made interesting contributions. See, in addition, Clough and Halley's edited collection *The Affective Turn*. See also the discussion in Chapter 4 of this volume.
4 In *Reality Hunger*, David Shields deliberately 'plagiarises' his sources, and then declares that he has done this towards the end of his book, confessing that his manifesto for the greater purchase of the real in contemporary culture is a pastiche of quotes mixed in with occasional formulations of his own. He acknowledges, therefore, that a great many of the sentences and paragraphs in the book are lifted straight from the work of other writers, explaining further that his publishers insisted he cite these sources, which he does reluctantly at the close of the book. Shields uses Picasso's line 'Art is theft' as an epigraph and stoutly defends it throughout. (The words attributed to Picasso are usually rendered as 'Good artists borrow, great artists steal'.)
5 'Citizen scholarship' is a method widely used and championed in the digital humanities, as is 'crowdsourcing', i.e. widespread engagement, via digital technologies, with the aim of sourcing data from ordinary citizens. For example, one might research a book on the Namibian war in the 1980s by 'crowdsourcing' – calling for testimony, facts and stories via digital means, including social media, email and other forms of electronic communication. 'Citizen scholarship' allows non-scholars a stake in research. Digital humanist Alex Gill describes 'citizen scholarship' as follows: 'In the Caribbean, for example, most scholars/writers/artists don't work for the academy. Many have affiliations to cultural groups of different sorts or freelance. A great deal of them work at banks, advertisement agencies, you name it. Beyond them, though, we have a cadre of aficionados, a wiki-like crowd that engages with the preservation and critique of our cultural heritage. Citizen scholarship refers to the aggregate activities of these groups and individuals. I know of very good scholars who never had a PhD. What we count as a scholarship is also important here. Sonya Monjar for example directs a great project in Puerto Rico, "Esta Vida Boricua", which focuses on life narratives. Some may say that

this is mostly biographical work, but I see it as archival synthesis. Hers is just one example of many outside of our traditional fields of vision that push the boundary between citizen engagement and scholarship' (Priego n.p.).

6   See Bob Hanke, who notes that Virilio's writings on old and new media 'are extensions of and deviations from McLuhan's thesis on acceleration' (204–205). Hanke writes: 'McLuhan was already aware, at the time of the publication of his first book *The Mechanical Bride* in 1951, that mid-twentieth-century media culture was a "whirling phantasmagoria that can be grasped only when arrested for contemplation"' (207). Of course, all of this plays into the condition identified by Zygmunt Bauman as 'liquid modernity'.

7   Explicating Virilio in new-media terms, Gregory Ulmer writes: 'Virilio introduces the neologism *dromosphere* [from *dromos*, meaning a race or racetrack in Ancient Greece, related to *dramein*, "to run"] to name the conditions likely to produce the General Accident. The dromosphere refers to the pollution of dimensions that follows from electronic augmentation of human thought and language. Instant communication is constricting time, eliminating the past and the future, reducing human temporality to Now-time. If the oral apparatus ran on cyclical time, and literacy on linear time, electracy operates within the moment of Now. All trajectory disappears, eliminating the journey with its departure and passages, leaving us only with pure arrival. The mood of this condition is claustrophobic, a sense of being trapped. The human condition in the dromosphere is that of being caught and held within Now-time. The paradox of this confinement is that, augmented by the technologies of telepresence, the experience of Now is separated from place, even from being-there (*Dasein*)' ('Avatar Emergency' 7). Ulmer adds: 'Virilio's argument is that teletechnologies through their instantaneous interactivity have produced a "single time" – Real Time – whose milieu is speed. This unprecedented immediacy and ubiquity makes democracy impossible, he argues. Public space in Real Time becomes an image in some medium — photography, cinema, television. These images replace the "trajectories" of the city, the face-to-face interaction of the public sphere and the encounter of subject with object in the agora, the forum' (8).

8   There are, of course, still many thinking people who do not use social media, but their numbers are in decline. Research suggests that academics are making increasing use of social media, in their personal as much as in their working lives. Deborah Lupton writes as follows about scholars in the US: 'Regular surveys using representative samples of American faculty members conducted by the educational publishing company Pearson continue to find that their respondents use social media far more in their personal lives than for professional purposes. However, their latest report notes that the professional use of social media has increased since their surveying began in 2009. More than half (55 per cent) of their respondents said that they used social media for professional purposes

other than teaching at least monthly, but only 41 per cent did so for teaching purposes' (4). See also Richard Van Noorden.

9   See Andrea Ochsner's *Lad Trouble: Masculinity and Identity in the British Male Confessional Novel of the 1990s*; Emily Fox-Gordon, 'Confessing and Confiding'.

10 See Lauren Berlant's critique of an 'intimate public sphere' in the US (Berlant, *The Queen of America*; see also Eng and Kazanjian, *Loss*).

11 For example, when mid-level police detective Jeffrey Benzien demonstrated, or mimed, his suffocating 'wet bag' interrogation technique of Tony Yengeni, who was later to become an ANC MP. See Daley.

12 An especially powerful example of this is Pumla Gobodo-Madikizela's *A Human Being Died that Night*.

13 In an email communication, Seltzer added this clarification on the media a priori: 'What [Niklas] Luhmann calls "communication media" are the conditions of social systems. In the systems epoch the media a priori is the ground of a social life that presupposes the "reality of the mass media" – the reality of mass media is premised on the condition in which not only is the copresence of communicants "effectively and *visibly* rendered impossible"; but also and beyond that, the success of communication no longer depends on it. One of the basic paradoxes of the media a priori is, thus, not only that it is constitutive but that it is "visibly" so – that is to say, it is self-exposing and it works via its self-exposition.'

14 These examples are based on real events reported in the South African media. See, for example, Koyana. See also Sacks.

15 CNN, 'Andries Tatane Dies Following Police Beating'.

16 See Mbembe's 2015 Facebook post, taken up by the website Africa is a Country as 'Achille Mbembe on the State of South African Political Life', in which he writes: 'But behind whites trial looms a broader indictment of South African social and political order [*sic*]. South Africa is fast approaching its Fanonian moment. A mass of structurally disenfranchised people have the feeling of being treated as "foreigners" on their own land. Convinced that the doors of opportunity are closing, they are asking for firmer demarcations between "citizens" (those who belong) and "foreigners" (those who must be excluded). They are convinced that as the doors of opportunity keep closing, those who won't be able to "get in" right now might be left out for generations to come – thus the social stampede, the rush to "get in" before it gets too late, the willingness to risk a fight because waiting is no longer a viable option. The old politics of waiting is therefore gradually replaced by a new politics of impatience and, if necessary, of disruption. Brashness, disruption and a new *anti-decorum* ethos are meant to bring down the pretence of normality and the logics of normalization in this most "abnormal" society...The age of impatience is an age when a lot is said – all sorts of things we had hardly heard about during the last twenty years; some ugly, outrageous, toxic things, including calls for murder, atrocious things that speak to everything except to the project of freedom, in this age of fantasy and hysteria, when the gap between psychic realities and actual material

realities has never been so wide, and *the digital world only serves as an amplifier of every single moment, event and accident. The age of urgency is also an age when new wounded bodies erupt and undertake to actually occupy spaces they used to simply haunt.* They are now piling up, swearing and cursing, speaking with excrements, asking to be heard' (n.p., emphasis added).

17 Seltzer's words here (*True Crime* 48) reveal a notable similarity with the italicised phrases in Mbembe's 'State of South African Political Life' in note 16 directly above. Mbembe adds: 'Psychic bonds – in particular bonds of pain and bonds of suffering – more than lived material contradictions are becoming the real stuff of political inter-subjectivity. "I am my pain" – how many times have I heard this statement in the months since #RhodesMustFall emerged? "I am my suffering" and this subjective experience is so incommensurable that "unless you have gone through the same trial, you will never understand my condition" – the fusion of self and suffering in this astonishing age of solipsism and narcissism ... In the bloody miasma of the Zuma years, the discourse of black power, self-affirmation and worldliness of the early 1990s is in danger of being replaced by the discourse of fracture, injury and victimization – identity politics and the resentment that always is its corollary' (n.p.).

18 Marikana was the scene of a massacre, in August 2012, of 34 protesting miners from the Lonmin platinum mine in Rustenburg, South Africa, by the postapartheid South African Police Service (SAPS). See Greg Marinovich, *Murder at Small Koppie* and 'Marikana Killings'.

19 The 'Fallists', however, dismiss Mandela as a sell-out, and so the myth of a 'better' future is unavailable to them. Scholars, too, are sceptical of the Mandela 'myth', but it remains a powerful mobilising trope, for or against, or a key reference point, in popular as well as less popular forms of discourse.

20 For an analysis of the case involving Anene Booysen's rape and disembowelment, see Munusamy, 'The Agony'.

21 See Warner's *Publics and Counterpublics*.

22 In postapartheid writing, forensic realism is consummately embodied in works such as Altbeker's *Fruit of a Poisoned Tree* and Gevisser's *Lost and Found in Johannesburg*, not to mention Jacob Dlamini's and Jonny Steinberg's acutely probing, investigative works of literary nonfiction.

23 See Dlamini's *Askari* and Altbeker's *Fruit of a Poisoned Tree*. Fred van der Vyver was acquitted on a charge of murdering Inge Lotz after a hearing in which it became clear that police misrepresented expert evidence to fabricate 'proof' that Van der Vyver was guilty. Going against the grain of public opinion concerning Van der Vyver's alleged guilt, Altbeker contextualises the court case within the wider failure of criminal justice in South Africa in the mid-2000s.

24 On this 'reflexive gap', see explanation, above, of Seltzer's notion of the 'murder of reality'. Seltzer talks about 'self-parrying of the media within the media and ... the ways in which this media reflexivity holds in place what has come to be called reflexive modernity' (Murder/Media/

Modernity 15). Gevisser, then, in the medium of his book, parries the various media of maps, one of the most widely consulted sources on Johannesburg, the city that is the subject of his book.

25 See Sarah Nuttall and Achille Mbembe, *The Elusive Metropolis*.

26 The late 'alternative' Afrikaans lyricist Johannes Kerkorrel, like Gevisser an openly gay man, also wrote about Estoril Books in Hillbrow: *'Vra 'n man op die stoep, | Tussen Hillbrow records en Estoril Books | En dis lank na twaalfuur, | En die Hillbrow toring stuur | Sy seine in die nag, sy sein in die nag, | Sy sein vir die junkies wat wag'* (LyricsFreak, 'Johannes Kerkorrel – Hillbrow Lyrics').

27 In *A Thousand Plateaus*, Deleuze and Guattari set out their concept of the rhizome, in which the phrase 'line of flight' is key: 'Unlike a structure, which is defined by a set of points and positions, with binary relations between the points and biunivocal relationships between the positions, the rhizome is made only of lines: lines of segmentarity and stratification as its dimensions, and the line of flight or deterritorialization as the maximum dimension after which the multiplicity undergoes metamorphosis, changes in nature...Unlike the graphic arts, drawing, or photography, unlike tracings, the rhizome pertains to a map that must be produced, constructed, a map that is always detachable, connectable, reversible, modifiable, and has multiple entryways and exits and its own lines of flight' (21). The fact that Gevisser's revisionary invocation of Johannesburg street maps is central to his book makes this especially pertinent. See also my essay 'Sharp-Sharp: Joburg Refractions', in Graeme Williams's *A City Refracted*.

28 JG Ballard's phrase, from his novel *The Atrocity Exhibition*. See discussion of Seltzer's use of this phrase in the opening section of this chapter, and also note 16. Mark Fisher comments as follows: 'In a sense, the phrase "atrocity exhibition" is a strictly literal description of this media landscape as it emerged in the early 1960s, populated by images of Vietnam, the Kennedys, Martin Luther King and Malcolm X... [F]or Ballard, the events of 1969 are merely the culmination of a decade whose guiding logic has been one of violence; a mediatized violence...As they begin to achieve the instantaneous speed Virilio thinks characteristic of postmodern communication, media (paradoxically) immediatize trauma, making it instantly available even as they prepackage it into what will become increasingly preprogrammed stimulus-response circuitries' (qtd. in Sellars n.p.).

29 See, for example, Brand and Heyns, *Socio-Economic Rights*; section 27(1)(c) of the Constitution of South Africa.

30 Reviewing Chipkin's work, JH Sweet writes: '[Chipkin] is especially interested in trying to understand the peculiarities of a nationalist politics in which the presidency and the government have become "quasi-religious objects", infallible before the eyes of the nation's "true believers", who he labels "authentic national subjects". For Chipkin, "the measure of citizenship in South Africa is the degree to which one is a bearer of this or that mark of national belonging" (60). Those who fail to adhere to the

strict demarcations of the nation are considered disloyal, even unpatri-
otic' (143). Chipkin's argument, Sweet writes, shows how the postapartheid inheritors of the 'intellectual' tradition of struggle in South Africa
'remained committed to a particular form of "modernity" that, even
today, continues to exclude from full citizenship women, workers, and
certain rural folk deemed insufficient in their nationalist political consciousness' (143). Chipkin himself finds such a measure of citizenship
deeply problematic.

31 Bethlehem's critique of the representational fixity of such an 'empirical
dominant' notwithstanding, the fact remains that writers felt a strong
need to bear witness to a world out there about what was 'really' going
on, behind the propaganda wars of the apartheid state, and behind the
disinformation spread by the ruling white establishment.

32 This has been widely documented. See Chris van Wyk's widely antholo-
gised poem 'In Detention'. See also the South African History Archive's
'Detention without Trial in John Vorster Square'.

33 See Chapter 7 of this volume, in which I suggest that leading writers in the
postapartheid period nevertheless continue the tradition of truth-telling
in works such as Coetzee's *Disgrace*; Coovadia's *Tales of the Metric System*;
Dangor's *Bitter Fruit*; Duiker's *The Quiet Violence of Dreams*; Gordimer's
The House Gun; Langa's *The Lost Colours of the Chameleon*; Mda's *Ways
of Dying*; Van Heerden's *30 Nights in Amsterdam*; Van Niekerk's *Agaat*;
Venter's *Wolf, Wolf*; Vladislavić's *The Restless Supermarket*; and Wicomb's
David's Story.

34 Another such writer is Raymond Suttner, whose book *Recovering
Democracy* also brings to light the perceived failure of the ruling party to
act in accordance with the democratic spirit and principles to which it
had committed itself long before the fall of apartheid.

35 Not his given name; his father's surname was Ndzhukula.

36 See Feinstein, *After the Party*. Other examples include the scandal in
which National Police Commissioner Bheki Cele facilitated an irregular
deal with a businessman for a R500 million building lease; and the exposure of former police commissioner and Interpol president Jackie Selebi,
who was sentenced to imprisonment for accepting R1.2 million in bribes.

37 Researcher David Bruce estimates that there have been at least 450 political killings in KwaZulu-Natal since April 1994 ('Political Killings' 16).
These numbers have grown as the 2016 local elections loom, with ANC
cadres coming into conflict with comrades from their alliance partner
the South African Communist Party (see Madlala).

38 See Susan D Moeller's book *Compassion Fatigue*, in which she writes that
compassion fatigue 'ratchets up the criteria for stories that get coverage'
(2), so that journalists reject events 'that aren't more dramatic and lethal
than their predecessors' in order to avoid the 'I've-seen-it-all-before-
syndrome' (2). For a critique of Moeller, see Simon Cottle, *Global Crisis
Reporting* 132.

39 Munusamy writes: 'There is a pattern to how government scandals generally unfold in South Africa. The media breaks the story after a lengthy

investigation. The Democratic Alliance issues a media statement, shrieking with disapproval and vowing to turn Parliament upside down to get answers. Other opposition parties join the chorus. The ANC and its allies ignore the allegations but attack the opposition for milking the scandal for publicity. They also attack the media and accuse it of having dubious intentions by chasing such stories – the most popular range from hatred of President Jacob Zuma and the ANC, neo-liberal, anti-majoritarian tendencies or that old favourite, a racist agenda. And all this before even accusing the newspaper of muckraking to boost copy sales. At the same time, government's default position is to remain silent. Evidence mounts, the media and opposition parties hound government for answers, all of which usually culminates in an obfuscation-laced question session in Parliament. By this time, public interest is already flagging but the opposition tries to keep the matter alive. The Public Protector and/or Auditor General is called in to investigate. Months later the findings are released, by which time the nature and seriousness of the transgression is a vague memory in the public mind. In any event, during that time a series of new scandals is being managed in much the same manner' (n.p.).

40 Delivered in May 2013, the speech focused on union politics, supporting the National Union of Mineworkers (NUM) against the dissident Association of Mineworkers and Construction Union (Amcu). Shabangu was speaking to NUM shop stewards and leaders at their central committee meeting held in Irene, near Pretoria. See Marinovich, 'NUM, AMCU, Marikana: 'Tis the Season to be Bloody'.

41 Bayart, Ellis, and Hibou's term (1–31, 49–68); see also Comaroff, Jean and John, *Law and Disorder* 7–8, 16.

42 See Rehad Desai's Emmy Award-winning documentary *Miners Shot Down*, and Greg Marinovich's book *Murder at Small Koppie*, which originated in Marinovich's extensive photojournalistic reports for the *Daily Maverick*, discussed below. See also Peter Alexander, Thapelo Lekgowa, Botsang Mmope, Luke Sinwell and Bongani Xezwi, *Marikana: Voices from South Africa's Mining Massacre*. The event was widely reported in the media and narrated in a documentary by Aryan Kaganof, and its aftermath given detailed attention in a multimedia *Mail & Guardian* online 'project'. This digital work, 'Marikana: One Year after the Massacre', the labour of reporter Niren Tolsi and photographer Paul Botes, is elegantly presented in well-styled text and is the length of a modest book.

43 See Media24's reports, 'Farlam Commission Hearing Final Arguments'; 'Marikana: Mr X Denies Being a Police Informer'; 'Marikana: Mr X Converts to Christianity'; 'Mr X is Lying, Lawyers Tell Marikana Commission'; 'Marikana Commission: Mr X's Testimony Collapses under Cross-Examination'. The Commission found that Mr X was an unreliable witness in all but one aspect of his testimony (see Marikana Commission of Inquiry: Report, paragraphs 108–116, pp. 642–645).

44 There are conflicting reports on what the miners actually earned. Many news sources, including the *Guardian*, quote a figure of R4 000 per

month (about US$250), but this has been disputed (see Ratcatcher, 'How much'). *Daily Maverick* reporter Sipho Hlongwane, with photo-journalist Greg Marinovich, scrutinised a rock-drill operator's payslip in the Wonderkop shantytown near Lonmin's Marikana platinum mine ('Malema Fans the Flames'). It showed gross earnings of R8 124.80 (US$508) per month, and net pay of just over R5 000 (US$312). According to Hlongwane and Marinovich, however, this miner noted that he had worked a lot of overtime during the month in question. The miners wanted R12 500 per month, or R150 000 per year. This is roughly US$9 375 or, in Australian dollars, A$13 600 per year (at current exchange rate of R16 to US$1, or R11 to A$1). In Australia, a rock driller earns A$100 692 per year (about ZAR1 million), nearly ten times the annual wage sought by the South African miners. In the USA, the median wage for rock drillers is US$21.89 per hour, totalling US$175 for an eight-hour workday. This translates into about US$3 700 per month, or R59 200. Annually, this equals about R710 000 per year.

45 See, for example, 'Anele' (real name withheld by the *Mail & Guardian* to protect the witness): 'August 16 [Marikana] reminds me of June 16,' says Anele. 'It was like a dream, maybe a nightmare, this failure by government and Lonmin' (Tolsi and Botes n.p.). See also Tolsi's explicit comparisons with June 1976, Sharpeville and Bisho, in 'Marikana: One Year after the Massacre'.

46 I am here invoking Jürgen Habermas, for whom relations between citizens (or 'intersubjective' relations) in what he called the 'bourgeois public sphere' were ideally based on rational deliberation between individuals in 'public places or public houses' (Habermas 1) – such as, for example, parliaments, coffee-houses and pubs – and in public newspapers and journals. See Simon Susen, 'Habermas's Public Sphere', 46–47 ff. Describing Habermas's thinking on intersubjectivity, Susen writes: 'The bourgeois public sphere is critical not only of premodern and modern states, but also of itself, for it constitutes an intersubjectively constructed realm based on open and reflexive discourses' (46). In the digitally driven wound culture of the dromosphere, if one follows Seltzer, all of this changes for the worse: '[W]e have been tracing the pathologization of public space in a wound culture. This is a world in which...public space and the scene of the crime appear as two ways of saying the same thing. This is a world, that is, in which openness to another (intimacy) and openness to others (sociality) are experienced in terms of woundedness. This is the double logic of the pathological public sphere. The torn and open body, the torn and exposed psyche, becomes the measure of publicness (it will be recalled that *Öffentlichkeit*, Habermas's term for the public sphere, means openness). And, collaterally, publicness itself is criminalized and pathologized' (*True Crime* 80).

47 Similarly, *The Seed is Mine* by Charles van Onselen must be counted as one of the great nonfiction epics of the struggle period, setting out in minutely detailed and meticulously micro-narrativised form the material

and affective conditions of a peasant sharecropper's life during a time of legislated segregation. The overemphasis in South African literary-critical studies on the work of a single writer, JM Coetzee, is matched here by lack of attention to the importance of this work from a literary-critical point of view.

48 When the Marikana massacre occurred, Ramaphosa was a non-executive director of Lonmin and executive chairman of the Shanduka Group, which (through Shanduka Resources) held 50.03% of Incwala Resources, Lonmin's Black Economic Empowerment partner. Ramaphosa founded Shanduka in 2001, but sold his stake in 2014 after becoming deputy president of the ANC. Ramaphosa, former general secretary of the National Union of Mineworkers and now deputy president of South Africa, is widely regarded as a prime candidate to become the country's next president.

49 See Tolsi, 'SAPS Rot Runs Deep'.

50 See Thulani Gqirana, 'IPID Briefs MPs on Riah Phiyega Charge'. Reporting for the *Mail & Guardian*, Gqirana noted that the cases related to Phiyega's and Mbombo's alleged contravention of section 6(2) of the Commissions Act.

51 Letsoalo and Evans report: 'Buhlungu described Marikana as a calculated use of brutal force. "Mortuary vans were ordered before the shooting [took place]. It's a premeditated [killing]," Buhlungu told the Numsa delegates shortly before they were shown a new DVD on the massacre' (n.p.). Alexander, Lekgowa, Mmope, Sinwell and Xezwi write as follows: 'On the basis of evidence presented, we maintain that Marikana was not just a human tragedy, but rather a sober undertaking by powerful agents of the state and capital who consciously organised to kill workers who had temporarily stopped going underground in order to extract the world's most precious metal – platinum' (21).

52 Wikipedia provides a concise snapshot of Marinovich's credentials: 'Greg Sebastian Marinovich (born 1962) is a South African photojournalist, film maker, photo editor, and member of the Bang-Bang Club. He co-authored the book *The Bang Bang Club: Snapshots from a Hidden War*, which details South Africa's transition to democracy [turned into a Canadian-South African film production, *The Bang-Bang Club*, by Steven Silver in 2010]. In the 1990s, Marinovich worked as the chief photographer for the Associated Press in Israel/Palestine. He was awarded the Pulitzer Prize for Spot News Photography in 1991 for his coverage of ANC supporters brutally murdering a man they believed to be an Inkatha spy. He has also received a Leica Award and a Visa d'Or.'

53 Corregido is here following linguist Teun van Dijk.

7 Fiction's response

1 See Twidle, 'Literary Non-Fiction' 5–6. Twidle writes: 'In and around 2010, with the end of a decade perhaps demanding appropriately

sweeping or summative statements, there was a claim made repeatedly and in various South African cultural forums. It was that fiction in this part of the world was being outstripped, outdone or overpowered by non-fiction' (5). Twidle goes on to discuss arguments to this effect by Marlene van Niekerk, Antjie Krog, Rian Malan, Antony Altbeker and Jonny Steinberg. Malan's argument (at a panel in Cape Town) about 'kingdoms of consciousness' existing in a country of historically enforced apartness (Twidle, 'Literary Non-Fiction' 16) is pertinent. Steinberg was also on the panel and said he was 'very taken' with Malan's metaphor, adding that it suggested 'the particular and uniquely challenging kind of work required by the writer of non-fiction in seeking to negotiate between different life-worlds: an exercise in cultural transfer and translation which, if pulled off, might be uniquely rewarding for the reader' (16).

2   As extracted from a review and reproduced as a blurb on the cover of Altbeker's book, and quoted by Twidle ('Literary Non-Fiction' 5).

3   See note 31, Chapter 3, on publishers agreeing that nonfiction outsells fiction, both in South Africa and elsewhere. The Publishers' Association of South Africa's 'Annual Book Publishing Industry Survey Report 2010', published in 2011, for example, pegs the sales of 'Local Adult Fiction' in 2010 at R59 029 000 (25.6% of the local market) and 'Local Adult Non-fiction' at sales of R171 211 000 (74.4% of the market). See 'Annual Book Book Publishing Industry Survey Report 2010' 38.

4   Of course, fictive writing has had its ups and downs before and after apartheid, as can be seen in the ascendancy of autobiography and memoir in the 1950s and 1960s, for example. My argument is that the trend towards nonfiction, always powerful in South African literary history, has accelerated significantly in the postapartheid period.

5   See Chapter 1 in this volume, under the heading 'The politics of (true) stories', and also note 40 of Chapter 1.

6   The essay title: '"In a Country Where You Couldn't Make This Shit Up?" Literary Non-Fiction in South Africa'.

7   See note 42, Chapter 1, on how the debate about the relative truth-telling valence of fictive and non-fictive forms stretches from Aristotle through to Foucault. The categories 'fiction' and 'nonfiction' are codependent, mutually constitutive and never entirely separate from each other. See also note 2, Chapter 6.

8   While this is of course true also of certain nonfiction forms, such as Marinovich's work (see previous chapter), fictive writing allows for greater freedom in its range of imaginative exploration of the depth and extent of 'real' feelings. This is clearly evident in the work of André Brink, for example, both before and after the fall of apartheid, in works that range from *Looking on Darkness* (1974) to *Philida* (2012).

9   Interestingly, it would be accurate to argue that Duiker's novel is heavily autobiographical, making it a fictionalised memoir.

10   See Coetzee, *Inner Workings: Literary Essays 2000–2005*, consisting of essays on various writers that were published in the *New York Review of Books*, and some as introductions to texts.

11   Concerning ekphrasis, Ryan Welsh contends: 'If the dialectic of word and image is central to the study of media, then the term ekphrasis ... must also be a crucial part of understanding media as the intersection of verbal and visual' ('Ekphrasis').

12   The panharmonicon, an instrument that plays the sounds made by all other instruments, was famously used as an analogy by Ralph Waldo Emerson for a form of writing that builds from oratory (the lecture and the sermon), and in which, according to an entry in Emerson's journal, 'everything is admissible, philosophy, ethics, divinity, criticism, poetry, humor, fun, mimicry, anecdotes, jokes, ventriloquism' (Ellison 229).

13   For Imraan Coovadia in *Tales of the Metric System* and *High Low In-Between*, Sally-Ann Murray in *Small Moving Parts* and Ingrid Winterbach in *The Road of Excess*, it is Durban; for Finuala Dowling in *Homemaking for the Down-at-Heart*, Henrietta Rose-Innes in *Nineveh* and Eben Venter in *Wolf, Wolf*, it is Cape Town; to name some of the most important examples of this trend.

14   At a factual level, for example, the claim that Vladislavić's lens is a 'nostalgic vision of the Johannesburg of his childhood': Vladislavić grew up not in Johannesburg but in Verwoerdburg – now Centurion – near Pretoria.

15   Goldblatt in fact advocated that artists should penetrate beyond mere surface. According to South African History Online, '[h]e argued that the role of a photographer was to go beyond the surface of things and to make a far more compelling argument against the system of white rule' ('David Goldblatt' n.p.).

16   An exception here is artist William Kentridge, as is JM Coetzee. Kentridge's conceptually daring multimedia productions evoke, rupture and combine various surfaces as well as their 'underneath'.

17   See also Vladislavić's *The Exploded View*, which juxtaposes postapartheid metropolitan surfaces and 'exploded', or diagrammatically enlarged, micro-views; in so doing, Vladislavić accentuates rather than delves below such surfaces, emphasising the *relation* of surface to a presumed underneath.

18   Here is an example from *Portrait with Keys*: 'There was a fad for Ndebele painting at the time. A woman called Esther Mahlangu had been commissioned to coat a BMW 525 in Ndebele colours as part of an advertising campaign. Or was it an art project? Either way, it was a striking symbolic moment in the invention of the new South Africa, a supposedly traditional, indigenous culture laying claim to one of the most desirable products our consumer society had to offer, smoothly wrapping this contemporary symbol of status, wealth and sophisticated style in its colours ... My friend Liz said the whole Ndebele fad was kitsch. "It's like that braai sauce people slosh over everything to give it an African flavour. Tomato and onions and too much chilli. Someone just made it up"' (*Portrait with Keys* 27).

19   The idea of a 'thick medium' plays on anthropologist Clifford Geertz's idea of 'thick description', which he borrows from Gilbert Ryle, and

about which he writes: 'The point for now is only that ethnography is thick description. What the ethnographer is in fact faced with ... is a multiplicity of complex conceptual structures, many of them superimposed upon or knotted into one another, which are at once strange, irregular, and inexplicit, and which he must contrive somehow first to grasp and then to render ... Doing ethnography is like trying to read (in the sense of "construct a reading of") a manuscript – foreign, faded, full of ellipses, incoherencies, suspicious emendations, and tendentious commentaries, but written not in conventionalized graphs of sound but in transient examples of shaped behavior' (*The Interpretation of Cultures* 9–10).

20 This setting is remarkably similar to the funeral-parlour machinations depicted in Marlene van Niekerk's play *Die Kortstondige Raklewe van Anastasia W.*

21 The novel in question is *Dukhless: Povest o nenastoiaschem cheloveke* (*Douh-Less: The Tale of an Unreal Person*) by Sergey Minaev.

22 See Forman's PowerPoint display, available online.

23 In *Breaking the Silence*, author Ellen Grünkemeier writes about several cases in which prominent southern Africans, including Mpe, Parks Mankahlana and Yvonne Vera, are thought to have died of AIDS, though no one dares say this in public (47).

24 Much the same might be said of Coetzee's *Disgrace*, Moele's *Book of the Dead*, Mhlongo's *Way Back Home*, Van Niekerk's *Agaat* and Venter's *Trencherman*.

25 The list includes Annari van der Merwe (Duiker's erstwhile publisher at Kwela Books), Siphiwo Mahala, Kagiso Lesego Molope, Fanuel JC Chaane Motsepe, and (in Mpe's case) Siphiwo Mahala, Nokuthula Mazibuko, Michelle McGrane and Niq Mhlongo, among others.

26 Tshabalala-Msimang, known by some as 'Dr Beetroot' for promoting garlic, beetroot and similar foods rather than antiretrovirals to combat AIDS, resisted the roll-out of antiretrovirals right up to 2004. Tshabalala-Msimang was the public voice of Mbeki's AIDS policy.

27 According to Bloomberg, Zwelinzima Vavi, who was at the time general secretary of the Congress of South African Trade Unions (Cosatu), said in 2006 that South Africa's approach to the AIDS epidemic was akin to genocide. 'At least 350,000 people died in just 10 years while the government was dilly-dallying and sending confused messages,' Vavi is reported to have said in an interview with Johannesburg's *Sunday Independent*. 'It was an act of genocide.' (Sguazzin n.p.). See also Kylie Thomas's *Impossible Mourning*.

28 Pamela Nichols recalls: 'Many times, Phaswane publicly commented that he wrote *Welcome to Our Hillbrow* as an alternative to committing suicide' (176).

29 See De Kock and Pieterse, 'A Vast Domain of Death'.

30 The numerous examples of postapartheid works that foreground collapse, decay and degeneration include also the works of Van Heerden (*In Love's Place; 30 Nights in Amsterdam*); Venter (*Wolf, Wolf*); Anker (*Siegfried; Buys*); Beukes (*Zoo City*); Coovadia (*High Low In-Between;*

Tales of the Metric System); Galgut (*The Good Doctor, The Impostor*); Langa (*The Lost Colours of the Chameleon*); Mhlongo (*Way Back Home*); Moele (*Book of the Dead*); Mzobe (*Young Blood*); SJ Naudé (*The Alphabet of Birds*); Rose-Innes (*Nineveh*) and Tlholwe (*Counting the Coffins*); as well as Finuala Dowling's book of poems *Notes from the Dementia Ward*.

31 Melanie Lamaga, 'A Noir Detective' (n.p.).

32 In the novel, those who have found themselves on the wrong side of the law become 'animalled', meaning they must carry an animal on their bodies wherever they go, and turning them into recognisable social outcasts. See *Zoo City* (8 ff.).

33 This is done à la Philip Pullman's daemons in the trilogy *His Dark Materials*, except that Beukes's creatures are not quite as cute as they are in Pullman's children's fantasy.

34 Says Beukes herself, in conversation with Gwen Ansell: 'I wrote the story that was nagging at the back of my head. It turned out to be *Zoo City*, which turned out to be SF. Or speculative fiction. Or New Weird. Or urban fantasy. Or whatever the hell you want to call it. No-one's picking up on my muti noir tag, dammit!' (Ansell and Beukes, 'Monkey Business' n.p.).

35 See, for example, Jeanne-Marie Jackson, *South African Literature's Russian Soul*, and Isabel Hofmeyr, 'The Complicating Sea'.

36 For a counter-view in this regard, see Ashraf Jamal, 'Global Invasion'.

37 See Angela Makholwa's comment, quoted earlier (Chapter 5): 'I think the frustration for me with much of apartheid-era literature is that it was grounded in race...The feedback I get from many readers is: "I never used to read South African fiction"...The South African books I read were the classics like *Cry, the Beloved Country* and I loved them, but I guess they framed South African fiction for me, which was race, race – all the time. I was, like, "what about the other stuff?" I guess there were other people out there thinking like me' (Gedye n.p.). See also De Kock, 'Does South African Literature Still Exist?'

38 SJ Naudé's *Alphabet of the Birds* performs a similar transnational 'escape act', finding a diaspora of South Africans everywhere in the world and nowhere in particular. Though in a more mimetic vein than Beukes, Naudé works also within a fluid set of global locations, transnational affinities, and networks which, incidentally, characterise (Afrikaans) precursors such as Van Heerden's *In Love's Place* and *30 Nights in Amsterdam*.

39 The man who was found by a South African High Court to have conducted a corrupt relationship with Jacob Zuma, and who benefited from the notorious arms deal, the new South Africa's first major corruption scandal.

40 The brand that has been the subject of several sentimental rainbow-nation television adverts.

Works cited

'Abahlali baseMjondolo'. *en.wikipedia.org*. Wikimedia Foundation Inc., 18 January 2016. Web.

Abrahams, Peter. *Mine Boy*. London: Heinemann, 1946.

Accone, Darryl. *All under Heaven: The Story of a Chinese Family in South Africa*. Cape Town: David Philip, 2004.

Adler, Glen, and Jonny Steinberg, eds. *From Comrades to Citizens: The South African Civics Movement and the Transition to Democracy*. London and New York: Macmillan and St. Martin's Press, 2000.

Agamben, Giorgio. *Homo Sacer: Sovereign Power and Bare Life*. Trans. Daniel Heller-Roazen. Stanford, CA: Stanford University Press, 1998.

Alexander, Peter. 'Rebellion of the Poor: South Africa's Service Delivery Protests – A Preliminary Analysis'. *Review of African Political Economy* 37.123 (2010): 25–40.

Alexander, Peter, Thapelo Lekgowa, Botsang Mmope, Luke Sinwell, and Bongani Xezwi. *Marikana: Voices from South Africa's Mining Massacre*. Athens, OH: Ohio University Press, 2013.

Al Jazeera. 'Xenophobia Plagues "Rainbow Nation"'. *america.aljazeera.com*. Aljazeera America LLC, 20 April 2015. Web.

Allen, Michael H. *Globalization, Negotiation, and the Future of Transformation in South Africa: Revolution at a Bargain?* New York: Palgrave Macmillan, 2006.

Allison, Simon. 'Young Lions Roar No More'. *gga.org*. Good Governance Africa, 1 July 2014. Web.

Altbeker, Antony. *Fruit of a Poisoned Tree: A True Story of Murder and the Miscarriage of Justice*. Johannesburg: Jonathan Ball, 2010.

———. *A Country at War with Itself: South Africa's Crisis of Crime*. Johannesburg: Jonathan Ball, 2007.

———. 'Puzzling Statistics: Is South Africa Really the World's Crime Capital?' *South African Crime Quarterly* 11.5 (2005): 1–8.

Amid, Jonathan, and Leon de Kock. 'The Crime Novel in Post-Apartheid South Africa: A Preliminary Investigation'. *scrutiny2: issues in english studies in southern africa* 19.1 (2014): 52–68.

Anderson, Muff. 'Watching the Detectives'. *Social Dynamics* 30.2 (2004): 141–153.

Anker, Willem. *Buys: 'n Grensroman*. Cape Town: Kwela, 2014.

———. *Siegfried*. Cape Town: Kwela, 2007.

'Annual Book Publishing Industry Survey Report 2010'. *publishsa.co.za*. Publishers' Association of South Africa, November 2011. Web.

Ansell, Gwen, and Lauren Beukes. 'Behind All the Monkey Business'. *mg.co.za*. Mail & Guardian Online, 6 May 2011. Web.

Appiah, Kwame Anthony. *In My Father's House: Africa in the Philosophy of Culture*. New York: Oxford University Press, 1992.

Arendt, Hannah. *The Human Condition*. 2nd ed. Chicago: University of Chicago Press, 2013 [1958].

Attree, Lizzy. 'AIDS, Space and the City in Phaswane Mpe's *Welcome to Our Hillbrow*'. *Words Gone Two Soon: A Tribute to Phaswane Mpe & K. Sello Duiker*. Ed. Mbulelo Vizikhungo Mzamane. Pretoria: Umgangatho Media & Communications, 2005. 187–193.

Attridge, Derek, and Rosemary Jolly. *Writing South Africa: Literature, Apartheid, and Democracy, 1970–1995*. Cambridge: Cambridge University Press, 1998.

Attwell, David. *Rewriting Modernity: Studies in Black South African Literary History*. Athens, OH: Ohio University Press, 2006.

Attwell, David, and Derek Attridge, eds. *The Cambridge History of South African Literature*. Cambridge: Cambridge University Press, 2012.

Attwell, David, and Barbara Harlow. 'Introduction: South African Fiction after Apartheid'. *Modern Fiction Studies* 46.1 (2000): 1–9.

Awerbuck, Diane. *Gardening at Night*. Cape Town: Umuzi; London: Secker & Warburg, 2003.

Baderoon, Gabeba. *Regarding Muslims: From Slavery to Post-Apartheid*. Johannesburg: Wits University Press, 2014.

Ballard, JG. *The Atrocity Exhibition*. London: Jonathan Cape, 1969.

Barker, Derek Alan. 'Escaping the Tyranny of Magic Realism? A Discussion of the Term in Relation to the Novels of Zakes Mda'. *Postcolonial Text* 4.2 (2008): 1–20.

Barnard, Rita. 'Rewriting the Nation'. *The Cambridge History of South African Literature*. Eds David Attwell and Derek Attridge. Cambridge: Cambridge University Press, 2012. 652–675.

———. 'Tsotsis: On Law, the Outlaw, and the Postcolonial State'. *Contemporary Literature* 49.4 (2008): 541–572.

———. 'On Laughter, the Grotesque, and the South African Transition: Zakes Mda's *Ways of Dying*'. *Novel: A Forum on Fiction* 37.3 (2004): 277–304.

Barris, Ken. 'That Loose Canon: Rumours of South African Writing'. *English Academy Review: Southern African Journal of English Studies* 32.1 (2015): 41–53.

Bauman, Zygmunt. *Consuming Life*. Cambridge: Polity Press, 2007.

———. *Liquid Modernity*. Cambridge: Polity Press, 2000.

Bayart, Jean-François, Stephen Ellis, and Béatrice Hibou. *The Criminalization of the State in Africa*. Oxford: James Currey, 1999.

Beall, Jo, Stephen Gelb, and Shireen Hassim. 'Fragile Stability: State and Society in Democratic South Africa'. *Journal of Southern African Studies* 31.4 (2005): 681–700.

Bell, David, and JU Jacobs, eds. *Ways of Writing: Critical Essays on Zakes Mda*. Pietermaritzburg: University of KwaZulu-Natal Press, 2009.

Bell, Duncan. 'What is Liberalism?' *Political Theory* 42.6 (2014): 682–715.

Berlant, Lauren. 'A Properly Political Concept of Love: Three Approaches in Ten Pages'. *Cultural Anthropology* 26.4 (2011): 683–691.

———. *The Female Complaint: The Unfinished Business of Sentimentality in American Culture*. Durham, NC: Duke University Press, 2008.

———. *The Queen of America Goes to Washington City: Essays on Sex and Citizenship*. Durham, NC: Duke University Press, 1997.

Best, Stephen, and Sharon Marcus. 'Surface Reading: An Introduction'. *Representations* 108 (Fall 2009): 1–21.

Bethlehem, Louise. *Skin Tight: Apartheid Literary Culture and Its Aftermath*. Pretoria: Unisa Press, 2006.

———. '"A Primary Need as Strong as Hunger": The Rhetoric of Urgency in South African Literary Culture under Apartheid'. *Poetics Today* 22.2 (2001): 365–389.

Beukes, Lauren. *Zoo City*. Johannesburg: Jacana, 2011.

Bhabha, Homi K. *The Location of Culture*. London and New York: Routledge, 1994.

———. ed. *Nation and Narration*. New York: Routledge, 1990.

Bloom, Kevin. *Ways of Staying*. Johannesburg: Picador Africa; London: Portobello, 2009.

Boehmer, Elleke. 'Endings and New Beginning: South African Fiction in Transition'. *Writing South Africa: Literature, Apartheid, and Democracy, 1970–1995*. Eds Derek Attridge and Rosemary Jolly. Cambridge: Cambridge University Press, 1998. 43–56.

Bond, Patrick. 'The Mandela Years in Power: Did He Jump or Was He Pushed?' *counterpunch.org*. Counterpunch, 6–8 December 2013. Web.

———. 'From Racial to Class Apartheid: South Africa's Frustrating Decade of Freedom'. *Monthly Review* 55.10 (2004): 45–59.

———. *The Elite Transition: From Apartheid to Neoliberalism in South Africa*. London: Pluto Press, 2000.

Bosman, Herman Charles. *Makapan's Caves and Other Stories*. Ed. Stephen Gray. London: Penguin, 1987.

Botha, Dominique. *False River*. Cape Town: Umuzi, 2013.

Brand, Danie, and Christof H Heyns, eds. *Socio-Economic Rights in South Africa*. Pretoria: Pretoria University Law Press, 2005.

Breytenbach, Breyten. 'Mandela's Smile: Notes in South Africa'. *Harper's Magazine* December 2008: 39–48.

———. *Dog Heart: A Memoir*. London: Faber; New York: Harcourt Brace, 1999.

Brink, André. *Philida*. London: Harvill Secker, 2012.

———. *Devil's Valley*. London: Vintage, 2000 [1998].

———. *Imaginings of Sand*. London: Minerva, 1997 [1996].

———. Ed. *SA, 27 April 1994: An Authors' Diary / 'n Skrywersdagboek*. Pretoria and Cape Town: Queillerie, 1994.

———. *The First Life of Adamastor*. London: Vintage, 2000 [1993].

———. 'To Re-Imagine Our History'. *Weekly Mail & Guardian Review of Books* 24–30 September 1993: 1–2.

———. *Looking on Darkness*. London: WH Allen, 1974.

Brooks, Peter. *Reading for the Plot: Design and Intention in Narrative*. New York: Vintage, 1985.

Brown, Andrew. *Refuge*. Cape Town: Zebra Press, 2009.

Brown, Duncan. *Voicing the Text: South African Oral Poetry and Performance*. Cape Town: Oxford University Press, 1998.

Brown, Duncan, and Bruno van Dyk, eds. *Exchanges: South African Writing in Transition*. Pietermaritzburg: University of Natal Press, 1991.

Brown, Wendy. *Undoing the Demos: Neoliberalism's Stealth Revolution*. Cambridge, MA: Zone Books (MIT Press), 2015.

———. 'Neoliberalism and the End of Democracy'. *Theory & Event* 7.1 (2003): 1–29.

———. 'Wounded Attachments'. *Political Theory* 21.3 (1993): 390–410.

Brownlee, Russel. *Garden of the Plagues*. Cape Town: Human & Rousseau, 2005.

Bruce, David. 'A Provincial Concern? Political Killings in South Africa'. *South African Crime Quarterly* 45 (September 2013): 13–24.

Brynard, Karen. *Weeping Waters*. Trans. Maya Fowler and Isobel Dixon. Johannesburg: Penguin, 2014.

———. *Plaasmoord*. Cape Town: Human & Rousseau, 2009.

Burger, J. 'Worrying Trends: The Official 2008/09 South African Crime Statistics'. *South African Crime Quarterly* 30 (2009): 3–11.

Carr, Nicholas. *The Shallows: What the Internet is Doing to Our Brains*. New York: Norton, 2010.

Chakrabarty, Dipesh. *Provincializing Europe: Postcolonial Thought and Historical Difference*. Princeton, NJ: Princeton University Press, 2000.

Chapman, Audrey R, and Bernard Spong. *Religion & Reconciliation in South Africa: Voices of Religious Leaders*. Radnor, PA: Templeton Foundation Press, 2003.

Chapman, Audrey R, and Hugo van der Merwe. *Truth and Reconciliation in South Africa: Did the TRC Deliver?* Philadelphia, PA: University of Pennsylvania Press, 2008.

Chapman, Michael. 'Introduction: Conjectures on South African Literature'. *Current Writing: Text and Reception in Southern Africa* 21.1/2 (2009): 1–23.

Chapman, Michael, and Margaret Lenta, eds. *SA Lit: Beyond 2000*. Pietermaritzburg: University of KwaZulu-Natal Press, 2011.

Chipkin, Ivor. *Do South Africans Exist? Nationalism, Democracy, and the Identity of 'the People'*. Johannesburg: Wits University Press, 2007.

Clarkson, Carrol. *Drawing the Line: Toward an Aesthetics of Transitional Justice*. New York: Fordham University Press, 2013.

Clingman, Stephen. *Birthmark*. Johannesburg: Jacana, 2015.

———. *Bram Fischer: Afrikaner Revolutionary*. 2nd ed. Johannesburg: Jacana, 2013 [1998].

Clough, Patricia Ticineto, with Jean Halley, eds. *The Affective Turn: Theorizing the Social*. Durham, NC: Duke University Press, 2007.

CNN. 'CNN: Andries Tatane Dies Following Police Beating'. Online video clip. *youtube.com*. YouTube, 22 April 2011. Web.

Coetzee, JM. *Summertime*. New York: Viking, 2009.

———. *Inner Workings: Literary Essays 2000–2005*. London: Harvill Secker, 2007.

———. *Youth*. London: Secker & Warburg, 2002.

———. *Disgrace*. London: Viking, 1999.

———. *Doubling the Point: Essays and Interviews*. Ed. David Attwell. Cambridge, MA: Harvard University Press, 1992.

———. *Foe*. London: Penguin, 1987.

———. *Life & Times of Michael K*. New York: Viking, 1983.

———. *Dusklands*. Johannesburg: Ravan Press, 1974; London: Secker & Warburg, 1982.

Cohen, Michael. 'Rainbow Nation Betrayed as South Africans Attack Immigrants'. *bloomberg.com*. Bloomberg L.P., 17 April 2015. Web.

Comaroff, Jean, and John L, eds. 'Figuring Crime: Quantifacts and the Production of the Un/Real'. *Public Culture* 18.1 (2006): 209–246.

———. *Law and Disorder in the Postcolony*. Chicago: University of Chicago Press, 2006.

———. 'Criminal Obsessions, after Foucault: Postcoloniality, Policing, and the Metaphysics of Disorder'. *Critical Inquiry* 30.4 (2004): 800–824.

———. *Of Revelation and Revolution: Christianity, Colonialism, and Consciousness in South Africa, Volume 1*. Chicago: University of Chicago Press, 1991.

Conrad, Mark T, ed. *The Philosophy of Neo-Noir*. Lexington, KY: University of Kentucky Press, 2007.

Coovadia, Imraan. *Tales of the Metric System*. Cape Town: Umuzi, 2014.

———. *High Low In-Between*. Cape Town: Umuzi, 2009.

Cornwell, Gareth. 'South African Literature in English since 1945: Long Walk to Ordinariness'. *The Columbia Guide to South African Literature in English since 1945*. Eds Gareth Cornwell, Dirk Klopper and Craig MacKenzie. New York: Columbia University Press, 2010. 1–42.

Cornwell, Gareth, Dirk Klopper, and Craig MacKenzie, eds. *The Columbia Guide to South African Literature in English since 1945*. New York: Columbia University Press, 2010.

Corregido, Jerónimo. 'A Study of Genre in *In Cold Blood*: A Formal Perspective'. *academia.edu*. Academia.edu, n.d. Web.

Corrigall, Mary. 'Debate: Novels Have to Engage with Politics, Says Heyns'. *sundayindybooks.blogspot.com*. Blogspot, 27 June 2012. Web.

Cottle, Simon. *Global Crisis Reporting*. Berkshire: Open University Press / McGraw-Hill, 2009.

Coullie, Judith Lütge. *The Closest of Strangers: Women's Life Writing in South Africa*. Johannesburg: Wits University Press, 2004.

Czada, Roland. 'South African Exceptionalism: Does It Exist, Will It Survive?' University of Cape Town. Graduate School of Humanities, Cape Town. 26 July 2002. Seminar.

Daley, Suzanne. 'Apartheid Torturer Testifies, as Evil Shows Its Banal Face'. *nytimes.com*. The New York Times, 9 November 1997. Web.

Dangor, Achmat. *Bitter Fruit*. Cape Town: Kwela; London: Global, 2001.

'David Goldblatt'. *sahistory.org.za*. South African History Online, n.d. Web.

Davids, Nadia. *An Imperfect Blessing*. Cape Town: Umuzi, 2014.

Davids, Nashira. 'The Year that Anger Boils Over'. *sowetanlive.co.za*. The Sowetan, 11 October 2012. Web.

De Kock, Leon. 'Off-colour? Mike Nicol's Neo-Noir "Revenge Trilogy" and the Post-Apartheid Femme Fatale'. *African Studies* 75.1 (2016): 98–113.

———. 'Sharp-Sharp: Joburg Refractions'. *A City Refracted*. Graeme Williams. Johannesburg: Jacana, 2015. n. pag.

———. 'The "Confessio" of an Academic Ahab: Or, How I Sank My Own Disciplinary Ship'. *English in Africa* 40.1 (2013): 37–57.

———. 'Ethics Knot Leaves Poetry at Sea'. *mg.co.za*. Mail & Guardian Online, 17 May 2013. Web.

———. 'Hardboiled Noir that Appropriates Politics'. *leondekock.co.za*. n.p., 30 August 2012. Web.

———. 'Roger Smith and the "Genre Snob" Debate'. *slipnet.co.za*. SLiPnet, 9 January 2012. Web.

———. 'So, What Should Academic Critics Be Doing, on the Edge of the Now – Skimming the Surface or Plumbing Those Depths?' *English Studies in Africa* 55.2 (2012): 3–17.

———. 'High Noon in the Badlands'. *mg.co.za*. Mail & Guardian Online, 6 May 2011. Web.

———. 'Hits Keep Coming But It Ain't Enough'. *leondekock.co.za*. n.p., 2010. Web.

———. 'Judging "New" South African Fiction in the Transnational Moment'. *Current Writing: Text and Reception in Southern Africa* 21.1/2 (2009): 24–58.

———. 'A History of Restlessness: And Now for the Rest'. *English Studies in Africa* 50.2 (2008): 109–122.

———. 'Does South African Literature Still Exist? Or: South African Literature is Dead, Long Live Literature in South Africa'. *English in Africa* 32.2 (2005): 69–84.

———. 'Sitting for the Civilization Test: The Making(s) of a Civil Imaginary in Colonial South Africa'. *Poetics Today* 22.2 (2001): 391–412.

———. 'South Africa in the Global Imaginary: An Introduction'. *Poetics Today* 22.2 (2001): 263–298.

———. *Civilising Barbarians*. Johannesburg: Wits University Press; Alice: Lovedale Press, 1996.

De Kock, Leon, and Lucy Graham. '"A Candy Castle Built on a Septic Tank": Cape Town in Crime Fiction'. Yale University, New Haven, CT. Paper presented at a Yale University conference, Crime and Its Fictions in Africa, March 2012.

De Kock, Leon, and Annel Pieterse. 'A Vast Domain of Death: Decomposition and Decay in Marlene van Niekerk's *Die Kortstondige Raklewe van Anastasia W*'. *South African Theatre Journal* 26.1 (2012): 61–92.

De Kok, Ingrid, and Karen Press, eds. *Spring is Rebellious: Arguments about Cultural Freedom.* Cape Town: Buchu Books, 1990.

Deleuze, Gilles, and Felix Guattari. *A Thousand Plateaus.* Trans. Brian Massumi. Minneapolis, MN: University of Minnesota Press, 1987.

Desai, Ashwin, and Richard Pithouse. '"What Stank in the Past is the Present's Perfume": Dispossession, Resistance, and Repression in Mandela Park'. *South Atlantic Quarterly* 103.4 (2004): 841–875.

De Wet, Philip. 'Zuma Straddles SA's Bitter Xenophobic Divide'. *mg.co.za.* Mail & Guardian Online, 17 April 2015. Web.

——. 'Transparency Deferred: 14 Years On and Secrecy Still Rules'. *mg.co. za.* Mail & Guardian Online, 3 February 2015. Web.

Dickson, Jessica. 'Reading the (Zoo) City: The Social Realities and Science Fiction of Johannesburg'. *The Salon: Johannesburg Workshop in Theory and Criticism* 7 (2014): 67–78. Web.

Dietrich, Keith Hamilton. 'Of Salvation and Civilisation: The Image of Indigenous Southern Africans in European Travel Illustration from the Sixteenth to the Nineteenth Century'. Diss. University of South Africa, 1993.

Dlamini, Jacob. *Askari: A Story of Collaboration and Struggle in the Anti-Apartheid Struggle.* Johannesburg: Jacana, 2014; Oxford: Oxford University Press, 2015.

——. *Native Nostalgia.* Johannesburg: Jacana, 2009.

Dowling, Finuala. *Homemaking for the Down-at-Heart.* Cape Town: Kwela, 2011.

——. *Notes from the Dementia Ward.* Cape Town: Kwela, 2008.

Dubow, Saul. *Scientific Racism in Modern South Africa.* Cambridge: Cambridge University Press, 1995.

Duiker, K Sello. *The Quiet Violence of Dreams.* Cape Town: Kwela, 2001.

——. *Thirteen Cents.* Cape Town: David Philip, 2000.

During, Simon. 'Literature – Nationalism's Other? The Case for Revision'. *Nation and Narration.* Ed. Homi K. Bhabha. London: Routledge, 1990. 139–153.

Durkheim, Emile. *The Division of Labor in Society.* Trans. George Simpson. New York: The Free Press, 1960 [1893].

'EFF: The Nazi Debate'. *iol.co.za.* The Sunday Independent, 3 August 2014. Web.

Ellison, Julie K. *Emerson's Romantic Style.* Princeton, NJ: Princeton University Press, 2014.

Emdon, Erica. *Jelly Dog Days.* Johannesburg: Penguin, 2009.

Eng, David L, and David Kazanjian. *Loss: The Politics of Mourning.* Berkeley, CA: University of California Press, 2003.

Eze, Emmanuel Chukwudi. 'Transition and the Reasons of Memory'. *South Atlantic Quarterly* 103.4 (2004): 755–768.

'Farlam Commission Hearing Final Arguments'. *news24.com.* News24, 5 November 2014. Web.

Farred, Grant. 'The Not-Yet Counterpartisan: A New Politics of Oppositionality'. *South Atlantic Quarterly* 103.4 (2004): 589–605.

————. 'Mourning the Postapartheid State Already? The Poetics of Loss in Zakes Mda's *Ways of Dying*'. *Modern Fiction Studies* 46.1 (2000): 183–206.

Faull, Andrew. 'Corruption in the South African Police Service: Civilian Perceptions and Experiences'. Institute for Security Studies, Paper 226, November 2011.

Feinstein, Andrew. *After the Party: Corruption, the ANC and South Africa's Uncertain Future.* Johannesburg: Jonathan Ball; London: Verso, 2009.

Felski, Rita. 'Suspicious Minds'. *Poetics Today* 32.2 (2011): 215–234.

Fincham, Gail. *Dance of Life: The Novels of Zakes Mda in Post-Apartheid South Africa.* Cape Town: UCT Press; Athens, OH: University of Ohio Press, 2011.

Finlay, Alan. 'Staging Performance: Race, Authenticity and the Right to Speak'. *Ecquid Novi: African Journalism Studies* 32. 3 (2011): 34–44.

Forman, Ross. 'New Literatures in English'. University of Warwick, Coventry, UK. Lecture series.

Foster, Hal. 'Death in America'. *October* 75 (Winter 1996): 37–59.

Fox-Gordon, Emily. 'Confessing and Confiding'. *theamericanscholar.org.* The American Scholar, Spring 2015. Web.

Fraser, Nancy. 'Transnationalizing the Public Sphere: On the Legitimacy and Efficacy of Public Opinion in a Post-Westphalian World'. *Theory, Culture and Society* 24.4 (2007): 7–30.

Frenkel, Ronit. 'South African Literary Cartographies: A Post-Transitional Palimpsest'. *Ariel: A Review of International English Literatures* 44.1 (2013): 25–44.

Frenkel, Ronit, and Craig MacKenzie. 'Conceptualizing "Post-Transitional" South African Literature in English'. *English Studies in Africa* 53.1 (2010): 1–10.

Gagiano, Annie. '"...To Remember is Like Starting to See": South African Life Stories Today'. *Current Writing: Text and Reception in Southern Africa* 21.1/2 (2009): 261–285.

Galgut, Damon. *The Good Doctor.* London: Atlantic, 2003; Johannesburg: Penguin, 2010.

————. *The Impostor.* Johannesurg: Penguin, 2008.

Gandhi, Sita. *Sita – Memoirs of Sita Gandhi Growing Up at Phoenix and in the Shadow of the Mahatma.* Ed. Uma Dhupelia-Mesthrie. Pretoria: South African History Online; Durban: Durban Local History Museum, 2003.

Garman, Anthea. 'Antjie Krog, Self and Society: The Making and Mediation of a Public Intellectual in South Africa'. Diss. University of the Witwatersrand, 2009.

Gaylard, Gerald, ed. *Marginal Spaces: Reading Ivan Vladislavić.* Johannesburg: Wits University Press, 2011.

Gedye, Lloyd. 'The Interview – Angela Makholwa: Death Becomes Her'. *city-press.news24.com.* City Press, 24 March 2014. Web.

Geertz, Clifford. *The Interpretation of Cultures: Selected Essays.* New York: Basic Books, 1973.

Gevisser, Mark. *Lost and Found in Johannesburg: A Memoir*. Johannesburg: Jonathan Ball; New York: Farrar, Straus and Giroux; London: Granta, 2014.

———. *Thabo Mbeki: The Dream Deferred*. Johannesburg: Jonathan Ball; New York: Farrar, Straus and Giroux, 2007.

Ginzburg, Carlo. *Clues, Myths, and the Historical Method*. Trans. John and Anne C. Tedeschi. Baltimore, MD: Johns Hopkins University Press, 1989.

Glaser, Clive. *Bo-Tsotsi: The Youth Gangs of Soweto, 1935–1976*. London: James Currey, 2000.

Glenny, Misha. *McMafia: A Journey through the Global Criminal Underworld*. Toronto: Anansi; London: Bodley Head; New York: Knopf, 2008.

Gobodo-Madikizela, Pumla. *A Human Being Died that Night: A South African Story of Forgiveness*. Boston: Houghton Mifflin, 2003. Second edition: *A Human Being Died that Night: A Story of Forgiveness*. Cape Town: David Philip, 2013.

Goldblatt, David, and Ivan Vladislavić. *TJ-Johannesburg: Photographs 1948–2010 / Double Negative, a Novel*. Cape Town: Umuzi, 2010.

Gordimer, Nadine. *No Time Like the Present*. London: Bloomsbury, 2012.

———. *The House Gun*. New York: Farrar, Straus and Giroux, 1998.

———. *July's People*. New York: Viking, 1981.

———. *A World of Strangers*. London: Jonathan Cape, 1976.

———. *The Late Bourgeois World*. London: Gollancz, 1966.

Gqirana, Thulani. 'IPID Briefs MPs on Riah Phiyega Charge'. *mg.co.za*. Mail & Guardian Online, 2 February 2016. Web.

Gqola, Pumla Dineo. *What is Slavery to Me? Postcolonial/Slave Memory in Post-Apartheid South Africa*. Johannesburg: Wits University Press, 2010.

Graham, Lucy Valerie. *State of Peril: Race and Rape in South African Literature*. New York: Oxford University Press, 2012.

Graham, Shane. 'The Entropy of Built Things: Postapartheid Anxiety and the Production of Space in Henrietta Rose-Innes' *Nineveh* and Lauren Beukes' *Zoo City*'. *Safundi: The Journal of South African and American Studies* 16.1 (2015): 64–77.

———. *South African Literature after the Truth Commission: Mapping Loss*. New York: Palgrave Macmillan, 2009.

Green, Jeremy. *Late Postmodernism: American Fiction at the Millennium*. New York: Palgrave Macmillan, 2005.

'Greg Marinovich'. *en.wikipedia.org*. Wikimedia Foundation Inc., 27 July 2015. Web.

Grünkemeier, Ellen. *Breaking the Silence: South African Representations of HIV/AIDS*. London: James Currey, 2013.

Grzeda, Paulina. 'Magical Realism: A Narrative of Celebration or Disillusionment? South African Literature in the Transition Period'. *Ariel: A Review of International English Literature* 44.1 (2013): 153–183.

Guelke, Adrian. *South Africa in Transition: The Misunderstood Miracle*. London and New York: I.B. Tauris, 1999.

Gumede, William Mervin. *Thabo Mebki and the Battle for the Soul of the ANC*. Johannesburg: Zebra Press, 2005.

Habermas, Jürgen. *The Structural Transformation of the Public Sphere: An Inquiry into a Category of Bourgeois Society*. Trans. Thomas Burger with Frederick Lawrence. Cambridge, MA: MIT Press, 1989 [1962].

Habib, Adam. *South Africa's Suspended Revolution: Hopes and Prospects*. Johannesburg: Wits University Press; Athens, OH: Ohio University Press, 2013.

Hamilton, Lawrence. '"(I've Never Met) a Nice South African": Virtuous Citizenship and Popular Sovereignty'. *Theoria: A Journal of Social and Political Theory* 56.119 (2009): 57–80.

Hanke, Bob. 'McLuhan, Virilio and Speed'. *Transforming McLuhan: Critical, Cultural and Postmodern Perspectives*. Ed. Paul Grosswiler. New York: Peter Lang, 2010. 203–226.

Harber, Anton. *Diepsloot*. Johannesburg: Jonathan Ball, 2011.

Hardt, Michael. 'For Love or Money'. *Cultural Anthropology* 26.4 (2011): 676–682.

Harris, Peter. *In a Different Time: The Inside Story of the Delmas Four*. Cape Town: Umuzi, 2008.

Hassim, Shireen. 'The Limits of Popular Democracy: Women's Organisations, Feminism and the UDF'. *Transformation* 51 (2003): 48–73.

Heche, Anne. *Call Me Crazy: A Memoir*. New York: Scribner, 2001.

Heffernan, James AW. *Museum of Words: The Poetics of Ekphrasis from Homer to Ashbery*. Chicago: University of Chicago Press, 1993.

Hirsch, Foster. *Detours and Lost Highways: A Map of Neo-Noir*. Milwaukee, WI: Hal Leonard Corporation, 1999.

'His Role in the Truth and Reconciliation Commission'. *sahistory.org.za*. South African History Online, n.d. Web.

Hlongwane, Sipho, and Greg Marinovich. 'Lonmin: Malema Fans the Flames, But the Victims are Still Out in the Cold'. *dailymaverick.co.za*. Daily Maverick, 18 August 2012. Web.

Hofmeyr, Isabel. 'The Complicating Sea: The Indian Ocean as Method'. *Comparative Studies of South Asia, Africa and the Middle East* 32.3 (2012): 584–590.

———. *'We Spend Our Years as a Tale that is Told': Oral Historical Narrative in a South African Chiefdom*. Johannesburg: Wits University Press; Portsmouth, NH: Heinemann; London: James Currey, 1994.

Hook, Derek. *(Post)apartheid Conditions: Psychoanalysis and Social Formation*. Basingstoke: Palgrave Macmillan, 2013.

Hudelson, Richard. *Modern Political Philosophy*. New York and London: ME Sharpe, 1999.

Isaacs, Mandla Lionel. '"Xenophobia" in South Africa: It's More Complicated than You Think'. *dailymaverick.co.za*. Daily Maverick, 22 April 2015. Web.

Ivanchikova, Alla. 'Commodity and Waste as National Allegory in Recent South African and Post-Soviet Fiction'. *CLCWeb: Comparative Literature and Culture* 13.4 (2011): 1–9. Web.

Jackson, Jeanne-Marie. *South African Literature's Russian Soul.* New York and London: Bloomsbury, 2015.

'Jacob Gedleyihlekisa Zuma'. *sahistory.org.za.* South African History Online, n.d. Web.

Jamal, Ashraf. 'Lauren Beukes: At the Forefront of the Global Invasion'. *mg.co.za.* Mail & Guardian Online, 1 March 2013. Web.

———. 'Bullet through the Church: South African Literature in English and the Future-Anterior'. *English Studies in Africa* 53.1 (2010): 11–20.

———. *Predicaments of Culture in South Africa.* Pretoria: Unisa Press, 2005.

———. *Love Themes for the Wilderness.* Cape Town: Kwela, 1996.

Jamal, Ashraf, with Russel Brownlee. 'ABSA Chain: Russel Brownlee in Conversation with Ashraf Jamal'. *oulitnet.co.za.* LitNet Archive, 8 September 2006. Web.

Jansen, Anemari. *Eugene de Kock: Assassin for the State.* Cape Town: Tafelberg, 2015.

Jones, Gwyneth. '*Zoo City* by Lauren Beukes – Review'. *theguardian.com.* The Guardian News and Media Limited, 13 May 2011. Web.

Kane-Berman, John S. *South Africa's Silent Revolution.* Johannesburg: South African Institute of Race Relations, 1990.

Kannemeyer, JC. *JM Coetzee: A Life in Writing.* Johannesburg: Jonathan Ball, 2012.

Khumalo, Fred. *Touch My Blood: The Early Years.* Cape Town: Umuzi, 2006.

Kistner, Ulrike. *Commissioning and Contesting Post-Apartheid's Human Rights: HIV/AIDS – Racism – Truth and Reconciliation.* Münster: Lit Verlag Münster, 2003.

Koyana, Xolani. 'Gugulethu Boys Drown in Wetland'. *iol.co.za.* Cape Times, 3 December 2014. Web.

Krog, Antjie. *Begging to be Black.* Cape Town: Random House Struik, 2009.

———. *Country of My Skull: Guilt, Sorrow, and the Limits of Forgiveness in the New South Africa.* Johannesburg: Random House, 1998.

Kruger, Loren. *Imagining the Edgy City: Writing, Performing, and Building Johannesburg.* New York: Oxford University Press, 2013.

———. '"Black Atlantics", "White Indians", and "Jews": Locations, Locutions, and Syncretic Identities in the Fiction of Achmat Dangor and Others'. *scrutiny2: issues in english studies in southern africa* 7.2 (2002): 34–50.

Kynoch, Gary. 'Fear and Alienation: Narratives of Crime and Race in Post-Apartheid South Africa'. *Canadian Journal of African Studies* 47.3 (2013): 427–441.

———. 'Fear and Alienation: Narratives of Crime and Race in Post-Apartheid South Africa'. Paper presented at 'Crime and its Fictions in Africa' conference, Yale University, 22–23 March 2012.

La Caze, Marguerite, and Henry Martyn Lloyd. 'Editors' Introduction: Philosophy and the "Affective Turn"'. *Parrhesia: A Journal of Critical Philosophy* 13 (2011): 1–13.

Lamaga, Melanie. 'A Noir Detective Pagan Cyberpunk Novel: Review of *Zoo City*, by Lauren Beukes'. *melanielamaga.com*. n.p., 13 August 2012. Web.

Landon, Justin. '*Zoo City* – Lauren Beukes'. *staffersbookreview.com*. Staffer's Book Review, n.d. Web.

Landsman, Anne. *The Devil's Chimney*. Johannesburg: Jonathan Ball; New York: Soho Press, 1997.

Langa, Mandla. *The Lost Colours of the Chameleon*. Johannesburg: Picador Africa, 2008.

Lazarus, Neil. 'The South African Ideology: The Myth of Exceptionalism, the Idea of Renaissance'. *South Atlantic Quarterly* 103.4 (2004): 607–628.

Leggett, Ted. 'The Sieve Effect: South Africa's Conviction Rates in Perspective'. *SA Crime Quarterly* 5 (2003): 11–14.

Letsoalo, Matuma, and Sarah Evans. 'Ramaphosa Must Answer for "Premeditated" Marikana Killings'. *mg.co.za*. Mail & Guardian Online, 18 December 2013. Web.

Leys, Ruth. 'The Turn to Affect: A Critique'. *Critical Inquiry* 37.3 (2011): 434–472.

Linz, Juan. *The Breakdown of Democratic Regimes: Crisis, Breakdown, & Reequilibration*. Baltimore, MD: Johns Hopkins University Press, 1978.

Linz, Juan, and Alfred Stepan, eds. *The Breakdown of Democratic Regimes: Europe*. Baltimore, MD: Johns Hopkins University Press, 1978.

———. *The Breakdown of Democratic Regimes: Latin America*. Baltimore, MD: Johns Hopkins University Press, 1978.

Livingstone, David. *Missionary Travels and Researches in South Africa*. London: Murray, 1857.

Lodge, Tom. *Politics in South Africa: From Mandela to Mbeki*. Cape Town: David Philip, 2002.

Lupton, Deborah. '"Feeling Better Connected": Academics' Use of Social Media'. *canberra.edu.au*. Canberra: News & Media Research Centre, University of Canberra, 10 June 2014. Web.

LyricsFreak. 'Johannes Kerkorrel – Hillbrow Lyrics'. *lyricsfreak.com*. LyricsFreak, n.d. Web.

Mack, Katherine Elizabeth. *From Apartheid to Democracy: Deliberating Truth and Reconciliation in South Africa*. Philadelphia, PA: Pennsylvania State University Press, 2014.

Mackenzie, Jassie. *Random Violence*. Cape Town: Umuzi, 2008.

Madlala, Cyril. 'KwaZulu-Natal's Intra-ANC Violence: Killing Fields Redux?' *dailymaverick.co.za*. Daily Maverick, 9 February 2016. Web.

Magona, Sindiwe. *Mother to Mother*. Cape Town: David Philip; Boston: Beacon Press, 1998.

———. *To My Children's Children*. Cape Town: David Philip, 1990.

Magubane, Zine. 'The Revolution Betrayed? Globalization, Neoliberalism, and the Post-Apartheid State'. *South Atlantic Quarterly* 103.4 (2004): 659–673.

Makholwa, Angela. *Black Widow Society*. Johannesburg: Pan Macmillan, 2013.

Malala, Justice. *We Have Now Begun Our Descent.* Johannesurg: Jonathan Ball, 2016.

Malan, Rian. *Resident Alien.* Johannesburg: Jonathan Ball, 2009.

———. *My Traitor's Heart.* London: Bodley Head; New York: Atlantic Monthly, 1990.

Mamdani, Mahmood. *Citizen and Subject: Contemporary Africa and the Legacy of Late Colonialism.* Princeton, NJ: Princeton University Press, 1996.

Mandela, Nelson. *Long Walk to Freedom.* London: Little, Brown and Co, 1995.

Mangcu, Xolela. *The Colour of Our Future: Does Race Matter in Post-Apartheid South Africa?* Johannesburg: Wits University Press, 2015.

———. *To the Brink: The State of Democracy in South Africa.* Pietermaritzburg: University of KwaZulu-Natal Press, 2008.

'Marikana Commission: Mr X's Testimony Collapses under Cross-Examination'. *dailymaverick.co.za.* Daily Maverick, 4 July 2014. Web.

Marikana Commission of Inquiry: Report on Matters of Public, National and International Concern Arising out of the Tragic Incidents at the Lonmin Mine in Marikana, in the North West Province. *sahrc.org.za.* South African Human Rights Commmission, n.d. Web.

'Marikana Killings'. *en.wikipedia.org.* Wikimedia Foundation Inc., 17 July 2015. Web.

'Marikana: Mr X Converts to Christianity'. *mg.co.za.* Mail & Guardian Online, 21 July 2014. Web.

'Marikana: Mr X Denies Being a Police Informer'. *mg.co.za.* Mail & Guardian Online, 7 August 2014. Web.

Marinovich, Greg. *Murder at Small Koppie: The Real Story of the Marikana Massacre.* Johannesburg: Penguin, 2016.

———. 'NUM, AMCU, Marikana:'Tis the Season to be Bloody'. *dailymaverick .co.za.* Daily Maverick, 4 June 2013. Web.

———. 'Marikana: Police Torturing Their Way to Intimidation'. *dailymaverick .co.za.* Daily Maverick, 2 November 2012. Web.

———. 'The Murder Fields of Marikana. The Cold Murder Fields of Marikana'. *dailymaverick.co.za.* Daily Maverick, 8 September 2012. Web.

Marinovich, Greg, and Greg Nicolson. 'Marikana Massacre: SAPS, Lonmin, Ramaphosa & Time for Blood. Miners' Blood'. *dailymaverick.co.za.* Daily Maverick, 24 October 2013. Web.

Marnewick, Chris. *Shepherds and Butchers.* Cape Town: Umuzi, 2008.

Martin, Richard. *Mean Streets and Raging Bulls: The Legacy of Film Noir in Contemporary Cinema.* Lanham, MD: Scarecrow, 1999.

Massumi, Brian. *Parables for the Virtual: Movement, Affect, Sensation.* Durham, NC: Duke University Press, 2002.

Matlou, Joël. *Life At Home and Other Stories.* Johannesburg: Cosaw, 1991.

Mbao, Wamuwi. 'Mixed Report Card for Mzobe'. *slipnet.co.za.* SLiPnet, 19 August 2011. Web.

Mbembe, Achille. 'Achille Mbembe on the State of South African Political Life'. *africasacountry.com.* Africa is a Country, 19 September 2015. Web.

————. 'Consumed by Our Lust for Lost Segregation'. *mg.co.za*. Mail & Guardian Online, 28 March 2013. Web.

McCarthy, Tom. 'Writing Machines'. *London Review of Books* 36.24 (2014): 21–22.

McRobbie, Angela, and Sarah L Thornton. 'Rethinking "Moral Panic" for Multi-Mediated Social Worlds'. *The British Journal of Sociology* 46.4 (1995): 559–574.

Mda, Zakes. *Black Diamond*. Johannesburg: Penguin, 2009.

————. *She Plays with the Darkness*. Johannesburg: Vivlia, 1995; New York: Picador, 2004.

————. *The Heart of Redness*. Cape Town: Oxford University Press, 2000.

————. *Ways of Dying*. Cape Town: Oxford University Press, 1995.

Medalie, David. *The Mistress's Dog: Short Stories 1996–2010*. Johannesburg: Picador Africa, 2010.

————. 'The Uses of Nostalgia'. *English Studies in Africa* 53.1 (2010): 35–44.

Meer, Fatima. *Prison Diary: One Hundred and Thirteen Days 1976*. Cape Town: Kwela, 2001.

Meyer, Deon. *Devil's Peak*. Trans. KL Seegers. New York: Little, Brown and Co., 2007 [2004].

————. *Heart of the Hunter*. Trans. KL Seegers. New York: Little, Brown and Co., 2003.

Mhlongo, Niq. *Affluenza*. Cape Town: Kwela, 2015.

————. *Way Back Home*. Cape Town: Kwela, 2013.

————. *After Tears*. Cape Town: Kwela, 2007; Athens, OH: Ohio University Press, 2011.

————. *Dog Eat Dog*. Cape Town: Kwela, 2004.

Mkhondo, Rich. *Reporting South Africa*. London: James Currey; Portsmouth, NH: Heinemann, 1993.

Mngxitama, Andile. 'Our Corrupt Economy is Built on Theft'. *mg.co.za*. Mail & Guardian Online, 20 September 2013. Web.

Moele, Kgebetle. *Book of the Dead*. Cape Town: Kwela, 2009.

Moeller, Susan D. *Compassion Fatigue: How the Media Sell Disease, Famine, War, and Death*. New York: Routledge, 1999.

Mofolo, Thomas. *Chaka*. Trans. Daniel P Kunene. Oxford: Heinemann, 1995 [1946].

Morris, Rosalind C. 'The Mute and the Unspeakable: Political Subjectivity, Violent Crime, and "the Sexual Thing" in a South African Mining Community'. *Law and Disorder in the Postcolony*. Eds Jean Comaroff and John L Comaroff. Chicago: University of Chicago Press, 2006. 57–101.

Moslund, Sten. *Making Use of History in New South African Fiction: An Analysis of the Purposes of Historical Perspectives in Three Post-Apartheid Novels*. Copenhagen: Museum Tusculanum Press, 2003.

————. 'Chris van Wyk's *The Year of the Tapeworm*: Beyond the Realism of Struggle in South Africa'. *Journal of Cultural Studies* 3.2 (2001): 412–431.

Motuba, McQueen. 'Writer's Block'. *Words Gone Two Soon: A Tribute to Phaswane Mpe & K. Sello Duiker*. Ed. Mbulelo Vizikhungo Mzamane. Pretoria: Umgangatho Media & Communications, 2005. 161–163.

Mpe, Phaswane. *Welcome to Our Hillbrow*. Pitermaritzburg: University of Natal Press, 2001.

'Mr X is Lying, Lawyers Tell Marikana Commission'. *timeslive.co.za*. Times Media Group, 21 July 2014. Web.

Msimang, Sisonke. 'Caught between the Devil and the Deep Blue Sea: A Nation Beholden to Criminals'. *dailymaverick.co.za*. Daily Maverick, 31 July 2014. Web.

Mthethwa, Bongani. '2008 "ANC Will Rule until Jesus Comes" 2014 "God Must Send Jesus Again": Zuma'. *timeslive.co.za*. Times Media Group, 31 December 2014. Web.

Mukherjee, Neel. '*Double Negative* by Ivan Vladislavić: Incandescent South African Novel that Travels from Apartheid to Democracy'. *independent. co.uk*. The Independent, 15 November 2013. Web.

Munusamy, Ranjeni. 'A New South African Syndrome – Scandal Fatigue'. *dailymaverick.co.za*. Daily Maverick, 21 February 2015. Web.

———. 'The Agony of South Africa's Daughter Anene Booysen. The Agony of South Africa'. *dailymaverick.co.za*. Daily Maverick, 8 February 2013. Web.

Murray, Martin J. *City of Extremes: The Spatial Politics of Johannesburg*. Durham, NC: Duke University Press, 2011.

———. *Revolution Deferred: The Painful Birth of Post-Apartheid South Africa*. London and New York: *Verso*, 1994.

Murray, Sally-Ann. *Small Moving Parts*. Cape Town: Kwela Books, 2009.

Mzamane, Mbulelo Vizikhungo, ed. *Words Gone Two Soon: A Tribute to Phaswane Mpe & K. Sello Duiker*. Pretoria: Umgangatho Media & Communications, 2005.

Mzobe, Sifiso. *Young Blood*. Cape Town: Kwela, 2010.

Naidoo, Phyllis. *Footprints in Grey Street*. Durban: Far Ocean Jetty Publishing, 2002.

Naudé, SJ. *The Alphabet of Birds*. Cape Town: Umuzi, 2014.

Ndebele, Njabulo S. 'Liberation Betrayed by Bloodshed'. *njabulondebele. co.za*. n.p., 26 August 2012. Web.

———. *Fine Lines from the Box: Further Thoughts about Our Country*. Cape Town: Umuzi, 2007.

———. *The Cry of Winnie Mandela*. Cape Town: David Philip, 2003.

———. 'Memory, Metaphor, and the Triumph of Narrative'. *Negotiating the Past: The Making of Memory in South Africa*. Eds Sarah Nuttall and Cheryl-Ann Michael. Cape Town: Oxford University Press, 2000. 19–28.

———. 'The Rediscovery of the Ordinary: Some New Writings from South Africa'. *South African Literature and Culture: Rediscovery of the Ordinary*. Manchester: Manchester University Press, 1994 [1991]. 41–59.

Ndlovu-Gatsheni, Sabelo J. *Tracking the Historical Roots of Postapartheid Citizenship Problems: The Native Club, Restless Natives, Panicking Settlers and the Politics of Nativism in South Africa*. Leiden: African Studies Centre, 2007.

Newman, Katherine S, and Ariane De Lannoy. *After Freedom: The Rise of the Post-Apartheid Generation in Democratic South Africa*. Boston: Beacon Press, 2014.

Ngcobo, Lauretta. *Prodigal Daughters: Stories of South African Women in Exile.* Pietermaritzburg: University of Kwa-Zulu Natal Press, 2012.

Nichols, Pamela. 'The Clarity of Fiction: The Case of Phaswane and Sello'. *Words Gone Two Soon: A Tribute to Phaswane Mpe & K. Sello Duiker.* Ed. Mbulelo Vizikhungo Mzamane. Pretoria: Umgangatho Media & Communications, 2005. 176–179.

Nicol, Mike. *Black Heart.* Cape Town: Umuzi, 2011.

———. *Killer Country.* Cape Town: Umuzi, 2010.

———. *Payback.* Cape Town: Umuzi, 2008.

———. *The Ibis Tapestry.* New York: Knopf, 1998.

Noseweek. 'Trapped in Pollsmoor'. *noseweek.co.za.* Noseweekonline, 1 December 2009. Web.

Nuttall, Sarah. 'The Rise of the Surface: Emerging Questions for Reading and Criticism in South Africa'. *Print, Text and Book Cultures in South Africa.* Ed. Andrew van der Vlies. Johannesburg: Wits Univeristy Press, 2012. 408–421.

———. 'The Way We Read Now.' *slipnet.co.za.* SLiPnet, 14 March 2011. Web.

———. *Entanglement.* Johannesburg: Wits University Press, 2009.

Nuttall, Sarah, and Achille Mbembe, eds. *Johannesburg: The Elusive Metropolis.* Durham, NC: Duke University Press, 2008.

Nuttall, Sarah, and Cheryl-Ann Michael, eds. *Senses of Culture: South African Culture Studies.* Oxford and New York: Oxford University Press, 2000.

O'Brien, Anthony. *Against Normalization: Writing Radical Democracy in South Africa.* Durham, NC: Duke University Press, 2001.

Ochsner, Andrea. *Lad Trouble: Masculinity and Identity in the British Male Confessional Novel of the 1990s.* Bielefeld: Transcript, 2009.

Orford, Margie. *Gallows Hill.* Johannesburg: Jonathan Ball, 2011.

Oxford University Press Southern Africa. 'Zakes Mda: The Story behind *Ways of Dying*'. *youtube.com.* Online video clip. YouTube, 23 May 2013. Web.

Paton, Alan. *Cry, the Beloved Country.* New York: Scribner, 1948.

Pauw, Jacques. *Little Ice Cream Boy.* Johannesburg: Penguin, 2009.

Pechey, Graham. 'Post-Apartheid Narratives'. *Colonial Discourse / Postcolonial Theory.* Eds Francis Barker, Peter Hulme and Margaret Iversen. Manchester: Manchester University Press, 1994. 151–171.

Perry, Alex. 'South Africa: Over-Exposing the President'. *world.time.com.* Time Inc., 23 May 2012. Web.

Petersen, Kirsten Holst. 'Introduction: An Altered Aesthetics?' *On Shifting Sands: New Art and Literature from South Africa.* Eds Kirsten Holst Petersen and Anna Rutherford. Portsmouth, NH: Dangaroo Press, 1991. i–viii.

Phalime, Maria. *Postmortem: The Doctor Who Walked Away.* Cape Town: Tafelberg, 2014.

Piketty, Thomas. *Capital in the Twenty-first Century.* Cambridge, MA: Harvard University Press, 2014.

Pinnock, David. *The Brotherhoods: Street Gangs and State Control in Cape Town*. Cape Town: David Philip, 1984.

Plaatje, Sol T. *Mhudi: An Epic of Native South African Life a Hundred Years Ago*. Johannesburg: Ad Donker, 1989 [1930].

Polela, McIntosh. *My Father, My Monster*. Johannesburg: Jacana, 2011.

Posel, Deborah. 'The People's Paper, the People's Crimes'. WISER Crime Stories Colloquium, University of the Witwatersrand, Johannesburg. June 2009. Unpublished paper.

Posel, Deborah, and Graeme Simpson, eds. *Commissioning the Past: Understanding South Africa's Truth and Reconciliation Commission*. Johannesburg: Wits University Press, 2002.

Priego, Ernesto. 'Global Perspectives: Interview with Alex Gil'. *4humanities. org*. 4 Humanities, 11 January 2013. Web.

Primorac, Ranka. *Whodunnit in Southern Africa*. London: African Research Institute, 2011.

Prose, Francine. 'Future Imperfect: *No Time Like the Present* by Nadine Gordimer'. Review. *nytimes.com*. The New York Times, 6 April 2012. Web.

Ramphele, Mamphela. *A Life*. Cape Town: David Philip, 1995.

Ratcatcher, The. 'How Much Do Rock Drillers at Lonmin Really Earn?' *politicsweb.co.za*. Politicsweb, 20 August 2012. Web.

Richman, Tim, ed. *Should I Stay or Should I Go? To Live in or Leave South Africa*. Cape Town: Two Dogs, 2010.

Robertson, Claire. *The Spiral House*. Cape Town: Umuzi, 2013.

Robins, Steven. *Letters of Stone: From Nazi Germany to South Africa*. Johannesburg: Penguin, 2016.

Rose-Innes, Henrietta. *Nineveh*. Cape Town: Umuzi, 2011.

Rossouw, Rehana. *What Will People Say?* Johannesburg: Jacana, 2015.

Roux, Daniel. 'A Post-Apartheid Canon?' *Pretexts: Literary and Cultural Studies* 9.2 (2000): 243–246.

Russell, Alec. *Bring Me My Machine Gun: The Battle for the Soul of South Africa from Mandela to Zuma*. New York: Public Affairs, 2009.

Sachs, Albie. 'Preparing Ourselves for Freedom: Culture and the ANC Constitutional Guidelines'. *TDR* 35.1 (1991): 187–193.

———. *The Soft Vengeance of a Freedom Fighter*. Cape Town: David Philip; London: Paladin, 1990.

Sacks, Jared. 'Shack Fires: A Devil in the Detail of Development'. *dailymaverick.co.za*. Daily Maverick, 7 January 2013. Web.

Said, Edward. *Orientalism*. London: Routledge and Kegan Paul, 1978.

Salazar, Philippe-Joseph. *An African Athens: Rhetoric and the Shaping of Democracy in South Africa*. Mahwah, NJ, and London: Lawrence Erlbaum, 2002.

Samuelson, Meg. 'Scripting Connections: Reflections on the "Post-Transitional"'. *English Studies in Africa* 53.1 (2010): 113–117.

———. 'Walking through the Door and Inhabiting the House: South African Literary Culture and Criticism after the Transition'. *English Studies in Africa* 51.1 (2008): 130–137.

———. *Remembering the Nation, Dismembering Women? Stories of the South African Transition.* Pietermaritzburg: University of KwaZulu-Natal Press, 2007.

———. 'Crossing Borders with Words: Sello Duiker, Phaswane Mpe and Yvonne Vera'. *Words Gone Two Soon: A Tribute to Phaswane Mpe & K. Sello Duiker.* Ed. Mbulelo Vizikhungo Mzamane. Pretoria: Umgangatho Media & Communications, 2005. 194–199.

Sanders, Mark. *Ambiguities of Witnessing: Law and Literature in the Time of a Truth Commission.* Johannesburg: Wits University Press; Stanford, CA: Stanford University Press, 2007.

Saul, John. 'Starting from Scratch? A Reply to Jeremy Cronin'. *Monthly Review* 54.7 (2002): 43.

Schmid, David. 'The Nonfiction Novel'. *The Cambridge History of the American Novel.* Eds Leonard Cassuto, Claire Eby and Benjamin Rciss. Cambridge: Cambridge University Press, 2011. 986–1001.

Schoeman, Karel. *Die Laaste Afrikaanse Boek: Outobiografiese Aantekeninge.* Cape Town: Human & Rousseau, 2002.

———. *Promised Land.* Trans. Marion Friedmann. London: Julian Friedmann, 1978.

Schreiner, Olive. *The Story of an African Farm.* London: Chapman, 1883.

Schrire, Robert, ed. *Critical Choices for South Africa.* Cape Town: Oxford University Press, 1990.

Sedgwick, Eve Kosofsky. 2003. *Touching Feeling: Affect, Pedagogy, Performativity.* Durham, NC: Duke University Press, 2003.

Seema, Johannes. 'Serote's *Come and Hope with Me* as "Testimony"'. *South African Journal of African Languages* 31.2 (2011): 218–228.

Sellars, Simon. 'The Atrocity Exhibition (1970)'. *ballardian.com.* Ballardian, 8 October 2006. Web.

Seltzer, Mark. 'Murder/Media/Modernity'. *Canadian Review of American Studies* 38.1 (2008): 11–41.

———. *True Crime: Observations on Media and Modernity.* New York: Routledge, 2007.

———. *Serial Killers: Death and Life in America's Wound Culture.* New York: Routledge, 1998.

———. 'Wound Culture: Trauma in the Pathological Public Sphere'. *October* 80 (1997): 3–26.

Serino, Kenichi, and Stella Mapenzauswa. 'South Africa's "Rainbow Nation" Turns Dark as Immigrant Attacks Rise'. *reuters.com.* Thomson Reuters, 19 April 2015. Web.

Sguazzin, Antony. 'Mbeki Government's AIDS Approach an "Act of Genocide", Vavi Says'. *bloomberg.com.* Bloomberg L.P., 6 December 2010. Web.

Sher, Antony. 'A Tidal Wave of Violence'. *theguardian.com.* The Guardian News and Media Limited, 19 September 2007. Web.

Shields, David. *Reality Hunger: A Manifesto.* New York: Knopf, 2010.

Shore, Megan, and Scott Kline. 'The Ambiguous Role of Religion in the South African Truth and Reconciliation Commission'. *Peace & Change: A Journal of Peace Research* 31.3 (2006): 309–332.

Silber, Gavin, and Nathan Geffen. 'Race, Class and Violent Crime in South Africa: Dispelling the "Huntley Thesis"'. *South African Crime Quarterly* 30 (2009): 35–43.

Skotnes, Pippa. '"Civilised Off the Face of the Earth": Museum Display and the Silencing of the /Xam'. *Poetics Today* 22.2 (2001): 299–321.

Sleigh, Dan. *Eilande*. Cape Town: Tafelberg, 2002.

Slovo, Gillian. *Every Secret Thing: My Family, My Country*. London: Abacus, 1997.

Smith, Roger. *Dust Devils*. London: Serpent's Tail, 2011.

———. *Wake Up Dead*. New York: Henry Holt, 2010.

———. *Mixed Blood*. New York: Henry Holt, 2009.

'Something Very Rotten'. *economist.com*. The Economist, 23 June 2015. Web.

South African History Archive. 'Detention without Trial in John Vorster Square: 1968–1997'. *google.com/culturalinstitute*. South African History Archive, n.d. Web.

Soutphommasane, Tim. *The Virtuous Citizen: Patriotism in a Multicultural Society*. Cambridge: Cambridge University Press, 2012.

Spivak, Gayatri Chakravorty. *In Other Worlds: Essays in Cultural Politics*. London: Routledge, 1998.

Steenkamp, Lizel. 'Political Hyenas in Feeding Frenzy – Vavi'. *news24.com*. Beeld, 26 August 2010. Web.

Steinberg, Jonny. *A Man of Good Hope*. Johannesburg: Jonathan Ball; New York: Knopf; London: Jonathan Cape, 2014.

———. *Three Letter Plague: A Young Man's Journey through a Great Epidemic*. London: Vintage, 2009. (US title: *Sizwe's Test*. Simon & Schuster, 2010.)

———. 'Crime'. *New South African Keywords*. Eds Nick Shepherd and Steven Robins. Johannesburg: Jacana; Athens, OH: Ohio University Press, 2008. 25–34.

———. *Thin Blue: The Unwritten Rules of Policing South Africa*. Johannesburg: Jonathan Ball, 2008.

———. *The Number: One Man's Search for Identity in the Cape Underworld and Prison Gangs*. Johannesburg: Jonathan Ball, 2004.

———. *Midlands*. Johannesburg: Jonathan Ball, 2002.

Stobie, Cheryl. 'The Queer Celebratory in Ashraf Jamal's *Love Themes for the Wilderness*'. *English in Africa* 34.2 (2007): 5–18.

Stockenström, Wilma. *The Expedition to the Baobab Tree*. London: Faber, 1983.

Surette, Ray. *Media, Crime, and Criminal Justice: Images, Realities, and Policies*. 5th ed. Stamford, CT: Cengage Learning, 2014.

Susen, Simon. 'Critical Notes of Habermas's Theory of the Public Sphere'. *Sociological Analysis* 5.1 (2011): 37–62.

Suttner, Raymond. *Recovering Democracy*. Johannesburg: Jacana, 2015.

———. 'The Persistence of the Past in the Present'. *dailymaverick.co.za*. Daily Maverick, 5 March 2014. Web.

Swartz, Leslie. *Able-Bodied: Scenes from a Curious Life*. Cape Town: Zebra Press, 2010.

Sweet, James H. 'South Africans Exist: Identity, Nationalism, and Democracy'. *Safundi: The Journal of South African and American Studies* 11.1/2 (2010): 141–148.

Taylor, Jane. *Ubu and the Truth Commission*. Cape Town: UCT Press, 1998.

Thomas, Kylie. *Impossible Mourning: Visuality and HIV/AIDS after Apartheid*. Lewisburg, PA: Bucknell University Press, 2013; Johannesburg: Wits University Press, 2014.

Thurman, Chris. 'The Long and the Short of It: Reflections on "Form" in Recent South African Fiction'. *Kritika Kultura* 18 (2012): 177–196.

Titlestad, Michael. 'Afterword: Observations on Post-Apartheid Literature'. *The Mistress's Dog: Short Stories 1996–2010*. By David Medalie. Johannesburg: Picador Africa, 2010. 181–191.

———. 'Tales of White Unrest: David Medalie's *The Mistress's Dog: Short Stories 1996–2010*'. *English Studies in Africa* 53:1 (2010): 118–121.

———. 'Allegories of White Masculinity in Damon Galgut's *The Good Doctor*'. *Social Dynamics* 35.1 (2009): 111–122.

———. *Making the Changes: Jazz in South African Literature and Reportage*. Pretoria: Unisa Press, 2004.

Titlestad, Michael, and Ashlee Polatinsky. 'Turning to Crime: Mike Nicol's *The Ibis Tapestry* and *Payback*'. *The Journal of Commonwealth Literature* 45.2 (2010): 259–273.

Titlestad, Michael, Deborah Posel, and Achille Mbembe. 'Crime and Punishment'. *Wiser Review* 3 (June 2008): 2.

Tlholwe, Diale. *Counting the Coffins*. Cape Town: Kwela, 2011.

Tolsi, Niren. 'SAPS Rot Runs Deep in Marikana Cover-up'. *mg.co.za*. Mail & Guardian Online, 2 July 2015. Web.

Tolsi, Niren, and Paul Botes. 'Marikana: One Year after the Massacre'. *marikana.mg.co.za*. Mail & Guardian Supplement, 16 August 2013. Web.

Troost, Heinrich. *Plot Loss*. Cape Town: Umuzi, 2007.

'Truth in Translation – The "Truth" Behind the Play'. *truthintranslation.org*. The Colonnades Theatre Lab, n.d. Web.

Tsehloane, Thabo. 'The Tragic and the Comic: Sello Duiker's and Niq Mhlongo's Contrasting Visions of Post-Apartheid Society'. *English Studies in Africa* 53.1 (2010): 79–90.

Twidle, Hedley. '"In a Country Where You Couldn't Make This Shit Up?" Literary Non-Fiction in South Africa'. *Safundi: The Journal of South African and American Studies* 13.1/2 (2012): 5–28.

Ulmer, Gregory. 'Avatar Emergency'. *Digital Humanities Quarterly* (DHQ) 5.3 (2011): n.pag. Web.

Valenzuela, J Samuel. 'Democratic Consolidation in Post-Transitional Settings: Notion, Process, and Facilitating Conditions'. University of Notre Dame, Kelloggs Institute for International Studies, Working Paper 150, December 1990.

Van der Vlies, Andrew. 'On the Ambiguities of Narrative and of History: Writing (about) the Past in Recent South African Literary Criticism'. *Journal of Southern African Studies* 34.4 (2008): 949–961.

Van Heerden, Etienne. *In Love's Place*. Trans. Leon de Kock. Johannesburg: Penguin, 2013.

———. *Klimtol*. Cape Town: Tafelberg, 2013.

———. *30 Nights in Amsterdam*. Trans. Michiel Heyns. Johannesburg: Penguin, 2011.

———. *The Long Silence of Mario Salviati*. Trans. Catherine Knox. London: Sceptre; New York: HarperCollins, 2002.

———. *Ancestral Voices*. Trans. Malcom Hacksley. New York: Viking, 1992; London: Allison & Busby, 1994.

Van Niekerk, Marlene. 'Maak Só die Ruimte vir Gesprek Groter'. *netwerk24. com*. Media24, 25 March 2015. Web.

———. *Agaat*. Trans. Michiel Heyns. Johannesburg: Jonathan Ball, 2006; Portland, OR: Tin House Books, 2010.

———. *Die Kortstondige Raklewe van Anastasia W.* Dir. Marthinus Basson. Klein Karoo Nasionale Kunstefees (KKNK) and Aardklop, 2010.

———. *Triomf*. Trans. Leon de Kock. Johannesburg: Jonathan Ball; London: Little, Brown and Co, 1999; New York: Overlook, 2004.

Van Noorden, Richard. 'Scientists and the Social Network'. *Nature* 512 (2014): 126–129.

Van Onselen, Charles. *The Seed is Mine: The Life of Kas Maine, a South African Sharecropper, 1849–1985*. London: James Currey, 1985.

———. *The Small Matter of a Horse: The Life of 'Nongoloza' Mathebula, 1867–1948*. Johannesburg: Ravan Press, 1984.

———. *Studies in the Social and Economic History of the Witwatersrand, 1886–1914, Vol. II, New Nineveh*. Johannesburg: Ravan Press, 1982.

Van Wyk, Chris. *The Year of the Tapeworm*. Johannesburg: Ravan Press, 1996.

Van Wyk Smith, Malvern. *Grounds of Contest: A Survey of South African English Literature*. Kenwyn: Jutalit, 1990.

Venter, Eben. *Wolf, Wolf*. Trans. Michiel Heyns. Cape Town: Tafelberg, 2013.

———. *Trencherman*. Cape Town: Tafelberg, 2008.

Viljoen, Hein, and Chris N van der Merwe, eds. *Beyond the Threshold: Explorations of Liminality in Literature*. New York: Peter Lang, 2007.

Viljoen, Shaun. *Richard Rive: A Partial Biography*. Johannesburg: Wits University Press, 2013.

Virilio, Paul. *Polar Inertia*. Trans. Patrick Camiller. London: Sage, 2000.

———. *Open Sky*. Trans. Julie Rose. London: Verso, 1997.

Vladislavić, Ivan. *Double Negative*. Cape Town: Umuzi, 2011; London: & Other Stories, 2013.

———. *Portrait with Keys*. London: Portobello, 2006.

———. *The Exploded View*. New York: Random House, 2004.

———. *The Restless Supermarket*. Cape Town: David Philip, 2001; London and New York: & Other Stories, 2014.

———. *The Folly*. Cape Town: David Philip, 1993.

———. *Missing Persons*. Cape Town: David Philip, 1989.

Wa Afrika, Mzilikazi. *Nothing Left to Steal: Jailed for Telling the Truth*. Johannesburg: Penguin, 2014.

Wacquant, Loïc. 'Crafting the Neoliberal State: Workfare, Prisonfare, and Social Insecurity'. *Sociological Forum* 25.2 (2010): 197–220.

———. *Punishing the Poor: The Neoliberal Government of Social Insecurity*. Durham, NC, and London: Duke University Press, 2009.

Walsh, Richard. *The Rhetoric of Fictionality: Narrative Theory and the Idea of Fiction*. Columbus, OH: Ohio State University Press, 2007.

Warner, Michael. *Publics and Counterpublics*. New York: Zone Books, 2002.

———. 'The Mass Public and the Mass Subject'. *The Phantom Public Sphere*. Ed. Bruce Robbins. Minneapolis, MN: University of Minnesota Press, 1993. 234–256.

Warnes, Christopher. 'Writing Crime in the New South Africa: Negotiating Threat in the Novels of Deon Meyer and Margie Orford'. *Journal of Southern African Studies* 38.4 (2012): 981–991.

———. 'Chronicles of Belief and Unbelief: Zakes Mda and the Question of Magical Realism in South African Literature'. *Ways of Writing: Critical Essays on Zakes Mda*. Eds David Bell and Johan Jacobs. Pietermaritzburg: University of KwaZulu-Natal Press, 2009. 73–90.

Welsh, Ryan. 'Theories of Media Keywords Glossary: Ekphrasis'. *csmt.uchicago.edu*. The University of Chicago, 2007. Web.

Wentzel, Marita. 'Liminal Spaces and Imaginary Places in *The Bone People* by Keri Hulme and *The Folly* by Ivan Vladislavić'. *Literator* 27.7 (2006): 79–96.

West-Pavlov, Russ. *Temporalities*. The New Critical Idiom series. Ed. John Drakakis. London and New York: Routledge, 2013.

White, Hayden. *Tropics of Discourse: Essays in Cultural Criticism*. Baltimore, MD: Johns Hopkins University Press, 1978.

———. *Metahistory: The Historical Imagination in Nineteenth-Century Europe*. Baltimore, MD: Johns Hopkins University Press, 1973.

Whyle, James. *The Book of War*. Johannesburg: Jacana, 2012.

Wicomb, Zoë. *October: A Novel*. New York: New York Press, 2014.

———. *Playing in the Light: A Novel*. Cape Town: Random House Struik; New York: New Press, 2011.

———. *David's Story*. Cape Town: Kwela, 2002; New York: The Feminist Press at the City University of New York, 2007.

Wiener, Mandy. *Killing Kebble: An Underworld Exposed*. 2nd ed. Johannesburg: Macmillan, 2012.

Wines, Michael. 'Under Fire, South Africa Shakes Its Strategy against AIDS'. *nytimes.com*. The New York Times, 3 November 2006. Web.

Winterbach, Ingrid. *The Road of Excess*. Trans. Leon de Kock. Cape Town: Human & Rousseau, 2014.

———. *To Hell with Cronjé*. Trans. Elsa Silke, with the author. Cape Town: Human & Rousseau, 2007.

Wylie, Dan. *Savage Delight: White Myths of Shaka*. Pietermaritzburg: University of Natal Press, 2000.

Young, Robert JC. *Colonial Desire: Hybridity in Theory, Culture and Race*. London: Routledge, 1995.

———. *White Mythologies: Writing History and the West*. London: Routledge, 1990.

Index